Becker Professional Education, a global leader in professional for ACCA for more than 20 years, and thousands of candidate succeeded in their professional examinations through its Platir Eastern Europe and Central Asia.*

Becker Professional Education has also been awarded ACCA Approved Content Provider Status for materials for the Diploma in International Financial Reporting (DipIFR).

Nearly half a million professionals have advanced their careers through Becker Professional Education's courses. Throughout its more than 50-year history, Becker has earned a strong track record of student success through world-class teaching, curriculum and learning tools.

We provide a single destination for individuals and companies in need of global accounting certifications and continuing professional education.

*Platinum – Moscow, Russia and Kiev, Ukraine. Gold – Almaty, Kazakhstan

Becker Professional Education's ACCA Study Materials

All of Becker's materials are authored by experienced ACCA lecturers and are used in the delivery of classroom courses.

Study System: Gives complete coverage of the syllabus with a focus on learning outcomes. It is designed to be used both as a reference text and as part of integrated study. It also includes the ACCA Syllabus and Study Guide, exam advice and commentaries and a Study Question Bank containing practice questions relating to each topic covered.

Revision Question Bank: Exam style and standard questions together with comprehensive answers to support and prepare students for their exams. The Revision Question Bank also includes past examination questions (updated where relevant), model answers and alternative solutions and tutorial notes.

Revision Essentials*: A condensed, easy-to-use aid to revision containing essential technical content and exam guidance.

*Revision Essentials are substantially derived from content reviewed by ACCA's examining team.

Becker Professional Education
is an ACCA approved content provider

ACCA

PAPER P4

ADVANCED FINANCIAL MANAGEMENT

STUDY QUESTION BANK

For Examinations to June 2016

No responsibility for loss occasioned to any person acting or refraining from action as a result of any material in this publication can be accepted by the author, editor or publisher.

This training material has been prepared and published by Becker Professional Development International Limited:

16 Elmtree Road
Teddington
TW11 8ST
United Kingdom

ISBN: 978-1-78566-134-1

Copyright ©2015 DeVry/Becker Educational Development Corp. All rights reserved.
The trademarks used herein are owned by DeVry/Becker Educational Development Corp. or their respective owners and may not be used without permission from the owner.

No part of this training material may be translated, reprinted or reproduced or utilised in any form either in whole or in part or by any electronic, mechanical or other means, now known or hereafter invented, including photocopying and recording, or in any information storage and retrieval system without express written permission. Request for permission or further information should be addressed to the Permissions Department, DeVry/Becker Educational Development Corp.

Acknowledgement

Past ACCA examination questions are the copyright of the Association of Chartered Certified Accountants and have been reproduced by kind permission.

STUDY QUESTION BANK – ADVANCED FINANCIAL MANAGEMENT (P4)

CONTENTS

Question		Page	Answer	Marks	Date worked
Tables and formulae		(v)			

ROLE OF FINANCIAL STRATEGY

1	Agency relationships	1	1001	10	
2	Ethics *(ACCA D03)*	1	1002	15	

SECURITY VALUATION AND THE COST OF CAPITAL

3	Cost of capital	1	1003	15	
4	Gaddes *(ACCA J03)*	2	1005	15	
5	Stock market efficiency	3	1007	10	

WEIGHTED AVERAGE COST OF CAPITAL AND GEARING

6	Redskins	3	1008	15	
7	Berlan	4	1010	20	
8	Kulpar *(ACCA D00)*	5	1013	25	

PORTFOLIO THEORY AND CAPM

9	Maltec *(ACCA J01)*	6	1015	5	
10	Wemere	6	1016	25	
11	Crestlee *(ACCA D92)*	8	1018	25	
12	Hotalot *(ACCA J89)*	9	1021	25	

BASIC INVESTMENT APPRAISAL

13	Amble	10	1023	25	
14	Progrow *(ACCA D95)*	11	1025	40	

ADVANCED INVESTMENT APPRAISAL

15	Tampem *(ACCA D06)*	14	1030	15	
16	Project review *(ACCA J09)*	15	1032	25	

BUSINESS VALUATION

17	Daron *(ACCA D96)*	16	1036	40	
18	Mercury training *(ACCA J08)*	18	1041	25	

MERGERS AND ACQUISITIONS

19	Bigun	20	1043	25	
20	Demast *(ACCA J94)*	21	1046	25	
21	Laceto *(ACCA J01)*	23	1050	40	
22	Miniprice & Savealot *(ACCA PP)*	25	1053	25	

ADVANCED FINANCIAL MANAGEMENT (P4) – STUDY QUESTION BANK

Question		Page	Answer	Marks	Date worked
CORPORATE RECONSTRUCTION AND RE-ORGANISATION					
23	Dricom *(ACCA D97)*	27	1056	25	
24	Aster *(ACCA J97)*	29	1061	25	
25	MBO	31	1063	10	
EQUITY ISSUES AND DEBT ISSUES					
26	Equity and debt issues	31	1065	15	
27	IXT	31	1066	25	
28	New debt issue *(ACCA D07)*	33	1069	15	
DIVIDEND POLICY					
29	Pavlon	34	1071	15	
30	TYR *(ACCA D02)*	35	1073	15	
OPTIONS					
31	Uniglow *(ACCA J02)*	35	1075	15	
32	Bioplasm *(ACCA D03)*	36	1076	15	
FOREIGN EXCHANGE RISK MANAGEMENT					
33	Forun *(ACCA J94)*	37	1078	40	
34	Storace	39	1082	15	
35	Participating option *(ACCA D00)*	40	1085	10	
36	MJY *(ACCA D05)*	40	1086	15	
INTEREST RATE RISK MANAGEMENT					
37	Omnitown	41	1087	25	
38	Manling	42	1089	25	
39	Murwald *(ACCA D94)*	43	1093	25	
40	Turkey	44	1096	15	
THE ECONOMIC ENVIRONMENT FOR MULTINATIONALS					
41	Global debt *(ACCA J04)*	44	1098	15	
42	Beela Electronics *(ACCA D01)*	44	1099	15	
43	IMF *(ACCA PP)*	45	1100	10	
INTERNATIONAL OPERATIONS					
44	Polycalc	45	1101	15	
45	Avto *(ACCA D03)*	46	1103	40	
46	Servealot *(ACCA J06)*	48	1107	15	
47	Kandover *(ACCA D06)*	48	1108	15	
FINANCIAL STATEMENT ANALYSIS					
48	Noifa Leisure	49	1111	25	
49	Twello	51	1113	25	
50	Sparks	53	1115	12	
51	Wurrall *(ACCA J04)*	54	1118	40	

Formulae

Modigliani and Miller Proposition 2 (with tax)

$$k_e = k_e^i + (1 - T)(k_e^i - k_d)\frac{V_d}{V_e}$$

The Capital Asset Pricing Model

$$E(r_i) = R_f + \beta_i[E(r_m) - R_f]$$

The asset beta formula

$$\beta_a = \left[\frac{V_e}{(V_e + V_d(1-T))}\beta_e\right] + \left[\frac{V_d(1-T)}{(V_e + V_d(1-T))}\beta_d\right]$$

The Growth Model

$$P_O = \frac{D_0(1+g)}{(r_e - g)}$$

Gordon's growth approximation

$$g = br_e$$

The weighted average cost of capital

$$WACC = \left[\frac{V_e}{V_e + V_d}\right]k_e + \left[\frac{V_d}{V_e + V_d}\right]k_d(1-T)$$

The Fisher formula

$$(1 + i) = (1 + r)(1 + h)$$

Purchasing power parity and interest rate parity

$$S_1 = S_0 \times \frac{(1+h_c)}{(1+h_b)} \qquad F_0 = S_0 \times \frac{(1+i_c)}{(1+i_b)}$$

Modified Internal Rate of Return

$$\text{MIRR} = \left[\frac{PV_R}{PV_I}\right]^{\frac{1}{n}} (1+r_e) - 1$$

The Black-Scholes option pricing model

$$c = P_a N(d_1) - P_e N(d_2) e^{-rt}$$

Where:

$$d_1 = \frac{\ln(P_a/P_e) + (r + 0.5s^2)t}{s\sqrt{t}}$$

$$d_2 = d_1 - s\sqrt{t}$$

The Put Call Parity relationship

$$p = c - P_a + P_e e^{-rt}$$

Present value table

Present value of 1 i.e. $(1 + r)^{-n}$

where r = discount rate

n = number of periods until payment

Discount rate (r)

Periods (n)	1%	2%	3%	4%	5%	6%	7%	8%	9%	10%	
1	0.990	0.980	0.971	0.962	0.952	0.943	0.935	0.926	0.917	0.909	1
2	0.980	0.961	0.943	0.925	0.907	0.890	0.873	0.857	0.842	0.826	2
3	0.971	0.942	0.915	0.889	0.864	0.840	0.816	0.794	0.772	0.751	3
4	0.961	0.924	0.888	0.855	0.823	0.792	0.763	0.735	0.708	0.683	4
5	0.951	0.906	0.863	0.822	0.784	0.747	0.713	0.681	0.650	0.621	5
6	0.942	0.888	0.837	0.790	0.746	0.705	0.666	0.630	0.596	0.564	6
7	0.933	0.871	0.813	0.760	0.711	0.665	0.623	0.583	0.547	0.513	7
8	0.923	0.853	0.789	0.731	0.677	0.627	0.582	0.540	0.502	0.467	8
9	0.914	0.837	0.766	0.703	0.645	0.592	0.544	0.500	0.460	0.424	9
10	0.905	0.820	0.744	0.676	0.614	0.558	0.508	0.463	0.422	0.386	10
11	0.896	0.804	0.722	0.650	0.585	0.527	0.475	0.429	0.388	0.350	11
12	0.887	0.788	0.701	0.625	0.557	0.497	0.444	0.397	0.356	0.319	12
13	0.879	0.773	0.681	0.601	0.530	0.469	0.415	0.368	0.326	0.290	13
14	0.870	0.758	0.661	0.577	0.505	0.442	0.388	0.340	0.299	0.263	14
15	0.861	0.743	0.642	0.555	0.481	0.417	0.362	0.315	0.275	0.239	15
(n)	11%	12%	13%	14%	15%	16%	17%	18%	19%	20%	
1	0.901	0.893	0.885	0.877	0.870	0.862	0.855	0.847	0.840	0.833	1
2	0.812	0.797	0.783	0.769	0.756	0.743	0.731	0.718	0.706	0.694	2
3	0.731	0.712	0.693	0.675	0.658	0.641	0.624	0.609	0.593	0.579	3
4	0.659	0.636	0.613	0.592	0.572	0.552	0.534	0.516	0.499	0.482	4
5	0.593	0.567	0.543	0.519	0.497	0.476	0.456	0.437	0.419	0.402	5
6	0.535	0.507	0.480	0.456	0.432	0.410	0.390	0.370	0.352	0.335	6
7	0.482	0.452	0.425	0.400	0.376	0.354	0.333	0.314	0.296	0.279	7
8	0.434	0.404	0.376	0.351	0.327	0.305	0.285	0.266	0.249	0.233	8
9	0.391	0.361	0.333	0.308	0.284	0.263	0.243	0.225	0.209	0.194	9
10	0.352	0.322	0.295	0.270	0.247	0.227	0.208	0.191	0.176	0.162	10
11	0.317	0.287	0.261	0.237	0.215	0.195	0.178	0.162	0.148	0.135	11
12	0.286	0.257	0.231	0.208	0.187	0.168	0.152	0.137	0.124	0.112	12
13	0.258	0.229	0.204	0.182	0.163	0.145	0.130	0.116	0.104	0.093	13
14	0.232	0.205	0.181	0.160	0.141	0.125	0.111	0.099	0.088	0.078	14
15	0.209	0.183	0.160	0.140	0.123	0.108	0.095	0.084	0.074	0.065	15

Annuity table

Present value of an annuity of 1 i.e. $\dfrac{1-(1+r)^{-n}}{r}$

where r = discount rate
       n = number of periods

Discount rate (r)

Periods (n)	1%	2%	3%	4%	5%	6%	7%	8%	9%	10%	
1	0.990	0.980	0.971	0.962	0.952	0.943	0.935	0.926	0.917	0.909	1
2	1.970	1.942	1.913	1.886	1.859	1.833	1.808	1.783	1.759	1.736	2
3	2.941	2.884	2.829	2.775	2.723	2.673	2.624	2.577	2.531	2.487	3
4	3.902	3.808	3.717	3.630	3.546	3.465	3.387	3.312	3.240	3.170	4
5	4.853	4.713	4.580	4.452	4.329	4.212	4.100	3.993	3.890	3.791	5
6	5.795	5.601	5.417	5.242	5.076	4.917	4.767	4.623	4.486	4.355	6
7	6.728	6.472	6.230	6.002	5.786	5.582	5.389	5.206	5.033	4.868	7
8	7.652	7.325	7.020	6.733	6.463	6.210	5.971	5.747	5.535	5.335	8
9	8.566	8.162	7.786	7.435	7.108	6.802	6.515	6.247	5.995	5.759	9
10	9.471	8.983	8.530	8.111	7.722	7.360	7.024	6.710	6.418	6.145	10
11	10.37	9.787	9.253	8.760	8.306	7.887	7.499	7.139	6.805	6.495	11
12	11.26	10.58	9.954	9.385	8.863	8.384	7.943	7.536	7.161	6.814	12
13	12.13	11.35	10.63	9.986	9.394	8.853	8.358	7.904	7.487	7.103	13
14	13.00	12.11	11.30	10.56	9.899	9.295	8.745	8.244	7.786	7.367	14
15	13.87	12.85	11.94	11.12	10.38	9.712	9.108	8.559	8.061	7.606	15

(n)	11%	12%	13%	14%	15%	16%	17%	18%	19%	20%	
1	0.901	0.893	0.885	0.877	0.870	0.862	0.855	0.847	0.840	0.833	1
2	1.713	1.690	1.668	1.647	1.626	1.605	1.585	1.566	1.547	1.528	2
3	2.444	2.402	2.361	2.322	2.283	2.246	2.210	2.174	2.140	2.106	3
4	3.102	3.037	2.974	2.914	2.855	2.798	2.743	2.690	2.639	2.589	4
5	3.696	3.605	3.517	3.433	3.352	3.274	3.199	3.127	3.058	2.991	5
6	4.231	4.111	3.998	3.889	3.784	3.685	3.589	3.498	3.410	3.326	6
7	4.712	4.564	4.423	4.288	4.160	4.039	3.922	3.812	3.706	3.605	7
8	5.146	4.968	4.799	4.639	4.487	4.344	4.207	4.078	3.954	3.837	8
9	5.537	5.328	5.132	4.946	4.772	4.607	4.451	4.303	4.163	4.031	9
10	5.889	5.650	5.426	5.216	5.019	4.833	4.659	4.494	4.339	4.192	10
11	6.207	5.938	5.687	5.453	5.234	5.029	4.836	4.656	4.586	4.327	11
12	6.492	6.194	5.918	5.660	5.421	5.197	4.988	4.793	4.611	4.439	12
13	6.750	6.424	6.122	5.842	5.583	5.342	5.118	4.910	4.715	4.533	13
14	6.982	6.628	6.302	6.002	5.724	5.468	5.229	5.008	4.802	4.611	14
15	7.191	6.811	6.462	6.142	5.847	5.575	5.324	5.092	4.876	4.675	15

Standard normal distribution table

	0·00	0·01	0·02	0·03	0·04	0·05	0·06	0·07	0·08	0·09
0·0	0·0000	0·0040	0·0080	0·0120	0·0160	0·0199	0·0239	0·0279	0·0319	0·0359
0·1	0·0398	0·0438	0·0478	0·0517	0·0557	0·0596	0·0636	0·0675	0·0714	0·0753
0·2	0·0793	0·0832	0·0871	0·0910	0·0948	0·0987	0·1026	0·1064	0·1103	0·1141
0·3	0·1179	0·1217	0·1255	0·1293	0·1331	0·1368	0·1406	0·1443	0·1480	0·1517
0·4	0·1554	0·1591	0·1628	0·1664	0·1700	0·1736	0·1772	0·1808	0·1844	0·1879
0·5	0·1915	0·1950	0·1985	0·2019	0·2054	0·2088	0·2123	0·2157	0·2190	0·2224
0·6	0·2257	0·2291	0·2324	0·2357	0·2389	0·2422	0·2454	0·2486	0·2517	0·2549
0·7	0·2580	0·2611	0·2642	0·2673	0·2703	0·2734	0·2764	0·2794	0·2823	0·2852
0·8	0·2881	0·2910	0·2939	0·2967	0·2995	0·3023	0·3051	0·3078	0·3106	0·3133
0·9	0·3159	0·3186	0·3212	0·3238	0·3264	0·3289	0·3315	0·3340	0·3365	0·3389
1·0	0·3413	0·3438	0·3461	0·3485	0·3508	0·3531	0·3554	0·3577	0·3599	0·3621
1·1	0·3643	0·3665	0·3686	0·3708	0·3729	0·3749	0·3770	0·3790	0·3810	0·3830
1·2	0·3849	0·3869	0·3888	0·3907	0·3925	0·3944	0·3962	0·3980	0·3997	0·4015
1·3	0·4032	0·4049	0·4066	0·4082	0·4099	0·4115	0·4131	0·4147	0·4162	0·4177
1·4	0·4192	0·4207	0·4222	0·4236	0·4251	0·4265	0·4279	0·4292	0·4306	0·4319
1·5	0·4332	0·4345	0·4357	0·4370	0·4382	0·4394	0·4406	0·4418	0·4429	0·4441
1·6	0·4452	0·4463	0·4474	0·4484	0·4495	0·4505	0·4515	0·4525	0·4535	0·4545
1·7	0·4554	0·4564	0·4573	0·4582	0·4591	0·4599	0·4608	0·4616	0·4625	0·4633
1·8	0·4641	0·4649	0·4656	0·4664	0·4671	0·4678	0·4686	0·4693	0·4699	0·4706
1·9	0·4713	0·4719	0·4726	0·4732	0·4738	0·4744	0·4750	0·4756	0·4761	0·4767
2·0	0·4772	0·4778	0·4783	0·4788	0·4793	0·4798	0·4803	0·4808	0·4812	0·4817
2·1	0·4821	0·4826	0·4830	0·4834	0·4838	0·4842	0·4846	0·4850	0·4854	0·4857
2·2	0·4861	0·4864	0·4868	0·4871	0·4875	0·4878	0·4881	0·4884	0·4887	0·4890
2·3	0·4893	0·4896	0·4898	0·4901	0·4904	0·4906	0·4909	0·4911	0·4913	0·4916
2·4	0·4918	0·4920	0·4922	0·4925	0·4927	0·4929	0·4931	0·4932	0·4934	0·4936
2·5	0·4938	0·4940	0·4941	0·4943	0·4945	0·4946	0·4948	0·4949	0·4951	0·4952
2·6	0·4953	0·4955	0·4956	0·4957	0·4959	0·4960	0·4961	0·4962	0·4963	0·4964
2·7	0·4965	0·4966	0·4967	0·4968	0·4969	0·4970	0·4971	0·4972	0·4973	0·4974
2·8	0·4974	0·4975	0·4976	0·4977	0·4977	0·4978	0·4979	0·4979	0·4980	0·4981
2·9	0·4981	0·4982	0·4982	0·4983	0·4984	0·4984	0·4985	0·4985	0·4986	0·4986
3·0	0·4987	0·4987	0·4987	0·4988	0·4988	0·4989	0·4989	0·4989	0·4990	0·4990

This table can be used to calculate N(d), the cumulative normal distribution functions needed for the Black-Scholes model of option pricing. If $d_i > 0$, add 0·5 to the relevant number above. If $d_i < 0$, subtract the relevant number above from 0·5.

ADVANCED FINANCIAL MANAGEMENT (P4) – STUDY QUESTION BANK

STUDY QUESTION BANK – ADVANCED FINANCIAL MANAGEMENT (P4)

Question 1 AGENCY RELATIONSHIPS

Explain the term "agency relationships" and discuss the conflicts that might exist in the relationship between:

(a) shareholders and managers;
(b) shareholders and creditors.

Explain the steps that might be taken to overcome these conflicts.

(10 marks)

Question 2 ETHICS

Discuss, and provide examples of, the types of non-financial, ethical and environmental issues that might influence the objectives of companies. Consider the impact of these non-financial, ethical and environmental issues on the achievement of primary financial objectives such as the maximisation of shareholder wealth.

(15 marks)

Question 3 COST OF CAPITAL

(a) Calculate the current pre-tax cost of the following debts:

  (i) A 10% coupon irredeemable bond issued at par.
  (ii) A 10% irredeemable bond trading at $85 per $100 face value.
  (iii) A 10% redeemable bond trading at $74 with three years to redemption at par.
  (iv) A 10% redeemable bond trading at par, with three years to redemption at par.
  (v) A 5% irredeemable $1 preference share trading at $0.65.

(4 marks)

(b) Calculate the current post-tax cost of the debts in (a) above, assuming a corporate tax rate of 35%

(3 marks)

(c) Given the following data about share prices, compute the cost of equity in each case:

  (i) Market price per share $1.50 ex-dividend. Dividend just paid 7.5 cents, which is expected to remain constant.

  (ii) Market price per share $1.65 cum-dividend. Dividend about to be paid 15 cents, which is expected to remain constant.

  (iii) Market price per share $1.20 ex-dividend. Dividend just paid 24 cents, with expected annual growth rate of 5%.

  (iv) Market capitalisation of equity $10 million. Dividend just paid $1.5 million, which is expected to remain constant.

(4 marks)

(d) **Calculate the market price per share and total market value of the following companies:**

  (i)   W Co has 50,000 $1 ordinary shares in issue, current dividend per share 10 cents expected to remain constant; cost of equity 10%.

  (ii) X Co has 1,000 $1 ordinary shares in issue, total dividend $500, no growth expected; cost of equity 15%.

  (iii) Y Co has 1 million ordinary shares, the dividend just paid was 10 cents per share and it is expected to grow at 5% per year; cost of equity 15%.

  (iv) Z Co has 10,000 shares in issue, dividends for the next five years are expected to be constant at 10 cents per share and then grow at 5% per year to perpetuity; cost of equity 15%. **(4 marks)**

(15 marks)

Question 4 GADDES

(a) **Briefly discuss possible reasons for an upward sloping yield curve.** **(4 marks)**

(b) The financial manager of Gaddes Co's pension fund is reviewing strategy regarding the fund. Over 60% of the fund is invested in fixed rate long-term bonds. Interest rates are expected to be quite volatile for the next few years. It is currently June 20X3.

Among the pension fund's current investments are two AAA rated bonds:

(1) Zero coupon June 20Y8
(2) 12% Gilt June 20Y8 (interest is payable semi-annually)

The current annual redemption yield (yield to maturity) on both bonds is 6%. The semi-annual yield may be assumed to be 3%. Both bonds have a par value and redemption value of $100.

Required:

  (i) **Estimate the market price of each of the bonds if interest rates (yields):**

   (a) **increase by 1%;**
   (b) **decrease by 1%.**

   The changes in interest rates may be assumed to be parallel shifts in the yield curve (yield changes by an equal amount at all points of the yield curve). **(6 marks)**

  (ii) **Comment on and briefly explain the size of the expected price movements from the current prices and how such changes in interest rates might affect the strategy of the financial manager with respect to investing in the two bonds.**
  (3 marks)

  (iii) **Comment on how the bond investment strategy of the financial manager may be affected if the yield curve was expected to steepen (the gap between short- and long-term interest rates to widen) and interest rates are expected to rise.**
  (2 marks)

(15 marks)

STUDY QUESTION BANK – ADVANCED FINANCIAL MANAGEMENT (P4)

Question 5 STOCK MARKET EFFICIENCY

The following statement contains several errors with reference to the three levels of market efficiency:

> "According to the efficient market hypothesis all share prices are correct at all times. This is achieved by prices moving randomly when new information is publicly announced. New information from published accounts is the only determinant of the random movements in share price.
>
> "Fundamental and technical analysis of the stock market serves no function in making the market efficient and cannot predict future share prices. Corporate financial managers are also unable to predict future share prices."

Required:

Explain the errors in the above statement.

(10 marks)

Question 6 REDSKINS

Redskins Co is a parent company owning shares in various subsidiary companies. Its directors are currently considering several projects to increase the range of the business activities undertaken by Redskins and its subsidiaries. The directors would like to use discounted cash flow techniques in their evaluation of these projects but as yet no weighted average cost of capital has been calculated.

Redskins has an authorised share capital of 10 million 25 cents ordinary shares, of which 8 million have been issued. The current ex-div market price per ordinary share is $1.10. A dividend of 10 cents per share has been paid recently. The company's project analyst has calculated that 18% is the most appropriate cost of equity capital. Extracts from the latest statement of financial position for both the group and the parent company are given below:

	Redskins Group $000	Redskins $000
Issued share capital	2,000	2,000
Share premium	1,960	1,960
Reserves	3,745	708
Shareholders' funds	7,705	4,668

	Redskins Group	Redskins
Non-controlling interests	895	–
3% irredeemable bonds	1,400	–
9% bonds	1,500	1,500
6% loan stock	2,000	2,000
Bank loans	1,540	600
Non-current liabilities	6,440	4,100

All debt interest is payable annually and all the current year's payments will be made shortly. The cum-interest market prices for $100 nominal value debt are $31.60 and $103.26 for the 3% irredeemable and 9% bonds respectively. Both the 9% bonds and the 6% loan stock are redeemable at par in 10 years' time. The 6% loan stock is not traded on the open market but the analyst estimates that its actual pre-tax cost is 10% per year. The bank loans bear interest at 2% above base rate (which is currently 11%) and are repayable in six years. The effective corporation tax rate of Redskins is 30%.

ADVANCED FINANCIAL MANAGEMENT (P4) – STUDY QUESTION BANK

Required:

(a) **Calculate the weighted average cost of capital.** (6 marks)

(b) **Discuss the problems that are encountered in the estimation of a company's weighted average cost of capital when:**

   (i) **bank overdrafts; and**
   (ii) **convertible loan stock,**

   are used as sources of long-term finance. (4 marks)

(c) **Outline the fundamental assumptions that are made whenever the weighted average cost of capital of a company is used as the discount rate in project appraisal.** (5 marks)

(15 marks)

Question 7 BERLAN

(a) Berlan Co has annual earnings before interest and tax of $15 million. These earnings are expected to remain constant. The market price of the company's ordinary shares is 86 cents per share cum-dividend and of bonds $105.50 per bond ex-interest. An interim dividend of six cents per share has been declared. Corporate tax is at the rate of 35% and all available earnings are distributed as dividends.

Berlan's long-term capital structure is shown below:

	$000
Ordinary shares (25 cents par value)	12,500
Reserves	24,300
	36,800
16% bond 31 December 20X4 ($100 par value)	23,697
	60,497

Required:

Calculate the weighted average cost of capital of Berlan. Assume that it is now 31 December 20Xl. (7 marks)

(b) Canalot Co is an all equity company with an equilibrium market value of $32.5 million and a cost of capital of 18% per year.

The company proposes to repurchase $5 million of equity and to replace it with 13% irredeemable loan stock.

Canalot's earnings before interest and tax are expected to be constant for the foreseeable future. Corporate tax is at the rate of 35%. All profits are paid out as dividends.

STUDY QUESTION BANK – ADVANCED FINANCIAL MANAGEMENT (P4)

Required:

Use Modigliani and Miller's model with corporate tax to demonstrate how this change in the capital structure of Canalot Co will affect its:

(i) market value;
(ii) cost of equity; and
(iii) weighted average cost of capital. (7 marks)

(c) Explain how financial gearing affects a firm's weighted average cost of capital according to the traditional view and Modigliani and Miller's model with corporate tax. Suggest why, in practice, firms do not adopt the optimal capital structure as suggested by Modigliani and Miller. (6 marks)

(20 marks)

Question 8 KULPAR CO

The finance director of Kulpar Co is concerned about the impact of capital structure on the company's value, and wishes to investigate the effect of different capital structures.

He is aware that as gearing increases the required return on equity will also increase, and the company's interest cover is likely to decrease. A decrease in interest cover could lead to a change in the company's credit rating by the leading rating agencies. He has been informed that the following changes are likely:

Interest cover	Credit rating	Cost of long term debt
More than 6·5	AA	8·0%
4·0 – 6·5	A	9·0%
1·5 – 4·0	BB	11·0%

The company is currently rated A.

Summarised financial data

	$m
Net operating income	110
Depreciation	20
Earnings before interest and tax	90
Interest	22
Taxable income	68
Tax (30%)	20·4
Net income	47·6
Capital expenditure	20

Market value of equity is $458 million, and of debt $305 million.
Kulpar's equity beta is 1·4. The beta of debt may be assumed to be zero.
The risk free rate is 5·5% and the market return 14%.

The company's growth rate of cash flow may be assumed to be constant, and to be unaffected by any change in capital structure.

ADVANCED FINANCIAL MANAGEMENT (P4) – STUDY QUESTION BANK

Required:

(a) **Determine the likely effect on the company's cost of capital and corporate value if the company's capital structure was:**

    (i)   **80% equity, 20% debt by market values;**
    (ii)   **40% equity, 60% debt by market values.**

Recommend which capital structure should be selected.

Any change in capital structure would be achieved by borrowing to repurchase existing equity, or by issuing additional equity to redeem existing debt, as appropriate.

The current total firm value (market value of equity plus market value of debt) is consistent with the growth model ($CF_1 / (k - g)$) applied on a corporate basis. CF_1 is next year's free cash flow, k is the weighted average cost of capital (WACC), and g the expected growth rate. Company free cash flow may be estimated using EBIT $(1 - t)$ + depreciation – capital spending.

State clearly any other assumptions that you make.   **(18 marks)**

(b) **Discuss possible reasons for errors in the estimates of corporate value in part (a) above.**

    (7 marks)

(25 marks)

Question 9 MALTEC

Maltec Co is a company that has diversified into five different industries in five different countries. The investments are each approximately equal in value. The company's objective is to reduce risk through diversification and it believes that the return on any investment is not correlated with the return on any other investment.

Required:

Discuss the validity of Maltec's objective of risk reduction through international diversification.

(5 marks)

Question 10 WEMERE

The managing director of Wemere, a medium-sized private company, wishes to improve the company's investment decision-making process by using discounted cash flow techniques. He is disappointed to learn that estimates of a company's cost of capital usually require information on share prices which, for a private company, are not available. His deputy suggests that the cost of equity can be estimated by using data for Folten Co, a similar sized company in the same industry whose shares are listed on the AIM, and he has produced two suggested discount rates for use in Wemere's future investment appraisal. Both of these estimates are in excess of 17% per year which the managing director believes to be very high, especially as the company has just agreed a fixed rate bank loan at 13% per year to finance a small expansion of existing operations. He has checked the calculations, which are numerically correct, but wonders if there are any errors of principle.

STUDY QUESTION BANK – ADVANCED FINANCIAL MANAGEMENT (P4)

Estimate 1: capital asset pricing model

Data have been purchased from a leading business school:

Equity beta of Folten	1.4
Market return	18%
Treasury bill yield	12%

The cost of capital is 18% + (18% – 12%) 1.4 = 26.4%.

This rate must be adjusted to include inflation at the current level of 6%. The recommended discount rate is 32.4%.

Estimate 2: dividend valuation model

Year	Folten Average share price (cents)	Dividend per share (cents)
20X5	193	9.23
20X6	109	10.06
20X7	96	10.97
20X8	116	11.95
20X9	130	13.03
D_1		14.20
The cost of capital is		11.01%
P		138
g		9%

where D_1 = expected dividend
P = current ex-div share price
g = growth rate of dividends

When inflation is included the discount rate is 17.01%.

Other financial information on the two companies is presented below:

	Wemere $000	Folten $000
Non-current assets	7,200	7,600
Current assets	7,600	7,800
Less: Current liabilities	3,900	3,700
	10,900	11,700
Financed by:		
Ordinary shares (25 cents par value)	2,000	1,800
Reserves	6,500	5,500
Term loans	2,400	4,400
	10,900	11,700

Notes:

(1) Wemere's board of directors has recently rejected a take-over bid of $10.6 million.
(2) Corporate tax is at the rate of 35%.

ADVANCED FINANCIAL MANAGEMENT (P4) – STUDY QUESTION BANK

Required:

(a) **Explain any errors of principle that have been made in the two estimates of the cost of capital and produce revised estimates using both of the methods.**

State clearly any assumptions that you make. **(14 marks)**

(b) **Discuss which of your revised estimates Wemere should use as the discount rate for capital investment appraisal.** **(4 marks)**

(c) **Discuss whether discounted cash flow techniques, including discounted payback, are useful to small unlisted companies.** **(7 marks)**

(25 marks)

Question 11 CRESTLEE

Crestlee Co is evaluating two projects. The first involves a $4.725 million expenditure on new machinery to expand the company's existing operations in the textile industry. The second is a diversification into the packaging industry and will cost $9.275 million.

Crestlee's summarised statement of financial position, and those of Canall Co and Sealalot Co, two quoted companies in the packaging industry, are shown below:

	Crestlee $m	Canall $m	Sealalot $m
Non-current assets	96	42	76
Current assets	95	82	65
Less: Current liabilities	(70)	(72)	(48)
	121	52	93
Financed by:			
Ordinary shares[1]	15	10	30
Reserves	50	27	50
Medium and long-term loans[2]	56	15	13
	121	52	93
Ordinary share price (cents)	380	180	230
Bond price ($)	104	112	–
Equity beta	1.2	1.3	1.2

[1] Crestlee and Sealalot 50 cents par value, Canall 25 cents par value.

[2] Crestlee 12% bonds, Canall 14% bonds, Sealalot medium-term bank loan.

Crestlee proposes to finance the expansion of textile operations with a $4.725 million 11% loan stock issue and the packaging investment with a $9.275 million rights issue at a discount of 10% on the current market price. Issue costs may be ignored.

Crestlee's managers are proposing to use a discount rate of 15% per year to evaluate each project.

The risk free rate of interest is estimated to be 6% per year and the market return 14% per year. Corporate tax is at a rate of 33% per year.

STUDY QUESTION BANK – ADVANCED FINANCIAL MANAGEMENT (P4)

Required:

(a) **Determine whether 15% per year is an appropriate discount rate to use for each of these projects. Explain your answer and state clearly any assumptions that you make.**

(19 marks)

(b) Crestlee's marketing director suggests that it is incorrect to use the same discount rate each year for the investment in packaging as the early stages of the investment are more risky and should be discounted at a higher rate. Another board member disagrees saying that more distant cash flows are riskier and should be discounted at a higher rate.

Discuss the validity of the views of each of the directors. (6 marks)

(25 marks)

Question 12 HOTALOT

Hotalot Co produces domestic electric heaters. The company is considering diversifying into the production of freezers. Data on four listed companies in the freezer industry and for Hotalot are shown below:

	Freezeup $000	Glowcold $000	Shiverall $000	Topice $000	Hotalot $000
Non-current assets	14,800	24,600	28,100	12,500	20,600
Working capital	9,600	7,200	11,100	9,600	12,700
	24,400	31,800	39,200	22,100	33,300
Financed by:					
Bank loans	5,300	12,600	18,200	4,000	17,400
Ordinary shares	4,000	9,000	3,500	5,300	4,000
Reserves	15,100	10,200	17,500	12,800	11,900
	24,400	31,800	39,200	22,100	33,300
Revenue	35,200	42,700	46,300	28,400	45,000
Earnings per share (cents)	25	53.3	38.1	32.3	106
Dividend per share (cents)	11	20	15	14	40
Price/earnings ratio	12	10	9	14	8
Equity beta	1.1	1.25	1.30	1.05	0.95

The par value per ordinary share is 25 cents for Freezeup and Shiverall, 50 cents for Topice and $1 for Glowcold and Hotalot.

Corporate debt may be assumed to be almost risk free and is available to Hotalot at 0.5% above the Treasury bill rate which is currently 9% per year. Corporate taxes are payable at a rate of 35%. The market return is estimated to be 16% per year. Hotalot does not expect its financial gearing to change significantly if the company diversifies into the production of freezers.

ADVANCED FINANCIAL MANAGEMENT (P4) – STUDY QUESTION BANK

Required:

(a) The equity beta of Hotalot is 0.95 and the alpha value is 1.5%. **Explain the meaning and significance of these values to the company.** (4 marks)

(b) **Estimate what discount rate Hotalot should use in the appraisal of its proposed diversification into freezer production.** (11 marks)

(c) Corporate debt is often assumed to be risk free. **Explain whether this is a realistic assumption and calculate how important this assumption is likely to be to Hotalot's estimate of a discount rate in (b) above.** (5 marks)

(d) **Discuss whether systematic risk is the only risk that Hotalot's shareholders should be concerned with.** (5 marks)

(25 marks)

Question 13 AMBLE

Amble Co is evaluating the manufacture of a new consumer product. The product can be introduced quickly and has an expected life of four years before it is replaced by a more efficient model. Costs associated with the product are expected to be:

Direct costs (per unit)

Labour

3.5 skilled labour hours at $5 per hour.
4 unskilled labour hours at $3 per hour.

Materials

6 kilos of material Z at $1.46 per kilo.
Three units of component P at $4.80 per unit.
One unit of component Q at $6.40.
Other variable costs: $2.10 per unit.

Indirect costs

Apportionment of management salaries $105,000 per year.
Tax allowable depreciation of machinery $213,000 per year.
Selling expenses (not including any salaries) $166,000 per year.
Apportionment of head office costs $50,000 per year.
Rental of buildings $100,000 per year.
Interest charges $104,000 per year.
Other overheads $70,000 per year (including apportionment of building rates $20,000).

(*Note:* rates are a local tax on property.)

If the new product is introduced it will be manufactured in an existing factory and will have no effect on rates payable. The factory could be rented for $120,000 per year (not including rates), to another company if the product is not introduced.

New machinery costing $864,000 will be required. The machinery is to be depreciated on a straight-line basis over four years and has an expected salvage value of $12,000 after four years. Amble's depreciation policy matches the allowances available for tax purposes. The machinery will be financed by a four year fixed rate bank loan, at an interest rate of 12% per year. Additional working capital requirements may be ignored.

The product will require two additional managers to be recruited at an annual gross cost of $25,000 each and one manager currently costing $20,000 will be moved from another factory where he will be replaced by a deputy manager at a cost of $17,000 per year. 70,000 kilos of material Z are already in inventory and are not required for other production. The realisable value of the material is $99,000.

The price per unit of the product in the first year will be $110 and demand is projected at 12,000, 17,500, 18,000 and 18,500 units in years 1 to 4 respectively.

The inflation rate is expected to be approximately 5% per year and prices will be increased in line with inflation. Wage and salary costs are expected to increase by 7% per year and all other costs (including rent) by 5% per year. No price or cost increases are expected in the first year of production.

Corporate tax is at the rate of 35% payable in the year the profit occurs. Assume that all sales and costs are on a cash basis and occur at the end of the year, except for the initial purchase of machinery which would take place immediately. No inventory will be held at the end of any year.

Required:

(a) **Calculate the expected internal rate of return (IRR) associated with the manufacture of the new product.** (15 marks)

(b) **Discuss what is meant by an asset beta.**

If you were told that the company's asset beta is 1.2, the market return is 15% and the risk free rate is 8%, discuss whether you would recommend introducing the new product. (5 marks)

(c) Amble is worried that the government might increase corporate tax rates.

Show by how much the tax rate would have to change before the project is not financially viable. A discount rate of 17% per year may be assumed for part (c).
(5 marks)

(25 marks)

Question 14 PROGROW

Progrow Co is a company with 350 employees located in Southern England. The company has two main products: a manually operated lifting jack for cars and a range of high quality metal gardening tools. The products are sold in car accessory shops, garden centres and "do it yourself" superstores.

The company's production manager has just learned that a new process incorporating new machines could be used in the manufacture of the jacks. The process would require some extra factory space, which is currently surplus to the company's needs (and could not be rented to an external user), and would require 25% less direct labour than current jack production techniques. No expansion in jack production from the current level of 250,000 units per year is proposed. The cost of the new machines would total $535,000 and the machines would require incremental annual maintenance costing approximately $45,000 in current prices. The existing machinery could be sold for $125,000 (after any tax effects including the balancing allowance on disposal). This amount would be received in one

ADVANCED FINANCIAL MANAGEMENT (P4) – STUDY QUESTION BANK

year's time. If the new machines are not purchased, the existing machinery is expected to be kept for a further five years after which time the after tax scrap value is expected to be negligible.

Prices and costs currently associated with the company's products are:

	Jacks $	Garden tools (average) $
Selling price (per unit)	11.20	7.80
Direct costs (per unit)		
Skilled labour	1.80	0.50
Unskilled labour	2.30	2.80
Materials	3.60	2.40
Indirect costs		
Apportionment of management salaries	0.43	0.26
Apportionment of head office overhead	0.54	0.44

Incremental annual interest costs associated with the finance of the new machines are $10,000.

As the company is located in a government approved development area, expenditure on any new machinery would be eligible for first year tax allowable depreciation of 50%, with a 25% reducing balance thereafter. The expected working life of the machines is five years at the end of which they are expected to have a scrap value of $40,000.

If the machines are purchased 26 skilled and 24 unskilled workers would be made redundant. Redundancy costs are on average $9,000 for skilled workers and $5,000 for unskilled workers. Twenty of the remaining skilled workers would need to retrain to use the new machines at a cost of $750 per person. These are all tax allowable costs.

As an alternative to buying the new machines the company could use the spare factory space to expand garden tool production. For a capital equipment expenditure of $200,000 the existing annual production of 400,000 garden tools could be increased by 70,000 units per year. Expenditure on this capital equipment is also eligible for 50% first year tax allowable depreciation and a 25% reducing balance thereafter. This new equipment would have a scrap value of $14,000 after five years.

The managing director of Progrow is concerned that failure to invest in the new jack manufacturing process might lead to the company losing significant market share in the jack market if competitors were able to reduce their prices in real terms as a result of introducing the new process.

If the new jack manufacturing process is introduced Progrow proposes that prices of jacks would be kept constant for the next few years. Garden tool prices are expected to increase by an average of 5% per year, wage and material costs by 6% per year. All other production and maintenance costs are expected to increase by 4% per year.

The financial gearing of Progrow is not expected to change with either the adoption of the new jack production process, or expansion of garden tool production.

The company is listed on the AIM[1] and its overall beta equity is 1.30. The average beta equity of other garden tool manufacturers is 1.4, but no data is available for jack manufacturers. The average market weighted gearing of other garden tool manufacturers is 50% equity and 50% debt.

The appropriate risk free rate is 7% and the estimated market return 14%. Corporate taxation is at the rate of 25% and is payable one year in arrears. It is now late in the current tax year.

---

[1] Alternative Investments Market

Summarised statement of financial position of Progrow as at 31 March

	$000
Non-current assets	2,800
Current assets	2,400
Less: Current liabilities	(1,950)
	3,250
Non-current liabilities	
Bank loan	400
15% secured bond (redeemable at par after 10 years)	1,000
Issued share capital (25 cents par)	700
Reserves	1,150
	3,250

The company's ex-div share price is 162 cents and bond price $125. Garden tool and jack manufacture represent 60% and 40% respectively of the company's total market value. All cash flows may be assumed to occur at year-ends.

Corporate debt may be assumed to be risk free.

Required:

(a) **Prepare a report advising the directors of Progrow whether to purchase the new machines or to expand garden tool production. Highlight in your report any further information requirements, or other factors that might influence the decision process. Relevant calculations, including expected net present values, should form an appendix to your report. State clearly any assumptions that you make.** (28 marks)

(Approximately 20 marks are available for calculations and 8 for discussion)

(b) The managing director's daughter is attending a university degree course in accounting and finance. During a telephone call to his daughter the managing director mentioned the possible alternative investments. She replied that she had learned that:

   (i) Net present value is not an appropriate technique to use for strategic investment decisions as it ignores any future options that might occur due to the use of the new machines, or from the expansion of garden tool production.

   (ii) The use of betas is suspect, as the capital asset pricing model (CAPM) has significant theoretical and practical weaknesses. She suggested consideration of the arbitrage pricing theory as an alternative to using CAPM.

The managing director has only recently been convinced of the benefit of using net present value and is left confused by his daughter's comments.

Required:

Discuss the validity of the comments made by the managing director's daughter and whether or not the managing director should take them into account in the investment decision process. (12 marks)

(40 marks)

ADVANCED FINANCIAL MANAGEMENT (P4) – STUDY QUESTION BANK

Question 15 TAMPEM

The financial management team of Tampem Co is discussing how the company should appraise new investments. There is a difference of opinion between two managers:

> Manager A believes that net present value should be used as positive NPV investments are quickly reflected in increases in the company's share price.
>
> Manager B states that NPV is not good enough as it is only valid in potentially restrictive conditions and should be replaced by APV (adjusted present value).

Tampem has produced estimates of relevant cash flows and other financial information associated with a new investment. These are shown below:

Year	1	2	3	4
	$000	$000	$000	$000
Pre-tax operating cash flows	1,250	1,400	1,600	1,800

Notes:

(i) The investment will cost $5,400,000 payable immediately, including $600,000 for working capital and $400,000 for issue costs. $300,000 of issue costs is for equity and $100,000 for debt. Issue costs are not tax allowable.

(ii) The investment will be financed 50% equity, 50% debt which is believed to reflect its debt capacity.

(iii) Expected company gearing after the investment will change to 60% equity, 40% debt by market values.

(iv) The investment's equity beta is 1·5.

(v) Debt finance for the investment will be an 8% fixed rate bond.

(vi) Tax-allowable depreciation is 25% per year on a reducing balance basis.

(vii) The corporate tax rate is 30%. Tax is payable in the year that the taxable cash flow arises.

(viii) The risk free rate is 4% and the market return 10%.

(ix) The after tax realisable value of the investment as a continuing operation is estimated to be $1·5 million (including working capital) at the end of year 4.

(x) Working capital may be assumed to be constant during the four years.

Required:

(a) Calculate the expected NPV and APV of the proposed investment. (10 marks)

(b) Discuss briefly the validity of the views of the two managers. Use your calculations in (a) to illustrate and support the discussion. (5 marks)

(15 marks)

STUDY QUESTION BANK – ADVANCED FINANCIAL MANAGEMENT (P4)

Question 16 PROJECT REVIEW

You have been conducting a detailed review of an investment project proposed by one of the divisions of your business. The company's current weighted average cost of capital is 10% per annum.

The initial capital investment is for $150 million followed by $50 million one year later. The post-tax cash flows, for this project, in $million, including the estimated tax benefit from tax-allowable depreciation, are as follows:

Year	0	1	2	3	4	5	6
Capital investment (plant and machinery):							
First phase	–127·50						
Second phase		–36·88					
Project post-tax cash flow ($m)			44·00	68·00	60·00	35·00	20·00

Company tax is charged at 30% and is paid/recovered in the year in which the liability is incurred. The company has sufficient profits elsewhere to fully utilise tax-allowable depreciation on this project. Capital investment is eligible for initial tax-allowable depreciation of 50% followed by allowances of 25% per annum on a reducing balance basis.

You notice the following points when conducting your review:

(1) An interest charge of 8% per annum on a proposed $50 million loan has been included in the project's post-tax cash flow before tax has been calculated.

(2) Depreciation for the use of company shared assets of $4 million per annum has been charged in calculating the project post-tax cash flow.

(3) Activity based allocations of company indirect costs of $8 million have been included in the project's post-tax cash flow. However, additional corporate infrastructure costs of $4 million per annum have been ignored which would only be incurred if the project proceeds.

(4) It is expected that the capital equipment will be written off and disposed of at the end of year six. The proceeds of the sale of the capital equipment are expected to be $7 million which have been included in the forecast of the project's post-tax cash flow. You also notice that an estimate for site clearance of $5 million has not been included nor any tax saving recognised on the unclaimed balancing allowance on the disposal of the capital equipment.

Required:

(a) **Prepare a corrected project evaluation using the net present value technique supported by a separate assessment of the sensitivity of the project to a $1 million change in the initial capital expenditure.** (12 marks)

(b) **Estimate the discounted payback period and the duration for this project commenting on the relative advantages and disadvantages of each method.** (5 marks)

(c) **Draft a brief report for presentation to the board of directors with a recommendation on the acceptability of this project and on the techniques that the board should consider when reviewing capital investment projects in future.** (8 marks)

(25 marks)

ADVANCED FINANCIAL MANAGEMENT (P4) – STUDY QUESTION BANK

Question 17 DARON

The senior managers of Daron, a company located in a European country, are reviewing the company's medium term prospects. The company is in a declining industry and is heavily dependent on a single product. Sales volume is likely to fall for the next few years. A general election will take place in the near future and the managers believe that the future level of inflation will depend on the result of the election. Inflation is expected to remain at approximately 5% per year if political party A wins the election, or will quickly move to approximately 10% per year if party B wins the election. Opinion polls suggest that there is a 40% chance of party B winning. An increase in the level of inflation is likely to reduce the volume of sales of Daron.

Projected financial data for the next five years, including expected inflation where relevant, are shown below:

Political party A wins, inflation 5% per year
$million

	20X7	20X8	20X9	20Y0	20Y1
Operating cash flows:					
Sales	28	29	26	22	19
Variable costs	17	18	16	14	12
Fixed costs	3	3	3	3	3
Other financial data:					
Incremental working capital*	–	(1)	(2)	(3)	(3)
Tax-allowable depreciation	4	3	3	2	1

Political party B wins; inflation 10% per year million

	20X7	20X8	20X9	20Y0	20Y1
	$m	$m	$m	$m	$m
Operating cash flows:					
Sales	30	26	24	20	16
Variable costs	18	16	15	12	11
Fixed costs	3	3	4	4	4
Other financial data:					
Incremental working capital*	1	(2)	(2)	(3)	(3)
Tax-allowable depreciation	4	3	3	2	1

*A bracket signifies a decrease in working capital:

Tax-allowable depreciation will be negligible after 20Y1 in both cases.

Cash flows after year 20Y1, excluding tax savings from tax-allowable depreciation, are expected to be similar to year 20Y1 cash flows for a period of five years, after which substantial new fixed investment would be necessary in order to continue operations.

Working capital will remain approximately constant after the year 20Y1.

Corporate taxation is at a rate of 30% per year and is expected to continue at this rate. Tax may be assumed to be payable in the year that the income arises.

Daron's current ordinary share price is 92 centos (100 centos = $1).

Summarised statement of financial position of Daron as at 31 March 20X6

	$m
Tangible non-current assets	24
Net current assets	12
Total assets less current liabilities	36
Loans and other borrowings falling due after one year	14
Capital and reserves:	
Called up share capital (25 centos par value)	5
Reserves	17
	36

The company can currently borrow long term from its bank at an interest rate of 10% per year. This is likely to quickly rise to 15.5% per year if the political party B wins the election.

The real risk free rate (i.e. excluding inflation) is 4% and the real market return is 10%.

Daron's equity beta is estimated to be 1.25. This is not expected to significantly change if inflation increases.

Three alternatives are available to the managers of Daron:

(i) Recommend the sale of the company now. An informal, unpublicised, offer of $20 million for the company's shares has been received from a competitor.

(ii) Continue existing operations, with negligible capital investment for the foreseeable future.

(iii) If the political party A wins the election, diversify operations by buying a going concern in the hotel industry at a cost of $9 million. The purchase would be financed by the issue of 10% convertible bonds. Issue costs are 2% of the gross sum raised. Daron has no previous experience of the hotel industry.

Financial projections of the hotel purchase ($m)

	20X7	20X8	20X9	20Y0	20Y1
Revenue	9	10	11	12	13
Variable costs	6	6	7	7	8
Fixed costs	2	2	2	2	2
Other financial data:					
Incremental working capital	1	–	–	1	–

Tax-allowable depreciation is negligible for the hotel purchase. The after tax realisable value of the hotel at the end of year 20Y1 is expected to be $10 million, including working capital. The systematic risk of operating the hotels is believed to be similar to that of the company's existing operations.

ADVANCED FINANCIAL MANAGEMENT (P4) – STUDY QUESTION BANK

Required:

(a) Using the above data, prepare a report advising the managers of Daron which, if any, of the three alternatives to adopt. Include in your report comment on any weaknesses/ limitations of your data analysis. Relevant calculations, including:

  (i) estimates of the present values of future cash flows from existing operations; and

  (ii) the estimated adjusted present value (APV) of diversifying into the hotel industry

should form appendices to your report.

The book value and market value of debt may be assumed to be the same. State clearly any other assumptions that you make. (32 marks)

(Approximately 20 marks are available for calculations and 12 for discussion.)

(b) Details of the possible convertible bond issue for the purchase of the hotel are as follows:

10% $100 convertible bonds 20Y0, issued and redeemable at par. The bonds are convertible into 60 ordinary shares at any date between 1 January 20X2 and 31 December 20X4. The bonds are callable for conversion by the company subject to the company's ordinary share price exceeding 200 centos between 1 January 20X2 and 31 December 20X4 and puttable for redemption by the bond holders if the share price falls below 100 centos between the same dates.

Required:

Discuss the implications for Daron if the diversification is financed with convertible bonds with these terms. (8 marks)

(40 marks)

Question 18 MERCURY TRAINING

Mercury Training was established in 2006 and since that time it has developed rapidly. The directors are considering either a flotation or an outright sale of the company.

The company provides training for companies in the computer and telecommunications sectors. It offers a variety of courses ranging from short intensive courses in office software to high level risk management courses using advanced modelling techniques. Mercury employs a number of in-house experts who provide technical materials and other support for the teams that service individual client requirements. In recent years, Mercury has diversified into the financial services sector and now also provides computer simulation systems to companies for valuing acquisitions. This business now accounts for one third of the company's total revenue.

Mercury currently has 10 million, 50c shares in issue. Jupiter is one of the few competitors in Mercury's line of business. However, Jupiter is only involved in the training business. Jupiter is listed on a small company investment market and has an estimated beta of 1·5. Jupiter has 50 million shares in issue with a market price of 580c. The average beta for the financial services sector is 0·9. Average market gearing (debt to total market value) in the financial services sector is estimated at 25%.

Other summary statistics for both companies for the year ended 31 December 2014 are as follows:

	Mercury	Jupiter
Net assets at book value ($million)	65	45
Earnings per share (c)	100	50
Dividend per share (c)	25	25
Gearing (debt to total market value)	30%	12%
Five year historic earnings growth (annual)	12%	8%

Analysts forecast revenue growth in the training side of Mercury's business to be 6% per annum, but the financial services sector is expected to grow at just 4%.

Background information

The equity risk premium is 3·5% and the rate of return on short-dated government debt is 4·5%.
Both companies can raise debt at 2·5% above the risk free rate.
Tax on corporate profits is 40%.

Required:

(a) **Estimate the cost of equity capital and the weighted average cost of capital for Mercury Training. Explain the circumstances where each of the two rates would be used.**
(10 marks)

(b) **Advise the owners of Mercury Training on a range of likely issue prices for the company.** (8 marks)

(c) **Discuss the advantages and disadvantages, to the directors of Mercury Training, of a public listing versus private equity finance as a means of disposing of their interest in the company.** (7 marks)

(25 marks)

ADVANCED FINANCIAL MANAGEMENT (P4) – STUDY QUESTION BANK

Question 19 BIGUN

The acquisition committee of Bigun Co is considering making takeover bids for two competitors, Klein Co and PTT Co. Summarised financial data is given below for the three companies:

Statement of financial position as at 31 March 20Y2

	Bigun	$m	Klein	$m	PTT	$m
Non-current assets		50		8.6		6.4
Current assets	43[1]		6.7		9.5	
Less: Current liabilities	27		3.0		3.9	
		16		3.7		5.6
		66		12.3		12.0
Financed by						
Ordinary shares (50c)		17		5.0[2]		2.8[2]
Reserves		30		1.3		3.7
		47		6.3		6.5
Long term debt		19[3]		6.0[4]		5.5[5]
		66		12.3		12.0

1. of which $5 million cash
2. $1 ordinary shares
3. 8% bonds 20Z5 – 20Z8 currently trading at $80
4. 11% bonds 20Y2 – 20Y4 currently trading at $110
5. 7 year 10% bank loan

	Bigun	Klein	PTT
Average sales growth 20X8 – 20Y2	8%	10%	8%
Average growth in profit after tax and interest on medium and long-term debt 20X8 – 20Y2	6%	10.5%	9.5%
Average payout ratio 20X8 – 20Y2	60%	40%	75%
P/E ratio at 31 March 20Y2	18.4	18.6	–
Estimated required return on equity	9.5%	12%	13%
Profit before tax and interest on medium and long-term debt for year ended 31 March 20Y2	$10m	$1.5m	$1.4m

The corporation tax rate is 35%.

Required:

(a) **Prepare a report advising the main board of Bigun of the possible cost of acquiring each of the companies.** (15 marks)

(b) **Discuss alternative terms that might be offered to the shareholders of Klein and PTT and the implications of these terms for the shareholders of Bigun.** (10 marks)

(25 marks)

Question 20 DEMAST

Demast Co has grown during the last five years into one of the UK's most successful specialist games manufacturers. The company's success has been largely based on its Megaoid series of games and models, for which it holds patents in many developed countries. The company has attracted the interest of two companies, Nadion, a traditional manufacturer of games and toys, and BZO International, a conglomerate group that has grown rapidly in recent years through the strategy of acquiring what it perceives to be undervalued companies.

Summarised financial details of the three companies are shown below:

Demast Co

Summarised statement of financial position as at 31 December 20X3

	$000	$000
Non-current assets (net)		8,400
Current assets		
Inventory	5,500	
Receivables	3,500	
Cash	100	
		9,100
Less: Current liabilities		
Trade payables	4,700	
Tax payable	1,300	
Overdraft	1,200	
		(7,200)
		10,300
Medium and long term loans		(3,800)
Net assets		6,500
Financed by		
Ordinary shares (25 cents nominal)		1,000
Reserves		5,500
		6,500

Summarised statement of profit or loss for the year ended 31 December 20X3

	$000
Revenue	27,000
Profit before tax	4,600
Taxation	1,380
	3,220
Dividends	(1,500)
Retained earnings	1,720

ADVANCED FINANCIAL MANAGEMENT (P4) – STUDY QUESTION BANK

Additional information:

(1) The realisable value of inventory is believed to be 90% of its book value.
(2) Land and buildings, with a book value of $4 million were last revalued in 20X0.
(3) The directors of the company and their families own 25% of the company's shares.

	Demast	Nadion	BZO Int
Revenue ($m)	27	112	256
Profit before tax ($m)	4.6	11	24
Non-current assets ($m net)	8.4	26	123
Current assets ($m)	9.1	41	72
Current liabilities ($m)	7.2	33	91
Overdraft ($m)	1.2	6	30
Long term liabilities ($m)	3.8	18	35
Interest payable ($m)	0.5	3	10
Share price (cents)	–	320	780
EPS (cents)	80.5	58	51
Estimated required return on equity	16%	14%	12%
Growth trends per year			
Earnings	12%	6%	13%
Dividends	9%	5%	8%
Revenue	15%	10%	23%

Assume that the following events occurred shortly after the above financial information was produced:

7 September – BZO makes a bid for Demast of two ordinary shares for every three shares of Demast. The price of BZO's ordinary shares after the announcement of the bid is 710 cents. The directors of Demast reject the offer.

2 October – Nadion makes a counter bid of 170 cents cash per share plus one $100 10% convertible bond 20X8, issued at par, for every $6.25 nominal value of Demast's shares. Each convertible bond may be exchanged for 26 ordinary shares at any time between 1 January 20X7 and 31 December 20X9. Nadion's share price moves to 335 cents. This offer is rejected by the directors of Demast.

19 October – BZO offers cash of 600 cents per share. The cash will be raised by a term loan from the company's bank. The board of Demast are all offered seats on subsidiary boards within the BZO group. BZO's shares move to 680 cents.

20 October – The directors of Demast recommend acceptance of the revised offer from BZO.

24 October – BZO announces that 53% of shareholders have accepted its offer and makes the offer unconditional.

Required:

(a) **Discuss the advantages and disadvantages of growth by acquisition.** (4 marks)

(b) **Discuss whether or not the bids by BZO and Nadion are financially prudent from the point of view of the companies' shareholders. Relevant supporting calculations must be shown.** (16 marks)

(c) **Discuss problems of corporate governance that might arise for the shareholders of Demast and BZO.** (5 marks)

(25 marks)

STUDY QUESTION BANK – ADVANCED FINANCIAL MANAGEMENT (P4)

Question 21 LACETO

(a) Laceto Co, a large UK-based retail group specialising in the sale of clothing and electrical goods is currently considering a takeover bid for a competitor in the electrical goods sector, Omnigen Co, whose share price has fallen by 205 cents during the last three months.

Summarised data for the financial year to 31 March 20X1:

	Laceto $m	Omnigen $m
Revenue	420	180
Profit before tax (after interest payments)	41	20
Taxation	12	6
Non-current assets (net)	110	63
Current assets	122	94
Current liabilities	86	71
Medium and long-term liabilities	40	12
Shareholders' funds	106	74

The share price of Laceto is currently 380 cents and of Omnigen 410 cents. Laceto has 80 million issued ordinary shares and Omnigen 30 million. Typical of Laceto's medium and long-term liabilities is a 12% bond with three years to maturity, a par value of $100 and a current market price of $108·80.

The finance team of Laceto has produced the following forecasts of financial data for the activities of Omnigen if it is taken over:

Financial year	20X2 $m	20X3 $m	20X4 $m	20X5 $m
Net sales	230	261	281	298
Cost of goods sold (50%)	115	131	141	149
Selling and administrative expenses	32	34	36	38
Tax-allowable depreciation	40	42	42	42
Interest	18	16	14	12
Cash flow needed for asset replacement and forecast growth	50	52	55	58

Corporate taxation is at the rate of 30% per year, payable in the year that the taxable cash flow occurs.

The risk-free rate is 6% per year and market return 14% per year. Omnigen's current equity beta is 1·2. This is expected to increase by 0·1 if the company is taken over as Laceto would increase the current level of capital gearing associated with the activities of Omnigen. Laceto group's gearing post-acquisition is expected to be between 18% and 23% (debt to debt plus equity by market values), depending on the final price paid for Omnigen.

Post-takeover cash flows of Omnigen (after replacement and growth expenditure) are expected to grow at between 3% and 5% per year after 20X5.

Additional notes:

(i) The realisable value of Omnigen's assets, net of all debt repayments, is estimated to be $82 million.

(ii) The P/E ratios of two of Omnigen's quoted competitors in the electrical industry are 13 and 15 respectively.

Required:

Discuss and evaluate what price, or range of prices, Laceto should offer to purchase the shares of Omnigen. State clearly any assumptions that you make. (25 marks)

Approximately 17 marks are for calculations and 8 for discussion.

(b) Before making a bid for Omnigen the managing director of Laceto hears a rumour that a bid for Laceto might be made by Agressa.com Co, an Internet retailer specialising in the sale of vehicles and electrical goods. Summarised financial data for Agressa.com are shown below:

Agressa.com	$m
Revenue	190
Operating profit	12
Interest	4
Taxation	2
Non-current assets (net)	30
Current assets	80
Current liabilities	30
Medium and long-term liabilities	40
Shareholders' funds	40

Agressa's current share price is $26·50 and the company has 15 million issued ordinary shares.

Required:

Prepare a brief report for the managing director of Laceto which analyses how Laceto might defend itself from a takeover bid from Agressa.com. (8 marks)

(c) **Discuss how the method of payment for the potential takeovers in (a) and (b) above might affect the success or failure of the bids.** (7 marks)

(40 marks)

Question 22 MINPRICE & SAVEALOT

The directors of Minprice Co, a food retailer with 20 superstores, are proposing to make a takeover bid for Savealot Co, a company with six superstores in the north of England. Minprice will offer four of its ordinary shares for every three ordinary shares of Savealot. The bid has not yet been made public.

Summarised Accounts
Statements of financial position as at 31 March 20X0

			Minprice $m			Savealot $m
Land and buildings (net)			483			42·3
Non-current assets (net)			150			17·0
			633			59·3
Current assets						
Inventory	328			51·4		
Receivables	12			6·3		
Cash	44	384		5·3	63·0	
Current liabilities						
Payables	447			46·1		
Dividend	12			2·0		
Taxation	22	(481)	(97)	2·0	(50·1)	12·9
Non-current liabilities						
14% loan stock			(200)			–
Floating rate bank loans			(114)			(17·5)
			222			54·7
Shareholders' funds						
Ordinary shares (25 cents par)		75	Ordinary shares (50 cents par)	20·0		
Reserves			147			34·7
			222			54·7

Statement of profit or loss for the year ending 31 March 20X0

	$m	$m
Revenue	1,130	181
Earnings before interest and tax	115	14
Net interest	(40)	(2)
Profit before tax	75	12
Taxation	(25)	(4)
Available to shareholders	50	8
Dividends	(24)	(5)
Retained earnings	26	3

The current share price of Minprice is 232 cents and of Savealot 295 cents. The current loan stock price of Minprice is $125.

Recent annual growth trends:	Minprice	Savealot
Dividends	7%	8%
EPS	7%	10%

Rationalisation following the acquisition will involve the following transactions (all net of tax effects):

(i) Sale of surplus warehouse facilities for $6·8 million.

(ii) Redundancy payments costing $9·0 million.

(iii) Wage savings of $2·7 million per year for at least five years.

Minprice's cost of equity is estimated to be 14·5% and weighted average cost of capital 12%. Savealot's cost of equity is estimated to be 13%.

Required:

(a) **Discuss and evaluate whether or not the bid is likely to be viewed favourably by the shareholders of both Minprice and Savealot. Include discussion of the factors that are likely to influence the views of the shareholders.**

All relevant calculations must be shown. (12 marks)

(b) **Discuss the possible effects on the likely success of the bid if the offer terms were to be amended to a choice of one new Minprice 10 year zero coupon bond redeemable at $100 for every 10 Savealot shares, or 325 cents per share cash. Minprice could currently issue new 10 year loan stock at an interest rate of 10%.**

All relevant calculations must be shown. (8 marks)

(c) The directors of Savealot have decided to fight the bid and have proposed the following measures:

  (i) Announce that their company's profits are likely to be doubled next year.

  (ii) Alter the Articles of Association to require that at least 75% of shareholders need to approve an acquisition.

  (iii) Persuade, for a fee, a third party investor to buy large quantities of the company's shares.

  (iv) Introduce an advertising campaign criticising the performance and management ability of Minprice.

  (v) Revalue non-current assets to current values so that shareholders are aware of the company's true market values.

  Acting as a consultant to the company, give reasoned advice on whether or not the company should adopt each of these measures. (5 marks)

(25 marks)

Question 23 DRICOM

Dricom Co is a manufacturer of mobile phones. The company was successful in the early 20X0s and established a small chain of shops in major UK cities. In 20X5-6 the company's new products experienced reliability problems and competition from superior products, causing sales to fall by 40% from 20X4-5 levels. This lead to substantial losses being made in both 20X5–6 and 20X6–7.

The company's managers are confident that the technical problems can be overcome, but this will require an investment of $2.25 million for new automated equipment and quality monitoring machinery. Dricom's bank, BXT Bank, is concerned about the company's recent performance and a new debt or equity issue on the stock market is not possible. Without the new investment Dricom is unlikely to be competitive and might not survive the next year. With the new investment profits before interest and tax are forecast to be at least $750,000 per year from 20X8-9 for at least five years.

Dricom
Summarised statement of financial position as at 30 September 20X7

	$000
Land and buildings	1,500
Plant and machinery (net)	2,100
	3,600
Current assets	
Inventory	1,340
Receivables	1,090
Cash at bank and in hand	35
Total current assets	2,465
Liabilities: amounts falling due within one year	
Overdraft	620
Other payables	940
	1,560
Total assets less current liabilities	4,505
Liabilities: amounts falling due after more than one year	
Term loan (from BXT Bank)	800
9% bond 20Y0	500
8% convertible bond 20X9	1,000
10% loan stock 20Y5	500
	2,800
Capital and reserves	
Called up share capital ($1 par value)	1,000
Share premium account	945
Retained earnings	(240)
Total shareholders' funds	1,705
Total capital employed	4,505

ADVANCED FINANCIAL MANAGEMENT (P4) – STUDY QUESTION BANK

Notes:

(i) The 9% straight bond is secured by a fixed charge on the company's main factory building, the convertible bond and term loan by a floating charge on tangible non-current assets. The loan stock and overdraft are unsecured.

(ii) The land and buildings are believed to have a realisable value 20% less than their net book value.

(iii) If the company ceased trading inventory would be sold at 50% of their book value.

(iv) The new equipment would result in fifty staff being made redundant, with an immediate after tax cost of $500,000. If the company were to be liquidated after tax redundancy payments would total $1 million. Redundancy payments may be assumed to rank before unsecured creditors.

(v) Obsolete machinery with a net book value of $800,000 will be sold for $300,000 irrespective of whether or not the new investment takes place. The remainder of the plant and machinery could be disposed of at net book value. All disposal values are after tax.

(vi) The overdraft currently costs 10% per year and the bank term loan 12% per year.

(vii) The company's current share price is 23 cents, loan stock price $78, straight bond price $90 and convertible bond price $94. All marketable debt has a par and redemption value of $100.

Dricom's finance director believes that a corporate restructuring could solve the company's problems and has made the following proposals:

(i) Existing shareholders are to be offered 28 cents per share to redeem their shares, which would then be cancelled.

(ii) $1 million would be provided by a venture capital organisation in return for 700,000 new 25 cents par value ordinary shares.

(iii) The company's directors and employees would subscribe to 500,000 new 25 cents ordinary shares at a price of 150 cents per share.

(iv) The convertible bond is to be replaced by new ordinary shares (par value 25 cents), with 60 ordinary shares for every $100 nominal value loan stock.

(v) The term loan is to be renegotiated with the bank and the total amount of the loan increased to $2 million. This would have an expected interest charge of 13% per year. A floating charge on tangible non-current assets would be offered on the overdraft.

(vi) All other long-term loans would remain unchanged.

Apart from the directors, none of the above parties have yet been consulted regarding the proposed reconstruction.

Following a reconstruction no corporate tax is expected to be paid for at least two years. The corporate tax rate is 33%.

The average price/earnings ratio in Dricom's industry is 12:1.

Required:

Acting as a consultant to Dricom prepare a report evaluating whether or not the suggested scheme of reconstruction is likely to succeed.

A full pro forma statement of financial position is NOT required as part of your evaluation. State clearly any assumptions that you make.

(25 marks)

Question 24 ASTER

The directors of ASTER Co have decided to concentrate the company's activities on three core areas, bus services, road freight and taxis. As a result the company has offered for sale a regional airport that it owns. The airport handles a mixture of short-haul scheduled services, holiday charter flights and airfreight, but does not have a runway long enough for long-haul international operations.

The existing managers of the airport, along with some employees, are attempting to purchase the airport through a leveraged management buy-out and would form a new unquoted company, Airgo Co.

The total value of the airport (free of any debt) has been independently assessed at $35 million.

The managers and employees can raise a maximum of $4 million towards this cost. This would be invested in new ordinary shares issued at the par value of 50 cents per share. ASTER, as a condition of the sale, proposes to subscribe to an initial 20% equity holding in the company and would repay all debt of the airport prior to the sale.

EPP Bank is prepared to offer a floating rate loan of $20 million to the management team, at an initial interest rate of LIBOR plus 3%. LIBOR is currently at 10%. This loan would be for a period of seven years, repayable on maturity and would be secured against the airport's land and buildings. A condition of the loan is that gearing, measured by the book value of total loans to equity, is no more than 100% at the end of four years. If this condition is not met the bank has the right to call in its loan at one month's notice. Airgo would be able to purchase a four-year interest rate cap at 15% for its loan from EPP Bank for an upfront premium of $800,000.

A venture capital company, Allvent is willing to provide up to $15 million in the form of unsecured mezzanine debt with attached warrants. This loan would be for a five-year period, with principal repayable in equal annual instalments and have a fixed interest rate of 18% per year.

The warrants would allow Allvent to purchase 10 Airgo shares at a price of 100 cents each for every $100 of initial debt provided, any time after two years from the date the loan is agreed. The warrants would expire after five years.

Most recent annual statement of profit or loss of the airport

	$000
Landing fees	14,000
Other revenue	8,600
	22,600
Labour	5,200
Consumables	3,800
Central overhead payable to ASTER	4,000
Other expenses	3,500
Interest paid	2,500
	19,000
Taxable profit	3,600
Taxation (33%)	1,188
Retained earnings	2,412

ASTER has offered to continue to provide central accounting, personnel and marketing services to Airgo for a fee of $3 million per year, with the first fee payable in year one.

All revenues and costs (excluding interest) are expected to increase by approximately 5% per year.

Required:

(a) **Prepare a report for the managers of the proposed Airgo discussing the advantages and disadvantages for the management buy-out of the proposed financing mix. Include in your report an evaluation of whether or not the EPP Bank's gearing restriction in four years' time is likely to be a problem and, if so, suggest what actions might be taken to solve the problem.**

All relevant calculations must be shown. State clearly any assumptions that you make.

(20 marks)

(b) As a possible alternative to obtaining finance from Allvent, assume that a venture capital company that you are employed by has been approached by the management buy-out team for a $10 million loan.

Discuss what information, other than that provided above, would be required from the MBO team in order to decide whether or not to agree to the loan. (5 marks)

(25 marks)

STUDY QUESTION BANK – ADVANCED FINANCIAL MANAGEMENT (P4)

Question 25 MBO

You have been asked to advise on the financing of a management buy-out. The buy-out will cost a total of $5 million of which 60% will be financed by a 10% fixed rate loan and 40% by $1 ordinary shares. Half of the ordinary shares would be subscribed by the buy-out team at par, the other half by a venture capitalist also at par. The venture capitalist's shares have warrants attached which permit the purchase of an equal amount of ordinary shares at par any time up to seven years in the future. The 10% loan would be repayable over a period of four years in equal annual instalments comprising both interest and principal. As part of the proposed deal the buy-out team must also take over the responsibility of servicing an existing $2 million 8% loan which is due to mature in ten years' time with the principal repayable on maturity by the buy-out team. No dividends are expected to be paid during the next four years. The current earnings before interest and tax are $1·1 million, and the corporate tax rate is 30% per annum. If the buy-out occurs, operating efficiencies are expected to allow growth in earnings before interest and tax of 4% per year for up to four years, without additional capital investment.

Required:

(a) The management buy-out team hopes to achieve a listing on the Alternative Investments Market (AIM) in four years' time. They have been told that a successful AIM issue is likely to require a book value capital gearing level of not more than 40% debt to equity.

   Advise the buy-out team whether or not this is likely to be achieved. (7 marks)

(b) **Provide a reasoned estimate of the MINIMUM price per share that might be expected in four years' time if a successful AIM issue takes place.** (3 marks)

(10 marks)

Question 26 EQUITY AND DEBT ISSUES

(a) **Describe the methods of raising new equity finance that can be used by an unlisted company.** (8 marks)

(b) **Discuss the factors to be considered by a listed company when choosing between an issue of debt and an issue of equity finance.** (7 marks)

(15 marks)

Question 27 IXT

Mr Axelot has just inherited the controlling interest in IXT Co. At his first board of directors' meeting an item for discussion is the financing of a £5 million expansion scheme. Mr Axelot has read that debt finance is normally cheaper than equity finance and suggests that all external finance during the next five years should be in the form of debt. For the expansion scheme he has suggested using either-

(a) A fixed rate 10-year Swiss Franc (CHF) bond for 12.25 million CHF issued in Zurich at an interest rate of 8% per year or

(b) A 13% bond 20X4–20X6 issued at par of £100 with warrants to purchase ordinary shares in five years' time at a price of 450 pence per share.

A director has challenged Mr Axelot's five year financing strategy, saying that it would be too risky, and has suggested that the £5 million expansion scheme be financed using a placing of new ordinary shares at a price of 245 pence per share.

Financial details of IXT are summarised below. Earnings before interest payable and tax are expected to increase by 20% per year for the next five years, during which time approximately £5 million per year will be required from external financing sources. The company normally uses a dividend payout ratio of 40% and corporate tax rates are not expected to change. IXT's current share price is 250 pence ex-dividend.

The level of inflation in Switzerland is 2% per year and in the United Kingdom 8% per year. The current spot exchange rate is CHF 2.445 – 2.450 per £.

IXT summarised statement of financial position as at 31 March 20X1

	£000	£000
Non-current assets		
Tangible non-current assets		33,000
Investments		4,500
		37,500
Current assets		
Inventory	12,400	
Receivables	9,200	
Bank	1,400	
		23,000
Current liabilities		
Short-term loans	(4,200)	
Overdrafts	(6,400)	
Trade payables	(10,100)	
Other	(1,800)	
		(22,500)
Liabilities falling due after more than one year		
Bonds and loan stock	(5,000)	
Unsecured bank loans	(8,400)	
		(13,400)
		24,600
Capital and reserves		
Issued share capital (25 pence par value)		4,000
Share premium account		3,500
Revaluation reserve		3,900
Retained earnings		13,200
		24,600

IXT summarised statement of profit or loss for the year ending 31 March 20X1

	£000
Revenue	53,500
Operating profit	13,400
Investment income	350
Interest payable	3,000
Taxable income	10,750
Taxation	3,762
Profit after tax	6,988
Dividends	2,795
Profit retained for the year	4,193

Required:

(a) **Explain why the cost of debt finance for a company is normally less than the cost of equity finance.** (4 marks)

Relevant calculations should be included to your answers to *both* parts (b) and (c) of this question.

State clearly any assumptions that you make.

(b) **Appraise Mr Axelot's suggested strategy that all external financing during the next five years should be in the form of debt.** (8 marks)

(c) **Discuss whether IXT should finance the *current* £5 million expansion project with the Swiss franc bond, the 13% bond or the placing.** (9 marks)

(d) A non-executive director mentions that his company has recently used mezzanine financing and suggests that IXT might consider this form of financing.

Explain briefly what mezzanine financing is and how it might be useful to IXT. (4 marks)

(25 marks)

Question 28 NEW DEBT ISSUE

Your company, which is in the airline business, is considering raising new capital of $400 million in the bond market for the acquisition of new aircraft. The debt would have a term to maturity of four years. The market capitalisation of the company's equity is $1·2 billion and it has a 25% market gearing ratio (market value of debt to total market value of the company). This new issue would be ranked for payment, in the event of default, equally with the company's other long-term debt and the latest credit risk assessment places the company at AA. Interest would be paid to holders annually. The company's current debt carries an average coupon of 4% and has three years to maturity. The company's effective rate of tax is 30%.

The current yield curve suggests that, at three years, government treasuries yield 3·5% and at four years they yield 5·1%. The current credit risk spread is estimated to be 50 basis points at AA. If the issue proceeds, the company's investment bankers suggest that a 90 basis point spread will need to be offered to guarantee take up by its institutional clients.

ADVANCED FINANCIAL MANAGEMENT (P4) – STUDY QUESTION BANK

Required:

(a) Advise on the coupon rate that should be applied to the new debt issue to ensure that it is fully subscribed. **(4 marks)**

(b) Estimate the current and revised market valuation of the company's debt and the increase in the company's effective cost of debt capital. **(6 marks)**

(c) Discuss the relative advantages and disadvantages of this mode of capital financing in the context of the company's stated financial objectives. **(5 marks)**

(15 marks)

Question 29 PAVLON

(a) Pavlon Co has recently obtained a listing on a Stock Exchange. 90% of the company's shares were previously owned by members of one family but since the listing approximately 60% of the issued shares have been owned by other investors. Pavlon's earnings and dividends for the five years prior to the listing are detailed below.

Year prior to listing	Profit after tax $	Dividend per share cents
5	1,800,000	3.60
4	2,400,000	4.80
3	3,850,000	6.16
2	4,100,000	6.56
1	4,450,000	7.12
Current year	5,500,000	

The number of issued ordinary shares was increased by 25% three years prior to the listing and by 50% at the time of the listing. The company's authorised capital is currently $25 million in 25 cents ordinary shares, of which 40 million shares have been issued. The market value of the company's equity is $78 million cum-dividend.

The board of directors is discussing future dividend policy. An interim dividend of 3.16 cents per share was paid immediately after the listing and a final dividend of 2.34 cents per share has just been declared.

The company's stated objective is to maximise shareholder wealth.

Required:

(i) Comment on the nature of the company's dividend policy prior to the listing and discuss whether such a policy is likely to be suitable for a company listed on the Stock Exchange.

(ii) Discuss whether the proposed final dividend of 2.34 cents is likely to be an appropriate dividend if the majority of the shares are owned by:

(1) wealthy private individuals;
(2) institutional investors.

(8 marks)

(b) The company's profit after tax is generally expected to increase by 15% per year for three years and 8% per year after that. Pavlon's cost of equity capital is estimated to be 12% per year. Dividends may be assumed to grow at the same rate as profits.

STUDY QUESTION BANK – ADVANCED FINANCIAL MANAGEMENT (P4)

Required:

(i) Using the dividend valuation model, give calculations to indicate whether shares of Pavlon are currently undervalued or overvalued.

(ii) Briefly outline the weaknesses of the dividend valuation model. **(7 marks)**

(15 marks)

Question 30 TYR

Summarised financial data for TYR Co is shown below:

Year	Post-tax earnings ($m)	Dividends ($m)	Issued shares (million)	Share price (cents)
20X7	86·2	34·5	180	360
20X8	92·4	36·2	180	410
20X9	99·3	37·6	180	345
20Y0	134·1	51·6	240	459
20Y1	148·6	53·3	240	448

Year	S&P 500 index	Inflation rate
20X7	2895	6%
20X8	3300	5%
20X9	2845	4%
20Y0	2610	3%
20Y1	2305	3%

TYR's cost of equity is estimated to be 11%.

Required:

(a) Explain, with supporting numerical evidence, the current dividend policy of TYR and briefly discuss whether or not this appears to be successful. **(6 marks)**

(b) Identify and consider additional information that might assist the managers of TYR in assessing whether the dividend policy has been successful. **(4 marks)**

(c) Evaluate whether or not the company's share price at the end of 20Y1 was what might have been expected from the Dividend Growth Model. Briefly discuss the validity of your findings. **(5 marks)**

(15 marks)

Question 31 UNIGLOW

(a) Briefly discuss the meaning and importance of the terms "delta", "theta" and "vega" (also known as kappa or lamba) in option pricing. **(5 marks)**

(b) Assume that your company has invested in 100,000 shares of Uniglow Co, a manufacturer of light bulbs. You are concerned about the recent volatility in Uniglow's share price due to the unpredictable weather. You wish to protect your company's investment from a possible fall in Uniglow's share price until winter in three months' time, but do not wish to sell the shares at present. No dividends are due to be paid by Uniglow during the next three months.

ADVANCED FINANCIAL MANAGEMENT (P4) – STUDY QUESTION BANK

Market data:

Uniglow's current share price: 200 cents
Call option exercise price: 220 cents
Time to expiry: 3 months
Interest rates (annual): 6%
Volatility of Uniglow's shares 50% (standard deviation per year)

Assume that option contracts are for the purchase or sale of units of 1,000 shares.

Required:

(i) **Devise a delta hedge that is expected to protect the investment against changes in the share price until winter. Delta may be estimated using $N(d_1)$.** (8 marks)

(ii) **Comment on whether or not such a hedge is likely to be totally successful.**
(2 marks)

(15 marks)

Question 32 BIOPLASM

Bioplasm Co has completed the preliminary development of a new drug to combat a major disease. Initial clinical trials of the drug have been favourable and the drug is expected to receive approval from the regulatory authority in the near future. Bioplasm has taken out a patent on the drug that gives it the exclusive right to commercially develop and market the drug for a period of 15 years. Although it is difficult to produce precise estimates, the company believes that to commercially develop and market the drug for worldwide use will cost approximately $400 million at current prices. The expected present value from sales of the drug during the patent period could vary between $350 million and $500 million. The current long-term government bond yield is 5%. The annual variance (standard deviation squared) of returns on similar biotech companies is estimated to be 0·185.

The finance director of Bioplasm can see from the possible net present values that the company has a difficult decision as to whether or not to develop the drug and wonders if option pricing could assist the decision.

Required:

Using the Black-Scholes option pricing model for the life of the patent, estimate the call values of the option to commercially develop and market the drug. Provide a reasoned recommendation, based on your calculations and any other relevant information, as to whether or not Bioplasm should develop the drug.

Note: Because the value of the returns from the patent will fall over the period before the drug is commercially developed, it is necessary to adjust the expected present value from sales of the drug. In all relevant parts of the Black-Scholes model, the present value from sales of the drug should be multiplied by $\exp^{(-0.067)(15)}$ to reflect this potential reduction in value according to when the drug is developed.

(15 marks)

Question 33 FORUN

(a) Forun Co, a UK-registered company, operates in four foreign countries, with total foreign subsidiary revenue of the equivalent of £60 million. The managing director is conducting a strategic review of the company's operations, with a view to increasing operations in some markets and to reducing the scale of operations in others. He has assembled economic and other data on the four countries where subsidiaries are located which he considers to be of particular interest. His major concern is foreign exchange risk of overseas operations.

		Country			
	UK	1	2	3	4
Inflation rate (%)	4	8	15	9	6
Real GDP growth (%)	1	–2	3	2	2
Balance of payments ($b)	–12	3	–14	5	–2
Base rate (%)	6	10	14	10	8
Unemployment rate	12	8	17	4	9
Population (million)	56	48	120	29	9
Currency reserves ($b)	35	20	18	26	3
IMF loans ($b)	–	4	20	5	5

On the basis of this information the managing director proposes that activity is concentrated in countries 1 and 4 and operations are reduced in countries 2 and 3.

A non-executive director believes that the meeting should not be focusing on such long-term strategic dimensions, as he has just read the report of the finance director who has forecast a foreign exchange loss on net exposed assets on consolidation of £15 million for the current financial year. The non-executive director is concerned with the detrimental impact he expects this loss to have on the company's share price. He further suggests a number of possible hedging strategies to be undertaken by Forun's foreign subsidiaries in order to reduce the exposure and the consolidated loss. These include:

(i) early collection of foreign currency receivables;
(ii) early repayment of foreign currency loans;
(iii) reducing inventory levels in foreign countries.

Required:

(i) **Discuss whether or not you agree with the managing director's proposed strategy with respect to countries 1 to 4.** (8 marks)

(ii) **Give advice as to the benefit of the non-executive director's suggested hedging strategies.** (10 marks)

(b) Forun has a number of intra-group transactions with its four foreign subsidiaries in six months' time and several large international trade deals with third parties. These are summarised below. Intra-group transactions are denominated in US dollars. All third party international trade is denominated in the currency shown.

Intra-group transactions

Receiving company	Paying company				
	UK	Sub 1	Sub 2	Sub 3	Sub 4
			US $000		
UK	–	300	450	210	270
1	700	–	420	–	180
2	140	340	–	410	700
3	300	140	230	–	350
4	560	300	110	510	–

Exports to third parties: Receipts due in six months (today is 1 June):

£2,000,000 from Australia
A$3,000,000 from Australia
$12 million from the US
£1,800,000 from Germany

Imports from third parties: Payments due in six months:

£3,000,000 to the US
A$3,000,000 to Australia
NZ$13 million to New Zealand
£2,000,000 to France

Foreign exchange rates

	Spot	3 month forward	6 month forward
US$ per £	1.4960 – 1.4990	1.4720 – 1.4770	1.4550 – 1.4600
A$ per £	2.1460 – 2.1500	2.1780 – 2.1840	2.2020 – 2.2090
NZ$ per £	2.4560 – 2.4590	2.4140 – 2.4180	2.3830 – 2.3870

Futures market rates
Sterling £62,500 contracts

	US$ per £	NZ$ per £
September	1.4820	2.4510
December	1.4800	2.4480

Minimum price movements are: US$ per £ 0.01 cents, NZ$ per £ 0.01 cents

Foreign currency option rates
Sterling £31,250 contracts (cents per £)

	Calls		Puts	
Exercise price	September	December	September	December
US$1.450 per £	3.50	5.75	4.80	7.90
US$1.475 per £	1.86	3.42	6.95	9.08
US$1.500 per £	0.82	1.95	9.80	11.53
US$1.525 per £	0.38	0.90	12.16	14.70

Required:

(i) **Explain and demonstrate how multilateral netting might be of benefit to Forun.** (5 marks)

STUDY QUESTION BANK – ADVANCED FINANCIAL MANAGEMENT (P4)

(ii) **Recommend, with supporting calculations, alternative hedging strategies that the company might adopt to protect itself against short-term foreign exchange exposure. You can assume no change in basis on futures contracts.** (17 marks)

(40 marks)

Question 34 STORACE

Storace, a UK-based company, has recently finalised a contract with a US company, Jacquin Inc, for the supply of a machine. The selling price is £100,000. As this is the first export sale made by Storace, the currency settlement details were not discussed at the meeting when the sale of the machine was agreed. The management of Storace believes that Jacquin Inc will agree to whatever currency settlement is suggested, since Jacquin Inc is very anxious that the machine contract be finalised quickly. Delivery of the machine will take place in three months' time when the amount will be settled immediately by Jacquin Inc.

The management of Storace is considering three possible methods of invoicing Jacquin Inc for the machine.

(i) Prepare the invoice in sterling (i.e. £100,000) and request payment in sterling on the settlement date.

(ii) Convert the sterling price at the current sterling/dollar spot rate and invoice Jacquin Inc in dollars. Buy sterling at the spot rate in three months' time when the dollar settlement is made by Jacquin Inc.

(iii) Invoice Jacquin Inc in dollars, converting the sterling price at the spot rate (as in (ii)). Storace will then immediately cover the position in the forward exchange market, by selling the dollars receivable forward at the three month forward exchange rate.

The current spot rate between sterling and dollars in London is £1 = $1.11. The premium for the dollar for three month forward exchange contracts is quoted as 1.20 – 1.15 cents. The management of Storace believes that the sterling/dollar spot rate will be somewhere in the range of £1 = $1.20 to £1 = $1.09 in three months' time.

Required:

(a) **Calculate the amount of sterling to be received by Storace under each of the three methods.** (4 marks)

(b) **Prepare a report to the management of Storace which sets out the advantages and disadvantages of each method and contains your recommendation on the choice of method.** (6 marks)

(c) **Outline the implications for corporate financial management of undertaking a major export sales drive.** (5 marks)

Ignore taxation.

(15 marks)

ADVANCED FINANCIAL MANAGEMENT (P4) – STUDY QUESTION BANK

Question 35 PARTICIPATING OPTION

Your UK-based company has won an export order worth $1·8 million from the US. Payment is due to be made to you in dollars in six months' time. It is now 15 November. You wish to protect the exchange rate risk with currency options, but do not wish to pay an option premium of more than £10,000.

Your bank has suggested using a participating currency option which has no premium. The option would allow a worst-case exchange rate at which the option could be exercised of $1·65 per £. If the contract moved in your favour then the bank would share (participate in) the profits and would take 50% of any gains relative to the current spot exchange rate.

You also have access to currency options on the Philadelphia Stock Exchange.

Current option prices are:

Sterling contracts, £31,250 contract size. Premium is US cents per £.

	Calls			Puts		
Exercise price	December	March	June	December	March	June
1·55	6·8	7·9	10·1	0·2	0·5	0·9
1·60	2·1	3·8	5·3	1·9	3·1	4·0
1·65	0·6	0·9	1·1	5·1	7·2	9·6
1·70	0·1	0·2	0·4	10·1	12·3	14·1

The current spot rate is $1·6055 – 1·6100 per £. Any option premium would be payable immediately.

Required:

Evaluate whether a participating option or traded option is likely to offer a better foreign exchange hedge.

(10 marks)

Question 36 MJY CO

Assume that it is now 31 December. MJY Co is a UK-based multinational company that has subsidiaries in two foreign countries. Both subsidiaries trade with other group members and with four third party companies (company 1 – company 4).

Projected trade transactions for three months' time are shown below. All currency amounts are in thousands.

	Payments (read down)						
Receipts (read across)	Co 1	Co 2	Co 3	Co 4	MJY	Subsidiary 1	Subsidiary 2
MJY	$90	£60	€75	–	–	£40	$50
Subsidiary 1	£50	€85	$40	$20	€72	–	€20
Subsidiary 2	£15	–	€52	$30	£55	€35	–
Company 1	–	–	–	–	–	–	–
Company 2	–	–	–	–	$170	–	–
Company 3	–	–	–	–	$120	€50	–
Company 4	–	–	–	–	–	–	€65

Foreign exchange rates

	$ per £	€ per £
Spot	1·7982 – 1·8010	1·4492 – 1·4523
3 months forward	1·7835 – 1·7861	1·4365 – 1·4390

$/£ options. £62,500 contract size. Premium in cents per £.

	Calls		Puts	
Strike price	February	May	February	May
1·80	1·96	3·00	3·17	5·34
1·78	2·91	3·84	2·12	4·20

Required:

Working from the perspective of a group treasurer, devise a hedging strategy for the MJY group, and calculate the expected outcomes of the hedges using forward markets, and, for the dollar exposure only, currency options.

(15 marks)

Question 37 OMNIOWN

(a) It is now 31 December 20X1 and the corporate treasurer of Omniown Co, a UK-based company, is concerned about the volatility of interest rates. His company needs in three months' time to borrow £5 million for a six month period. Current interest rates are 14% per year for the type of loan Omniown would use and the treasurer does not wish to pay more than this.

He is considering using:

(i) a forward rate agreement (FRA); or
(ii) interest rate futures; or
(iii) an interest rate cap.

Required:

Explain briefly how each of these three alternatives might be useful to Omniown.

(10 marks)

(b) The corporate treasurer of Omniown expects interest rates to increase by 2% during the next three months and has decided to hedge the interest rate risk using interest rate futures.

March three-month sterling futures are currently priced at 86.25. The standard contract size is £500,000 and the minimum price movement is one tick (the value of one tick is 0.01% per year of the contract size).

Required:

Show the effect of using the futures market to hedge against interest rate movements:

(i) **if interest rates increase by 2% and the futures market price also moves by 2%;**

(ii) **if interest rates increase by 2% and the futures market moves by 1.5%;**

(iii) **if interest rates fall by 1% and the future market moves by 0.75%.**

In each case estimate the hedge efficiency.

Taxation, margin requirements and the time value of money are to be ignored. (10 marks)

(c) As an alternative to interest rate futures, the corporate treasurer had been able to purchase an interest rate cap at 14% for a premium of 0.2% of the size of the loan to be protected. The cap would be effective for the entire six month period of the loan.

Required:

Calculate whether the total cost of the loan after hedging in each of the situations (b)(i) to (b)(iii) above would have been less with the futures hedge or with the cap.

Taxation, margin requirements and the time value of money are to be ignored. (5 marks)

(25 marks)

Question 38 MANLING

(a) **Explain and illustrate what is meant by disintermediation and securitisation. Discuss how disintermediation and securitisation can help the financial manager.** (8 marks)

(b) Manling Co, a UK-based company, has £14 million of fixed rate loans at an interest rate of 12% per year which are due to mature in one year. The company's treasurer believes that interest rates are going to fall, but does not wish to redeem the loans because large penalties exist for early redemption. Manling's bank has offered to arrange an interest rate swap for one year with a company that has obtained floating rate finance at London Interbank Offered Rate (LIBOR) plus $1\frac{1}{8}$%. The bank will charge each of the companies an arrangement fee of £20,000 and the proposed terms of the swap are that Manling will pay LIBOR plus $1\frac{1}{2}$% to the other company and receive from the company $11\frac{5}{8}$%.

Corporate tax is at 35% per year and the arrangement fee is a tax allowable expense. Manling could issue floating rate debt at LIBOR plus 2% and the other company could issue fixed rate debt at $11\frac{3}{4}$%. Assume that any tax relief is immediately available.

Required:

(i) **Evaluate whether Manling would benefit from the interest rate swap:**

    (1) **if LIBOR remains at 10% for the whole year;**
    (2) **if LIBOR falls to 9% after six months.** (6 marks)

(ii) **If LIBOR remains at 10% evaluate whether both companies could benefit from the interest rate swap if the terms of the swap were altered. Any benefit would be equally shared.** (6 marks)

(c) **Manling expects to have £1 million surplus funds for three months prior to making a tax payment. Discuss possible short-term investments for these funds.** (5 marks)

(25 marks)

Question 39 MURWALD

The corporate treasury team of Murwald Co, a UK-based company, is debating what strategy to adopt towards interest rate risk management. The company's financial projections show an expected cash deficit in three months' time of £12 million, which will last for a period of approximately six months. Base rate is currently 6% per year and Murwald can borrow at 1.5% over base, or invest at 1% below base. The treasury team believe that the European Central Bank will raise Euro-area interest rates by 2%, which could lead to a similar rise in UK interest rates.

The corporate treasury team believes that interest rates are more likely to rise than to fall and does not want interest payments during the six month period to increase by more than £10,000 from the amounts that would be paid at current interest rates. It is now 1 December.

LIFFE prices (1 December)

Futures

LIFFE £500,000 three month sterling interest rate (points of 100%):

December	93.75
March	93.45
June	93.10

Options

LIFFE £500,000 short sterling options (points of 100%):

Exercise price	Calls June	Puts June
9200	3.33	
9250	2.93	–
9300	2.55	0.92
9350	2.20	1.25
9400	1.74	1.84
9450	1.32	2.90
9500	0.87	3.46

Required:

(a) **Illustrate results of futures and options hedges if by 1 March:**

(i) Interest rates rise by 2%. Futures prices move by 1.8%;
(ii) Interest rates fall by 1%. Futures prices move by 0.9%.

Recommend with reason how Murwald should hedge its interest rate exposure. All relevant calculations must be shown. State clearly any assumptions you make.

Taxation, transactions costs and margin requirements may be ignored. **(20 marks)**

(b) **Discuss the advantages and disadvantages of other derivative products that Murwald might have used to hedge the risk.** **(5 marks)**

(25 marks)

ADVANCED FINANCIAL MANAGEMENT (P4) – STUDY QUESTION BANK

Question 40 TURKEY

On 1 December Turkey Co, a UK-based company, forecast a cash deficit of up to £3 million for the four-month period 1 February – 31 May and proposed to take out a loan for this amount on 1 February. The corporate treasurer is worried that in the intervening period interest rates might rise.

You are given the following information:

LIFFE £500,000 3 month sterling future prices:

December	91.25
March	91.44
June	91.33
September	91.18

Both 3-month and 6-month certificates of deposit (CDs) were quoted at 8.8% (annualised rate). The company can borrow at the CD rate.

On 1 February, the following prices prevailed:

March	89.34
June	89.01
September	88.92

The CD rate was 11.20% for both 3- and 6-month deposits. The loan was taken out as planned.

Required:

(a) **Provide a reasoned analysis of Turkey's problem and recommend a suitable hedging strategy as at 1 December, justifying the type and number of contracts chosen.** (8 marks)

(b) **Evaluate the success of your strategy using 1 February data and explain why the hedge was not perfect.** (7 marks)

(15 marks)

Question 41 GLOBAL DEBT

(a) **Discuss the reasons for the existence of the "global debt problem". Explain briefly what is meant by financial contagion and how financial contagion might affect the global debt problem.** (7 marks)

(b) **Explain the main attempts that have been made to resolve the global debt problem and how governments might try to limit financial contagion.** (8 marks)

(15 marks)

Question 42 BEELA ELECTRONICS

The finance department of Beela Electronics, a UK-based company, has been criticised by the company's board of directors for not undertaking an assessment of the political risk of the company's potential direct investments in Africa. The board has received an interim report from a consultant that provides an assessment of the factors affecting political risk in three African countries. The report assesses key variables on a scale of –10 to +10, with –10 the worst possible score and +10 the best.

	Country 1	Country 2	Country 3
Economic growth	5	8	4
Political stability	3	–4	5
Risk of nationalisation	3	0	4
Cultural compatibility	6	2	4
Inflation	7	–6	6
Currency convertibility	–2	5	–4
Investment incentives	–3	7	3
Labour supply	2	8	–3

The consultant suggests that economic growth and political stability are twice as important as the other factors.

The consultant states in the report that previous clients have not invested in countries with a total weighted score of less than 30 out of a maximum possible 100 (with economic growth and political stability double weighted). The consultant therefore recommends that no investment in Africa should be undertaken.

Required:

(a) **Discuss whether or not Beela electronics should use the technique suggested by the consultant in order to decide whether or not to invest in Africa.** (8 marks)

(b) **Discuss briefly how Beela might manage political risk if it decides to invest in Africa.**

(7 marks)

(15 marks)

Question 43 IMF

Discuss how a government might try to reduce a large, persistent, current account deficit on the balance of payments, and illustrate what impact such government action might have on a multinational company operating in the country concerned. Explain the possible role and impact of the International Monetary Fund (IMF) in this process.

(10 marks)

Question 44 POLYCALC

Polycalc Co is an internationally diversified company based in the UK. It is presently considering undertaking a capital investment in Australia to manufacture agricultural fertilisers. The project would require immediate capital expenditure of A$15 million, plus A$5 million of working capital which would be recovered at the end of the project's four year life. It is estimated that annual revenue of A$18 million would be generated by the project, with annual operating costs of A$5 million. Straight-line depreciation over the life of the project is an allowable expense against company tax in Australia which is charged at a rate of 50%, payable at each year-end without delay. The project can be assumed to have a zero scrap value.

Polycalc plans to finance the project with a £5 million 4-year loan at 10% plus £5 million of retained earnings. The proposed financing scheme reflects the belief that the project would have a debt capacity of two-thirds of capital cost. Issue costs on the debt will be 2½% and are tax deductible.

In the UK the fertiliser industry has an equity beta of 1.40 and an average debt: equity gearing ratio of 1:4. Debt capital can be assumed to be virtually risk-free. The current return on UK T-bills is 9% and the excess market return is 9.17%.

ADVANCED FINANCIAL MANAGEMENT (P4) – STUDY QUESTION BANK

Corporate tax in the UK is at 35% and can be assumed to be payable at each year-end without delay. Because of a double-taxation agreement, Polycalc will not have to pay any UK tax on the project. The company is expected to have a substantial UK tax liability from other operations for the foreseeable future.

The current spot rate is A$ 2.00 per £ and the A$ is expected to depreciate against the £ at an annual rate of 10%.

Required:

(a) **Using the Adjusted Present Value technique, advise the management of Polycalc on the project's desirability.** (8 marks)

(b) **Comment briefly on the company's intended financing plans for the Australian project. Suggest with reasons a more sensible alternative.** (2 marks)

(c) **Explain the limitations and difficulties of using the Capital Asset Pricing Model to generate discount rates for project appraisal.** (5 marks)

(15 marks)

Question 45 AVTO

Avto Co, a UK-based company, is considering an investment in Terrania, a country with a population of 60 million that has experienced twelve changes of government in the last 10 years. The investment would cost 580 million Terranian (T) francs for machinery and other equipment and an additional 170 million T francs would be necessary for working capital.

Terrania has a well-trained, skilled labour force and good communications infrastructure, but has suffered from a major disease in its main crop, the banana, and the effect of cheaper labour in neighbouring countries.

Terrania is heavily indebted to the IMF and the international banking system and it is rumoured that the IMF is unwilling to offer further assistance to the Terranian government. The Terranian government has imposed temporary restrictions on the remittance of funds from Terrania on three occasions during the last ten years.

The proposed investment would be in the production of recordable DVD players, which are currently manufactured in the UK, mainly for the European Union market. If the Terranian investment project was undertaken the existing UK factory would either be closed down or downsized. Avto hopes to become more competitive by shifting production from the UK.

Additional information:

(i) UK corporate tax is at the rate of 30% per year and Terranian corporate tax at the rate of 20% per year, both payable in the year that the tax charge arises. Tax-allowable depreciation in Terrania is 25% per year on a reducing balance basis. A bilateral tax treaty exists between Terrania and the UK.

(ii) The after-tax realisable value of the machinery and other equipment after four years is estimated to be 150 million T francs.

(iii) £140,000 has recently been spent on a feasibility study into the logistics of the proposed Terranian investment. The study reported favourably on this issue.

(iv) The Terranian government has offered to allow Avto to use an existing factory rent free for a period of four years on condition that Avto employs at least 300 local workers. Avto has estimated that the investment would need 250 local workers. Rental of the factory would normally cost 75 million T francs per year before tax.

(v) Almost all sales from Terranian production will be to the European Union priced in Euros.

(vi) Production and sales are expected to be 50,000 units per year. The expected year 1 selling price is 480 Euros per unit.

(vii) Unit costs throughout year 1 are expected to be:
Labour: 3,800 T francs based on using 250 workers
Local components: 1,800 T francs
Component from Germany: 30 Euros
Sales and distribution: 400 T francs

(viii) Fixed costs in year 1 are 50 million T francs

(ix) Local costs and the cost of the German component are expected to increase each year in line with Terranian and EU inflation respectively. Due to competition, the selling price (in Euros) is expected to remain constant for at least four years.

(x) All net cash flows arising from the proposed investment in Terrania would be remitted at the end of each year back to the UK.

(xi) If the UK factory is closed Avto will face tax allowable redundancy and other closure costs of £35 million. Approximately £20 million after tax is expected to be raised from the disposal of land and buildings.

(xii) If Avto decides to downsize rather than close its UK operations then tax allowable closure costs will amount to £20 million and after tax asset sales to £10 million. Pre-tax net cash flows from the downsized operation are expected to be £4 million per year, at current values. Manufacturing capacity in Terrania would not be large enough to supply the market previously supplied from the UK if downsizing does not occur.

(xiii) The estimated beta of the Terranian investment is 1·5 and of the existing UK investment 1·1.

(xiv) The relevant risk free rate is 4·5% and market return 11·5%.

(xv) Money market investment in Terrania is available to Avto paying a rate of interest equivalent to the Terranian inflation rate.

(xvi) Forecast % inflation levels:

	UK and the EU	Terrania
Year 1	2%	20%
Year 2	3%	15%
Year 3	3%	10%
Year 4	3%	10%
Year 5	3%	10%

(xvii) Spot exchange rates:

Terranian francs £	36·85
Terranian francs per €	23·32

ADVANCED FINANCIAL MANAGEMENT (P4) – STUDY QUESTION BANK

Required:

(a) Prepare a financial appraisal of whether or not Avto should invest in Terrania and close or downsize its UK factory. State clearly all assumptions that you make.

(b) Discuss the wider commercial issues that the company should consider, in addition to the financial appraisal, before making its decision on whether to invest.

(c) Estimate the possible impact of blocked remittances in Terrania for the planning horizon of four years and discuss how Avto might react to blocked remittances.

(28 marks in total are available for calculations and 12 for discussion) **(40 marks)**

Question 46 SERVEALOT

Servealot Co has issued the following statement as part of its annual report:

"This company aims at all times to serve its shareholders by paying a high level of dividends and adopting strategies that will increase the company's share price. Satisfying our shareholders will ensure our success. The company will reduce costs by manufacturing overseas wherever possible and will attempt to minimise the company's global tax bill by using tax haven facilities."

Required:

Discuss the validity and implications of each of the comments and strategies in the above statement.

(15 marks)

Question 47 KANDOVER

Kandover Co, a UK company, has recently established a subsidiary in another country, Petronia. An essential component that is produced in the UK by Kandover will need to be provided to the subsidiary in Petronia. The finance team are discussing what transfer price should be set for sales between the parent company and subsidiary. Three suggestions have been made:

(i) Use the estimated UK market price of the component as the transfer price. This is £18 per unit.

(ii) Use fixed cost per year plus variable cost per unit.

(iii) Use a negotiated price of UK total cost plus 25%

The following is a breakdown of the cost structure of an important component that must be sent between parent company and the overseas subsidiary. Annual sales are 50,000 units.

Parent company costs	£
Variable costs	13 per unit
Fixed cost	£120,000

Once received by the subsidiary the component undergoes further processing and is sold locally at P$250 per unit.

Costs in Petronia	P$
Local variable costs	82
Local fixed cost	351,000

The current exchange rate is P$7·8 per £.

The corporate tax rate in Petronia is 25% and in the UK 30%.

A 15% withholding tax is levied on all dividend payments in Petronia.

A bilateral tax treaty exists between the UK and Petronia. This allows tax paid on income and distributions in one country to be credited against a tax liability on the same income in the other country.

Assume that all available profits in Petronia are to be remitted back to the UK.

Required:

(a) **Calculate the expected after-tax profits that would result from each of the three transfer pricing methods.** (9 marks)

(b) **Discuss the advantages and disadvantages of each of the methods.** (6 marks)

(15 marks)

Question 48 NOIFA LEISURE

Chairman's report

"The group's financial position has never been stronger. Revenue has risen 209% and the share price has almost doubled during the last four years. Since the end of the year the company has acquired Beddall Hotels for £100 million, financed at only 9% per year by a euro floating rate loan which has little risk. Our objective is to become the largest hotel group in the United Kingdom within five years."

Statement of profit or loss summaries – Years ending 31 December

	20X6 £m	20X7 £m	20X8 £m	20X9 £m
Revenue	325	370	490	680
Operating profit	49	60	75	92
Investment income	18	10	3	1
	67	70	78	93
Interest payable	14	16	24	36
Profit before tax	53	54	54	57
Taxation	20	19	19	20
Profit after taxation	33	35	35	37
(Loss)/gain on disposal of tangible non-current assets	(3)	–	–	4
Profit after tax	30	35	35	41
Dividends	12	12	12	12
Retained earnings	18	23	23	29

Statement of financial position summaries – At 31 December

	20X6 £m	20X7 £m	20X8 £m	20X9 £m
Non-current assets				
Tangible assets	165	260	424	696
Investments	120	68	20	4
	285	328	444	700
Current assets				
Inventory	40	45	70	110
Receivables	56	52	75	94
Cash	2	3	4	5
	98	100	149	209
Less Current liabilities				
Trade payables	82	94	130	176
Taxation	18	19	19	20
Overdraft	–	–	42	68
Other	15	24	28	42
	115	137	219	306
Total assets less current liabilities	268	291	374	603
Financed by				
Ordinary shares (10 pence par)	50	50	50	50
Share premium	22	22	22	22
Revaluation reserve	–	–	–	100
Retained earnings	74	97	120	149
Shareholders' funds	146	169	192	321
Bank loans	42	42	102	102
13% bond	80	80	80	180
	268	291	374	603

Analysis by type of activity

	20X6		20X7		20X8		20X9	
	Revenue	Profit (Note 1)	Revenue	Profit	Revenue	Profit	Revenue	Profit
	£m	£m	£m	£m	£m	£m	£m	£m
Hotels	196	36	227	41	314	37	471	45
Theme park	15	(3)	18	(2)	24	3	34	5
Bus company	24	6	28	8	38	14	46	18
Car hire	43	7	45	8	52	12	62	15
Zoo (Note 2)	5	(1)	6	(1)	9	–	10	(1)
Waxworks	10	1	11	3	13	4	14	5
Publications	32	3	35	3	40	5	43	5
	325	49	370	60	490	75	680	92

Notes:
(1) Operating profit before taxation.
(2) The zoo was sold during 20X9.

	20X6	20X7	20X8	20X9
Noifa average share price (pence)	82	104	120	159
FT 100 share index	1,500	1,750	1,800	2,300
Leisure industry share index	178	246	344	394
Leisure industry P/E ratio	10:1	12:1	19:1	25:1

Required:

In his report the chairman stated that "the group's financial position has never been stronger". From the viewpoint of an external consultant appraise whether you agree with the chairman. Discussion of the group's financing policies and strategic objective, with suggestions as to how these might be altered, should form part of your appraisal.

Relevant calculations must be shown.

(25 marks)

Question 49 TWELLO

A four year summary of the financial accounts of Twello Co is shown below:

Consolidated statements of profit or loss for the years

	20X5 $m	20X6 $m	20X7 $m	20X8 $m
Revenue	742	859	961	1,028
Operating profit	22	25	40	54
Interest payable (net)	(2)	–	(5)	(6)
Profit before tax	20	25	35	48
Taxation	(7)	(8)	(12)	(17)
	13	17	23	31
Loss on disposal of tangible non-current assets	(4)	–	(2)	–
Dividends	(4)	(5)	(7)	(9)
Profit retained	5	12	14	22

Consolidated statement of financial position

	20X5 $m	20X6 $m	20X7 $m	20X8 $m
Non-current assets				
Tangible assets	142	168	189	225
Long-term investments	4	6	8	8
	146	174	196	233
Current assets				
Inventory	43	46	49	52
Receivables	18	24	26	31
Money market investments	11	20	20	12
Cash	4	4	8	6
	76	94	103	101
Less: Current liabilities				
Bank loans and overdrafts	8	8	20	18
Trade payables	66	60	84	89
Taxation	7	7	8	12
Dividends payable	2	2	3	4
Other short-term liabilities	21	26	35	40
	104	103	150	163
Total assets less current liabilities	118	165	149	171
Long-term liabilities				
11% convertible bond 20Z0-4 (Note 1)	17	17	17	17
4% deep discount loan stock (Note 2)	–	–	30	30
	17	17	47	47
Shareholders' funds				
Issued share capital (50 cents)	25	30	30	30
Share premium	30	60	–	–
Retained earnings	46	58	72	94
	118	165	149	171

Note 1 – Each $100 bond is convertible into 12.6 ordinary shares in any year up to 20Z0. The conversion rate has been adjusted for a rights issue in 20X6.

Note 2 – Redeemable at a total cost of $60 million in 20Y4 (at face value $100).

	20X5	20X6	20X7	20X8
Average share price (cents)	300	350	440	520
Average earnings yield of the industry	12%	11%	14%	12.5%

Additional notes:

(i) A 1 for 5 rights issue was made in 20X6.

(ii) The company made an acquisition in 20X7 costing $80 million. The book value of the tangible assets acquired was $20 million.

(iii) The directors estimate that the current market value of tangible non-current assets is $315 million.

Required:

(a) **Appraise the financial health of Twello, commenting on any possible financial weaknesses.** (13 marks)

(b) **Suggest what other information would be useful in your assessment of the company's financial health.** (5 marks)

(c) **Explain the advantages of deep discount bonds.**

If ordinary bonds have a redemption yield of 12% per year evaluate whether a second deep discount bond on the same terms as Twello's existing deep discount bond is likely to be attractive to investors.

Assume that interest is payable annually. Taxation may be ignored in your evaluation.

(7 marks)

(25 marks)

Question 50 SPARKS CO

Sparks Co is a large retailer which had seen many years of steady decline. However a new CEO, Dave Diamond, initiated a complex capital reconstruction programme and a highly aggressive business turnaround strategy. Profits subsequently started to rise and, with them, the firm's share price.

Some investors are of the opinion that the apparent improvement in the company's performance may have more to do with "accounting shenanigans" than any improvement in the underlying business. Dave Diamond, however, insists the improvement is genuine and sustainable. Shareholders will vote at the upcoming AGM as to whether the CEO should be awarded a large bonus.

Summary information from the most recent financial statements for Sparks Co is as follows:

	20X4 $m	20X3 $m
Statement of profit or loss		
Revenue	9,000	8,500
Cost of sales	5,500	5,250
Gross profit	3,500	3,250
less other operating costs	2,250	2,220
Operating profit	1,250	1,030
Finance costs	80	110
Profit before tax	1,170	920
Income tax expense (at 30%)	310	270
Profit for the period	860	650

Statement of financial position	$m	$m
Assets		
Non-current assets	4,980	4,540
Current assets	1,220	850
Total assets	6,200	5,390
Equity and liabilities		
Ordinary share capital (25c)	400	425
Share premium	230	200
Capital redemption reserve	2,300	2,300
Reconstruction reserve	(6,540)	(6,500)
Retained earnings	5,990	5,400
Dividends payable	(350)	(270)
Total equity	2,030	1,555
Non-current liabilities	1,900	1,865
Current liabilities	2,270	1,970
Total equity and liabilities	6,200	5,390

The firm's weighted average cost of capital has been estimated at 6.12%.

Required:

Summarise the performance of Sparks in 20X4 compared with 20X3 on the basis of the EVA® for each year and ratios you consider appropriate.

(12 marks)

Question 51 WURRALL CO

The board of directors of Wurrall Co has requested the production of a four-year financial plan. The key assumptions behind the plan are:

(i) Historically, sales growth has been 9% per year. Uncertainty about future economic prospects over the next four years from 20X5–20X8 however implies that this growth rate will reduce by 1% per year after the financial year 20X5 (e.g. to 8% in 20X6). After four years, growth is expected to remain constant at the 20X8 rate.

(ii) Cash operating costs are estimated to be approximately 68% of sales.

(iii) Tax allowable depreciation for the past few years has been approximately 15% of the net book value of plant and machinery at year end. This will continue for the next few years.

(iv) Inventories, receivables, cash in hand and "other payables" are assumed to increase in proportion to the increase in sales.

(v) Investment in, and net book value of, plant and machinery is expected to increase in line with sales. No investment is planned in other non-current assets other than a refurbishment of buildings at an estimated cost of $40 million in late 20X7.

(vi) Any change in interest paid as a result of changes in borrowing may be assumed to be effective in the next year. Wurrall plans to meet any changes in financing needs, with the exception of the repayment of the fixed rate loan, by adjusting its overdraft.

(vii) Wurrall currently pays 7% per annum interest on its short-term borrowing.

(viii) Corporation tax is expected to continue at its present rate over the next four years.

(ix) For the last few years the company's dividend policy has been to pay a constant percentage of earnings after tax. No changes in this policy are planned.

(x) Wurrall has borrowed extensively from the banking system, and covenants exist that prevent the company's gearing (book value of total loans to book value of total loans plus equity) exceeding 40% for a period of more than one year.

(xi) The company's managing director has publicly stated that both profits before tax and Wurrall's share price should increase by at least 100% during the next four years.

Statement of profit or loss for the year ended March 20X4

	$m
Revenue	1,639
Operating costs before depreciation	(1,225)
EBITDA	414
Tax-allowable depreciation	(152)
EBIT	262
Net interest payable	(57)
Profit before tax	205
Tax (30%)	(62)
Dividends	(80)
Amount transferred to reserves	63

ADVANCED FINANCIAL MANAGEMENT (P4) – STUDY QUESTION BANK

Statement of financial position as at 31 March 20X4

		$m
Non-current assets		
Land and buildings	310	
Plant and machinery (net)	1,012	
Investments[2]	32	1,354
Current assets		
Inventories	448	
Receivables	564	
Cash in hand and short-term deposits	20	1,032
Current liabilities:		
Short term loans and overdrafts	230	
Other payables	472	(702)
Non-current liabilities:		
Borrowings (8% fixed rate)[3]		(580)
		1,104
Capital and reserves		
Issued share capital (10 cents par)		240
Reserves		864
		1,104

The company's current share price is 210 cents, and its weighted average cost of capital is 11%.

Required:

(a) **Produce pro forma statements of financial position and statements of profit or loss for each of the next four years. Clearly state any assumptions that you make.** (12 marks)

(b) **Critically discuss any problems or implications of the assumptions that are made in each of points (i) to (iv) and point (ix) in the question.** (8 marks)

(c) **Using free cash flow analysis, evaluate and discuss whether or not the managing director's claims for the future share price are likely to be achievable. (The operating cash flow element of free cash flow may be estimated by: EBIT (1 - t) plus depreciation.)** (10 marks)

(d) **Using financial ratios or other forms of analysis, highlight any potential financial problems for the company during this period. Discuss what actions might be taken with respect to these problems.** (10 marks)

(40 marks)

---

[2] The investments yield negligible interest

[3] Borrowings are scheduled to be repaid at the end of 20X6 and will be refinanced with a similar type of loan in 20X6.

Answer 1 AGENCY RELATIONSHIPS

Agency relationships exist when one or more persons, the principal(s), hire another person, the agent, to perform some task on his (or their) behalf. The principal will delegate some decision-making authority to the agent. The problems of agency relationships occur when there is a conflict of interest between the principal(s) and the agent.

(a) **Shareholders and managers**

As the manager's share of total equity decreases (the divorce of ownership and control) the cost to him of decisions that are not optimal for other shareholders also decreases. Examples of possible conflict include the following:

- Managers might not work industriously to maximise shareholder wealth if they feel that they will not fairly share in the benefits of their labours.

- There might be little incentive for managers to undertake significant creative activities, including looking for profitable new ventures or developing new technology.

- Managers might award themselves high salaries or "perks".

- Managers might take a more short-term view of the firm's performance than the shareholders would wish.

(b) **Shareholders and creditors**

- Creditors (including the lenders of loan finance) provide funds for a company on the basis of the company's assets, gearing levels and cash flow (both present and anticipated). If the managers take on more risky projects than expected by the creditors, the burden of the extra risk will fall largely upon the creditors. Conversely, if the risky investments were successful, the benefits would accrue to the shareholders.

- If gearing is increased, the providers of "old debt" will face a greater risk of the company getting into financial distress or going into liquidation.

To try to ensure that managers act in the best interests of shareholders, the shareholders incur agency costs. Such costs include:

(1) cost of monitoring management actions (e.g. management audit);
(2) cost of structuring corporate organisations to minimise undesirable management actions.

If the remuneration of management is partially a function of the success of the firm, then conflict of interest should be reduced. This might involve share option schemes, performance shares (e.g. based on earnings per share) and profit based salaries or bonuses.

The threat of firing (including the board being "deposed" by discontented shareholders) is suggested to be an incentive for efficient management, as is the possibility of job loss if a company's share price through management action is low and a takeover occurs.

It has been suggested that the nature of the managerial labour market negates much of the agency problem. A manager's wealth is made up of present wealth plus the present value of future income. The better the manager's performance, the higher the company's share price, and the greater the salary, both now and in the future, the manager can obtain. The manager's desire for wealth maximisation will tend to cause him to act in the shareholders' interests.

The main way in which creditors might protect themselves against conflicts of interest with shareholders is to insist on restrictive covenants being incorporated into loan agreements. Such covenants might restrict the level of additional debt finance that might be raised, or prevent management (here acting on the shareholders' behalf) from disposing of major tangible assets without the agreement of the providers of debt, or restrict the level of dividends that can be paid. Additionally, if creditors perceive that they are being unfairly treated, they can either refuse to provide further credit, or only agree to provide future credit at higher than normal rates, both of which are likely to have adverse effects on shareholder wealth, and are deterrents to managers acting unfairly against the creditors' interests.

Answer 2 ETHICS

Non-financial issues, ethical and environmental issues in many cases overlap, and have become of increasing significance to the achievement of primary financial objectives such as the maximisation of shareholder wealth. Most companies have a series of secondary objectives that encompass many of these issues.

Traditional non-financial issues affecting companies include:

- Measures that increase the welfare of employees such as the provision of housing, good and safe working conditions, social and recreational facilities.

    These might also relate to managers and encompass generous perquisites.

- Welfare of the local community and society as a whole. This has become of increasing significance, with companies accepting that they have some responsibility beyond their normal stakeholders in that their actions may impact on the environment and the quality of life of third parties.

- Provision of, or fulfilment of, a service. Many organisations, both in the public sector and private sector provide a service, for example to remote communities, which would not be provided on purely economic grounds.

- Growth of an organisation, which might bring more power, prestige, and a larger market share, but might adversely affect shareholder wealth.

- Quality. Many engineering companies have been accused of focusing upon quality rather than cost effective solutions.

- Survival. Although to some extent linked to financial objectives, managers might place corporate survival (and hence retaining their jobs) ahead of wealth maximisation. An obvious effect might be to avoid undertaking risky investments.

Ethical issues of companies have been brought increasingly into focus by the actions of Enron and others. There is a trade-off between applying a high standard of ethics and increasing cash flow or maximisation of shareholder wealth. A company might face ethical dilemmas with respect to the amount and accuracy of information it provides to its stakeholders. An ethical issue attracting much attention is the possible payment of excessive remuneration to senior directors, including very large bonuses and "golden parachutes".

Should bribes be paid to facilitate the company's long-term aims? Are wages being paid in some countries below subsistence levels? Should they be? Are working conditions of an acceptable standard? Do the company's activities involve experiments on animals, genetic modifications, etc? Should the company deal with or operate in countries that have a poor record of human rights? What is the impact of the company's actions on pollution or other aspects of the local environment?

Environmental issues might have very direct effects on companies. If natural resources become depleted the company may not be able to sustain its activities, weather and climatic factors can influence the achievement of corporate objectives through their impact on crops, the availability of water etc. Extreme environmental disasters such as typhoons, floods, earthquakes, and volcanic eruptions will also impact on companies' cash flow, as will obvious environmental considerations such as the location of mountains, deserts, or communications facilities. Should companies develop new technologies that will improve the environment, such as cleaner petrol or alternative fuels? Such developments might not be the cheapest alternative.

Environmental legislation is a major influence in many countries. This includes limitations on where operations may be located and in what form, and regulations regarding waste products, noise and physical pollutants.

All of these issues have received considerable publicity and attention in recent years. Environmental pressure groups are prominent in many countries; companies are now producing social and environmental accounting reports, and/or corporate social responsibility reports. Companies increasingly have multiple objectives that address some or all of these three issues. In the short term non-financial, ethical and environmental issues might result in a reduction in shareholder wealth; in the longer term it is argued that only companies that address these issues will succeed.

Answer 3 COST OF CAPITAL

(a) **Cost of debt (pre-tax)**

(i) $\dfrac{\text{Annual interest payment}}{\text{Issue proceeds (or market price)}} = \dfrac{\$10}{\$100} = 10\%$

(ii) $\dfrac{\$10}{\$85} + 11.76\%$

(iii) The method is to find the IRR of the following cash flows:

t_0	t_1	t_2	t_3
(74)	$10	$10	$110

By trial and error, NPV of the four cash flows at:

25% NPV $= -\$74 + 1.440 \times \$10 + 0.512 \times \$110 = -\$3.28$
20% NPV $= -\$74 + 1.528 \times \$10 + 0.579 \times \$110 = \$4.97$

Therefore: $k_d = 20\% + \dfrac{4.97}{4.97 + 3.28} \times (25\% - 20\%) = 23\%$

(iv) As redeemable at current market price, then $\dfrac{\$10}{\$100} + 10\%$

(v) Irredeemable, $\dfrac{\$0.05}{\$0.65} + 7.7\%$

(b) Cost of debt (post-tax)

(i) $10\% (1 - 0.35) = 6.5\%$

(ii) $11.76\% (1 - 0.35) = 7.64\%$

(iii) The method is to find the IRR of the following cash flows:

t0	t1	t2	t3
$(74)	$6.5	$6.5	$106.5

By trial and error:

15%   NPV $= -\$74 + 1.626 \times \$6.5 + 0.658 \times \$106.5 = \$6.646$

20%   NPV $= -\$74 + 1.528 \times \$6.5 + 0.579 \times \$106.5 = -\$2.405$

Therefore: $k_d = 15\% + \dfrac{6.646}{6.646 + 2.405} \times (20\% - 15\%) = 19\%$

(iv) $10\% \times (1 - 0.35) = 6.5\%$

(v) 7.7% (no corporation tax relief on preference share dividend).

(c) Cost of equity

(i) $k_e = \dfrac{7.5}{150} \times 100 = 5\%$

(ii) $k_e = \dfrac{15}{165 - 15} \times 100 = 10\%$

(iii) $k_e = \dfrac{24 \times (1 + 0.05)}{120} \times 100 + 5 = 26\%$

(iv) $k_e = \dfrac{1.5}{10} \times 100 = 15\%$

(d) Dividend valuation model

(i) No growth, hence $P_0 = \dfrac{D}{k_e} = \dfrac{\$0.10 \times 50{,}000}{0.1} = \$50{,}000$

Per share $P_0 = \dfrac{\$50{,}000}{50{,}000} = \$1.00$

(ii) No growth, hence $P_0 = \dfrac{\$500}{0.15} = \$3{,}333$

Per share $P_0 = \dfrac{\$3{,}333}{1{,}000} = \$3.33$

(iii) Constant growth $P_0 = \dfrac{D_0(1+g)}{(k_e - g)}$

$= \dfrac{\$0.10 \times 1m \times (1.05)}{(0.15 - 0.05)} = \$1.05m$

Per share $= \$1.05$

(iv) P_0 = PV of future dividends

$= \$0.10 \times 10,000 \times 3.352 + \dfrac{\$0.10 \times 10,000 \times (1.05)}{(0.15 - 0.05)} \times 0.497$

$= \$8,570$

Per share $\approx \$0.86$

Answer 4 GADDES

(a) **Possible reasons for upward sloping yield curve**

- Future expectations. If future short-term interest rates are expected to increase then the yield curve will be upward sloping.

- Liquidity preference. It is argued that investors seek extra return for giving up a degree of liquidity with longer-term investments. Other things being equal, the longer the maturity of the investment, the higher the required return, leading to an upward sloping yield curve.

- Preferred habitat/market segmentation. Different investors are more active in different segments of the yield curve. For example banks would tend to focus on the short-term end of the curve, whilst pension funds are likely to be more concerned with medium and long term segments. An upward sloping curve could in part be the result of a fall in demand in the longer term segment of the yield curve leading to lower bond prices and higher yields.

(b)(i) **Market price**

Current market prices

(1) Zero coupon $\dfrac{\$100}{(1 \cdot 06)^{15}} = \$41 \cdot 73$

(2) 12% gilt with a semi-annual coupon

PV of an annuity for 30 periods at 3% is $\dfrac{1 - (1 \cdot 03)^{-30}}{0 \cdot 03} = 19 \cdot 6004$

		$
PV of interest payments	$6 \times 19 \cdot 6004 = $	117·60
PV of redemption using $\dfrac{1}{(1+0 \cdot 03)^{30}}$	$100 \times 0 \cdot 4120 = $	41·20
		158·80

(a) *If interest rates increase by 1%*

(1) Zero coupon $\dfrac{\$100}{(1\cdot07)^{15}} = \$36\cdot25$, a decrease of $\$5\cdot48$ or $13\cdot1\%$

(2) 12% gilt

PV of an annuity for 30 periods at $3\cdot5\%$ is $\dfrac{1-(1\cdot035)^{-30}}{0\cdot035} = 18\cdot3920$

		$
PV of interest payments	$\$6 \times 18\cdot3920 =$	110·35
PV of redemption using $\dfrac{1}{(1+0\cdot035)^{30}}$	$\$100 \times 0\cdot3563 =$	35·63
		145·98

This is a decrease of $\$12\cdot82$ or $8\cdot1\%$.

(b) *If interest rates decrease by 1%*

(1) Zero coupon $\dfrac{\$100}{(1\cdot05)^{15}} = \$48\cdot10$, an increase of $\$6\cdot37$ or $15\cdot3\%$

(2) 12% gilt with a semi-annual coupon:

PV of an annuity for 30 periods at $2\cdot5\%$ is $\dfrac{1-(1\cdot025)^{-30}}{0\cdot025} = 20\cdot9303$

		$
PV of interest payments	$\$6 \times 20\cdot9303 =$	125·58
PV of redemption using $\dfrac{1}{(1+0\cdot025)^{30}}$	$\$100 \times 0\cdot4767 =$	47·67
		173·25

This is an increase of $\$14\cdot45$ or $9\cdot1\%$.

(ii) *Expected price movements*

The price/yield relation is not linear; it has a convex shape. There is a bigger absolute movement in bond prices when interest rates fall than when they rise. The percentage movement is also higher for low coupon bonds than high coupon bonds. Other things being equal, a financial manager would prefer to hold high coupon bonds if interest rates are expected to increase and low or zero coupon bonds when interest rates are expected to decrease.

(iii) *Bond investment strategy*

If interest rates are expected to rise, and the gap between yields on short and long dated bonds to widen, the financial manager would not want to hold longer dated bonds as these would suffer a larger fall in price than short dated bonds. Short dated bonds, probably with high coupons, would be preferred.

Answer 5 STOCK MARKET EFFICIENCY

The efficient market hypothesis is often considered in terms of three levels of market efficiency:

(1) Weak form efficiency;
(2) Semi-strong form efficiency;
(3) Strong form efficiency.

The accuracy of the statement in the question depends in part upon which form of market efficiency is being considered. The first sentence states that all share prices are correct at all times. If "correct" means that prices reflect true values (the true value being an equilibrium price which incorporates all relevant information that exists at a particular point in time), then strong form efficiency does suggest that prices are always correct. Weak and semi-strong prices are not likely to be correct as they do not fully consider all information (e.g. semi-strong efficiency does not include inside information). It might be argued that even strong form efficiency does not lead to correct prices at all times as, although an efficient market will react quickly to new relevant information, the reaction is not instant and there will be a short period of time when prices are not correct.

The second sentence in the statement suggests that prices move randomly when new information is publicly announced. Share prices do not move randomly when new information is announced. Prices may follow a random walk in that successive price changes are independent of each other. However, prices will move to reflect accurately any new relevant information that is announced, moving up when favourable information is announced, and down with unfavourable information. If strong form efficiency exists, prices might not move at all when new information is publicly announced, as the market will already be aware of the information prior to public announcement and will have already reacted to the information.

Information from published accounts is only one possible determinant of share price movement. Other include the announcement of investment plans, dividend announcements, government changes in monetary and fiscal policies, inflation levels, exchange rates and many more.

Fundamental and technical analysts play an important role in producing market efficiency. An efficient market requires competition among a large number of analysts to achieve "correct" share prices, and the information disseminated by analysts (through their companies) helps to fulfil one of the requirements of market efficiency (i.e. that information is widely and cheaply available).

An efficient market implies that there is no way for investors or analysts to achieve consistently superior rates of return. This does not say that analysts cannot accurately predict future share prices. By pure chance some analysts will accurately predict share prices. However, the implication is that analysts will not be able to do so consistently. The same argument may be used for corporate financial managers. If, however, the market is only semi-strong efficient, then it is possible that financial managers, having inside information, would be able to produce a superior estimate of the future share price of their own companies and that if analysts have access to inside information they could earn superior returns.

ADVANCED FINANCIAL MANAGEMENT (P4) – STUDY QUESTION BANK

Answer 6 REDSKINS

(a) **Post-tax weighted average cost of capital**

The following calculations are based on the capital structure of the Redskins group which is deemed to be more appropriate for determining a discount rate to evaluate the projects available to Redskins and its subsidiaries.

Cost of debt

For irredeemable stock, k_d $= \dfrac{\text{Interest}(1-T)}{\text{Ex - interest market value}}$

Cost of 3% irredeemable stock $= \dfrac{\$3.00 \times (1-0.30)}{\$(31.60-3.00)} = 7.34\%$

For redeemable stock, to calculate k_d it is necessary to compute the internal rate of return of the after-tax cash flows:

		Cash flows $	PV at 5% $	PV at 10% $
Time 0	Ex-interest market price	(94.26)	(94.26)	(94.26)
Time 1–10	Interest (post-tax)	6.30	48.65	38.71
Time 10	Repayment of capital	100.00	61.40	38.60
Net present values			15.79	(16.95)

Cost of 9% debt $= 5\% + \left(\dfrac{\$15.79}{\$(15.79+16.95)}\right) \times 5\% = 7.41\%$

After-tax cost of bank loan $= (11\% + 2\%) \times (\$1 - 0.30) = 9.10\%$

Cost of 6% unquoted stock:

The value of the stock is the present value of the pre-tax cash flows discounted at 10%, i.e.

($6.00 × 6.145) + ($100 × 0.386) = $75.47

The after-tax cost is the discount rate which equates the after-tax cash flows to a present value of $75.47, i.e.

	Cash flows $	PV at 5% $	PV at 10% $
Time 0 Current value	(75.47)	(75.47)	(75.47)
Time 1–10 Post-tax interest	4.20	32.43	25.81
Time 10 Repayment	100.00	61.40	38.60
Net present values		18.36	(11.06)

By linear interpolation IRR $= 5\% + \dfrac{18.36}{29.42} \times 5\% = 8.12\%$

Cost of equity = 18% (given)

The values of the various sources of finance are as follows:

	$000	$000
Equity	8,000 × 1.1	8,800
3% debt	1,400 × 0.286	400
9% debt	1,500 × 0.9426	1,414
6% debt	2,000 × 0.7547	1,509
Bank loan		1,540

$$\text{WACC} = \frac{(0.18 \times 8{,}800) + (0.0734 \times 400) + (0.0741 \times 1{,}414) + (0.0812 \times 1{,}509) + (0.0910 \times 1{,}540)}{8{,}800 + 400 + 1{,}414 + 1{,}509 + 1{,}540}$$

$$= \frac{1{,}981}{13{,}663} = 14.5\%$$

(b) **Problems in estimating WACC**

(i) Where bank overdrafts are used as sources of long-term finance

Theoretically bank overdrafts are repayable on demand and therefore are current liabilities. However, it is undoubtedly true that many firms run more or less permanent overdrafts and effectively use them as a source of long-term finance. Where this is true, a case can be made for incorporating the cost of the overdraft into the calculation of the weighted average cost of capital. To do this it is necessary to know the interest rate and the size of the overdraft.

The first of these variables, the interest rate, presents no special problems. Overdraft rates are known and the quoted rate is the "true" rate. As with other interest payments, overdraft interest is an allowable expense for tax purposes and this must be incorporated in the calculation. Interest on overdrafts fluctuates through time and this presents a problem. However, it is not a problem unique to overdrafts as other interest rates are also likely to vary. The particular problem in incorporating the cost of an overdraft into the WACC is determining its magnitude for weighting purposes. By their very nature overdrafts vary in size on a daily basis. It would be necessary to separate the overdraft into two components. The first is the underlying permanent amount which should be incorporated into the WACC. The second component is that part which fluctuates on a daily basis with the level of activity. A technique similar to that used to identify the fixed and variable elements of semi-variable costs could be used to separate these two component parts.

(ii) Where convertible loan stocks are used as sources of long-term finance

The formula for determining the cost of a convertible loan stock derives from the basic valuation model for convertibles which is as follows:

$$Vc = \sum_{t=1}^{n} \frac{I(1-T)}{(1+kc)t} + \frac{MV}{(1+kc)n}$$

where
- I = Interest payable
- T = Rate of corporation tax
- n = Years to conversion
- MV = Market value of shares at the time of conversion
- Kc = Cost of convertible stock
- Vc = Market value of convertibles

ADVANCED FINANCIAL MANAGEMENT (P4) – STUDY QUESTION BANK

In principle the calculation of k_c is a simple IRR computation. In practice the difficulty is in knowing whether the investor will exercise his conversion right, which will depend upon the market value of the shares at the time of conversion. Therefore, to compute k_c requires a prediction of future share prices which obviously poses severe problems.

(c) **Use of WACC as a discount rate**

It can be shown that, in a perfect capital market in which the market value of an ordinary share is the discounted present value of the future dividend stream, acceptance of a project which has a positive NPV when discounted at the WACC will result in the share price increasing by the amount of the NPV. It is this relationship between the NPV and the market value which is the basis of the rationale for using the WACC in conjunction with the NPV rule. However, the use of the WACC in this way depends upon a number of assumptions:

- The objective of the firm is to maximise the current market value of the ordinary shares. If the firm is pursuing some other objective (e.g. sales maximisation subject to a profit constraint) some other discount rate may be more appropriate.

- The market is perfect and the share price is the discounted present value of the dividend stream. Market imperfections may undermine the relationship between NPV and the market value, and cast doubt upon the usefulness of WACC as a discount rate. Furthermore, if the market values shares in some other way (earnings multiplied by a P/E ratio?), then the link will also be broken.

- The current capital structure will be maintained and the existing capital structure is optimal.

- The risk of projects to be evaluated is the same as the average risk of the company as a whole. The discount rate has two components, namely the risk-free rate and a premium for risk. The weighted average cost of capital incorporates a risk premium which is appropriate to the risk of the company as a whole (i.e. the average risk of all its existing assets and projects). Where a project is to be considered which has a different level of risk, then the WACC is not the appropriate rate.

Answer 7 BERLAN

(a) **Weighted average cost of capital**

Cost of equity

	$000
Earnings before interest and tax	15,000
Interest 23,697 × 16%	(3,791)
	11,209
Corporation tax @ 35%	(3,923)
Available for dividend to equity	7,286

$$\text{Dividend per share} = \frac{7{,}286 \times 100}{12{,}500 \times 4} \qquad 14.57$$

$$k_e = \frac{D}{P_0} = \frac{14.57}{86.6} = 0.182$$

Cost of debt

Year	31 Dec 20X1 0	31 Dec 20X2 1	31 Dec 20X3 2	31 Dec 20X4 3
	(105.50)	16(1 – 0.35)	16(1 – 0.35)	16(1 – 0.35) + 100

The cost of debt is found by discounting the above cash flows, using trial discount rates.

Try 6%: $-105.5 + (10.4 \times 2.673) + (100 \times 0.84)$ = 6.3

Try 10%: $-105.5 + (10.4 \times 2.487) + (100 \times 0.751)$ = (4.5)

Post-tax cost of debt $= 6 + \dfrac{6.3}{6.3 + 4.5} \times (10\% - 6\%) = 8.3\%$

Weighted average cost of capital

	$000
Market value of equity = E = 12,500 × 4 × (0.86 – 0.06)	40,000
Market value of debt = D = 23,697 × 105.5/100	25,000
	65,000

Cost of capital = WACC = $(0.182 \times 40/65) + (0.083 \times 25/65) = 14.4\%$

(b) **Analysis of Canalot**

    (i)   Market value

Vg = Vu + Dt

= 32.5 + (5 × 0.35)

= $34.25m (i.e. an increase of $1.75m).

Tax relief is available on the interest on debt. Hence introduction of debt instead of equity reduces the company's tax liability. The present value of tax relief to perpetuity is Dt and this increase in value accrues to the equity shareholders.

    (ii)   Cost of equity

$k_e = k_e^i + (1 - T)(k_e^i - k_d) \dfrac{V_d}{V_e}$

$= 0.18 + (1 - 0.35)(0.18 - 0.13) \times \dfrac{5}{32.5 - 5 + 1.75}$

= 18.56% (i.e. an increase of 0.56%).

The introduction of debt increases the risk borne by the equity shareholders – this increase in risk is referred to as financial risk. This increase in risk (which is systematic) results in the equity holders demanding a higher return on their investment. Hence the cost of equity rises which, according to Modigliani and Miller (M&M) is at a linear rate.

(iii)   WACC

WACC = (0.1856 × 29.25 ÷ 34.25) + (0.13 × 0.65 ×5 ÷ 34.25)
     = 0.171 (i.e. 17.1%)

This is a decrease of 0.9%.

The introduction of debt has three effects:

- it increases the cost of equity;
- the cost of debt is less than the cost of equity which results in a saving;
- tax relief is available on debt interest.

M&M argue that the first two effects cancel out. The net effect of introducing debt is the benefit of tax relief which reduces the company's overall cost of capital.

(c)   Effect of financial gearing

The traditional theory suggests that at "low" levels of gearing the benefits (i.e. cost of debt < cost of equity and tax relief) from increasing debt outweigh the disadvantages (i.e. the increase in financial risk to the equity shareholders) and therefore the average cost of capital decreases. However, at "high" levels of gearing the costs start to outweigh the benefits causing the cost of capital to increase. Hence a "U" shaped cost of capital curve and an "optimum" level of gearing (i.e. the level of gearing can directly affect the value of the firm). This is not based on a theoretical model and no guidance is given how to identify this optimum. Therefore, the theory is of limited practical use although it suggests that managers should attempt to achieve a balance between the amount of debt and equity finance used.

M&M theory with corporate tax suggests that a company should gear up as much as possible since the benefits of debt always exceed the cost. This implies a gearing level approaching 100% which is clearly unrealistic in practice.

The reasons for the model being unrealistic are the assumptions on which it is based and the costs which are excluded from the model:

(i)   Assumptions

(1)   Individuals and companies borrow at the same interest rate for all levels of debt;

(2)   Personal gearing is viewed by shareholders as equivalent in risk terms to corporate borrowing;

(3)   There are no transaction costs and that information is freely available.

(ii)   Costs excluded

(1)   Bankruptcy costs. At high levels of gearing the probability of bankruptcy occurring increases and with it the expected cost of bankruptcy which can be a very significant amount from the shareholders' point of view.

(2)   Debt capacity. There is a restriction on the amount of debt that a company is able to raise. Lenders will not be prepared to lend beyond certain levels – often determined by the level of security required for a loan. This capacity will vary from company to company.

STUDY QUESTION BANK – ADVANCED FINANCIAL MANAGEMENT (P4)

(iii)   Personal tax

In a more recent article Miller argued that when personal tax is taken into account the introduction of debt has no effect on the value of the firm.

(iv)   Tax relief

At high levels of debt the firm may reach a stage where it has insufficient taxable profits against which to set off debt interest (i.e. it would not be able to utilise the tax relief and hence no cash benefit from introducing more debt). This is sometimes referred to as "tax exhaustion".

(v)   Agency costs

The managers of the company may impose limits on the level of debt to suit their requirements rather than the best interests of shareholders. Similarly providers of debt may restrict the actions of management.

These costs/restrictions tend to counteract the beneficial effect (tax relief) of introducing more debt. The impact of these various costs is to restrict the level of gearing below the 100% suggested by the M&M model, indicating again that an optimal level of gearing may exist.

Answer 8 KULPAR CO

(a)   Impact of capital structure on cost of capital and corporate value

The company's existing gearing is $458 million equity to $305 million debt, or 60% equity, 40% debt.

A change in gearing will result in a change in the equity beta. Assuming the beta of debt is zero, the equity beta with no gearing may be estimated by:

$$\beta \text{ ungeared} = \beta \text{ geared} \times \frac{E}{E + D(1-t)} \text{ or } 1.4 \times \frac{60}{60 + 40(1-0.3)} = 0.9545$$

If gearing was 80% equity, 20% debt by market values, the "ungeared" beta may be "regeared" to find the new equity beta:

$$\beta \text{ geared} = \beta \text{ ungeared} \times \frac{E + D(1-t)}{E} \text{ or } 0.9545 \times \frac{80 + 20(1-0.3)}{80} = 1.122$$

Using CAPM, $k_e = R_f + \beta(R_m - R_f)$ or $5.5\% + 1.122(14\% - 5.5\%) = 15.04\%$

If gearing was 40% equity, 60% debt by market values, this may be "regeared" to find the new equity beta:

$$\beta \text{ geared} = \beta \text{ ungeared} \times \frac{E + D(1-t)}{E} \text{ or } 0.9545 \times \frac{40 + 60(1-0.3)}{40} = 1.957$$

Using CAPM, $k_e = R_f + \beta(R_m - R_f)$ or $5.5\% + 1.957(14\% - 5.5\%) = 22.13\%$

The cost of debt depends on interest cover and the credit rating.

	80%E, 20%D	*40%E, 60%D*
Net operating income	110	110
Depreciation	20	20
Earnings before interest and tax	90	90
Interest	12·21 (approx $152·6m debt)	50·36 (approx $457·8m debt)
Interest cover	7·37	1·79
Cost of debt	8·0%	11·0%

The interest payable is found by examining different interest rate and interest cover possibilities.

80% equity 20% debt must fall into the AA rating (if the interest rate was 9%, interest would be $13·73 million and cover 6·55, still AA cover)

40% equity, 60% debt must fall into the BB rating (interest of 9% would be $41·20 million, and cover 2·18 still in the BB rating).

WACC at 80% equity, 20% debt = 15·04% × 0·80 + 8·0% (1 – 0·3) 0·20 = 13·15%

WACC at 40% equity, 60% debt = 22·13% × 0·40 + 11·0% (1 – 0·3) 0·60 = 13·47%

Existing cost of equity is: 5·5% + (14% – 5·5%) 1·4 = 17·4%

Existing WACC is 17·4% × 0·60 + 9% (1 – 0·3) 0·40 = 12·96%

The two alternative capital structures are expected to increase the cost of capital from its current level.

Corporate value

Using the suggested equation, company cash flow = 90 (1 – 0·3) + 20 – 20 = 63

The growth rate is unknown. However, existing corporate value, company cash flow and weighted average cost of capital are known, allowing the growth rate to be estimated.

$$763 = \frac{63(1+g)}{0·1296 - g} \text{ Solving } g = 0·043 \text{ or } 4·3\%$$

Assuming this growth rate remains unchanged corporate value with different gearing levels is estimated to be:

80% equity, 20% debt $\frac{63(1+0·043)}{0·1315 - 0·043} = \$742m$

40% equity, 60% debt $\frac{63(1+0·043)}{0·1347 - 0·043} = \$717m$

Altering the capital structure to either of the two suggested levels is expected to reduce corporate value from its current level of $763 million. It is recommended that the capital structure is kept at its current level of 60% equity, 40% debt.

(b)   Possible reasons for errors in the estimates of corporate value

The estimates of corporate value are only approximations and may be incorrect for many reasons including:

- The assumption of constant growth may be incorrect.

- Corporate value in this model is sensitive to the level of capital spending which might alter considerably from period to period.

- The model ignores the cash flow impact of any changes in working capital.

- Corporate cash flow would be better estimated by:

    (EBIT − depreciation)(1 − t) + depreciation − capital spending + or − change in working capital

- Any change in gearing would involve transactions costs as shares were repurchased or issued, and debt was issued or redeemed.

- Repurchases of shares might not be possible at the current market price.

- The corporate tax rate might change

- Credit rating agencies use other factors in addition to interest cover when deciding a company's rating, such as the quality of the company's management, or the volatility of a company's cash flows.

- Operating cash flow might itself be affected by a change in debt rating.

- The valuation does not take account of any additional costs that might exist at high levels of gearing such as direct and indirect bankruptcy costs.

- Tax exhaustion might exist at high gearing levels whereby the company can no longer benefit from tax relief on interest paid on incremental debt issues.

- Corporate debt is not risk free and does not have a beta of zero. A positive beta will alter the cost of capital estimates.

Answer 9 MALTEC

In theory, a well-diversified investor will not place any extra value on companies that diversify. On the contrary, as corporate diversification is expensive, and might move companies away from their core competence, a diversified company might have a relatively low market value. However, not all investors are well diversified, and even well diversified investors might benefit from a diversified company. A diversified company might have a less volatile cash flow pattern, be less likely to default on interest payments, have a higher credit rating and therefore lower cost of capital, leading to higher potential NPVs from investments and a higher market value.

If the diversification is international the benefits of diversification will depend upon whether the countries where the investments take place are part of any integrated international market, or are largely segmented by government restrictions (e.g. exchange controls, tariffs, quotas). If markets are segmented international diversification might offer the opportunity to reduce both systematic and unsystematic risk. An integrated market would only offer the opportunity to reduce unsystematic risk.

ADVANCED FINANCIAL MANAGEMENT (P4) – STUDY QUESTION BANK

Most markets are neither fully integrated nor segmented meaning that international diversification will lead to some reduction in systematic risk, which would be valued by investors.

It is to be hoped that risk reduction is not the only objective of Maltec; returns and shareholder utility are also important.

Answer 10 WEMERE

(a) **Errors of principle and revised estimates**

The first error made is to suggest using the cost of equity, whether estimated via the dividend valuation model or the capital asset pricing model (CAPM) as the discount rate. The company should use its overall cost of capital, which would normally be a weighted average of the cost of equity and the cost of debt.

Errors specific to CAPM

- The formula is wrong. It wrongly includes the market return twice. It should be:

  $E(r_i) = R_f + \beta_i(E(r_m) - R_f)$

- The equity beta of Folten reflects the financial risk resulting from the level of gearing in Folten. It must be adjusted to reflect the level of gearing specific to Wemere. It is also likely that the beta of an unlisted company is higher than the beta of an equivalent listed company.

- The return required by equity holders (i.e. the cost of equity) already includes a return to allow for inflation.

Errors specific to the dividend valuation model

- The formula is wrong. It should be: $\dfrac{D_1}{P_0} + g$

- Treatment of inflation – as for CAPM.

- Again the impact of the difference in the level of gearing of Wemere and Folten on the cost of equity has not been taken into account.

Revised estimates – CAPM

CAPM: required return $= R_f + \beta_i(E(r_m) - R_f)$

For Folten

Vd = 4,400

Ve = 1.38 × 1,800 × 4 = $9,936,000

Assume the debt of debt = 0

$$\beta a = \left[\dfrac{V_e}{(V_e + V_d(1-T))} \beta_e \right]$$

$$\beta a = \frac{9{,}936}{9{,}936 + 4{,}400(1 - 0.35)} \times 1.4 = 1.087$$

For Wemere

$$1.087 = \frac{10{,}600}{10{,}600 + 2{,}400(1 - 0.35)} \times \beta_e$$

$1.087 = 0.872\, \beta_e$
$\beta_e = 1.25$

Cost of equity = $12 + 1.25\,(18 - 12) = 19.5\%$

$$\text{WACC} = 19.5\% \times \frac{10{,}600}{10{,}600 + 2{,}400} + 13(1 - 0.35) \times \frac{2{,}400}{10{,}600 + 2{,}400} = 17.5\%$$

Revised estimate – Dividend valuation model

Folten

$$k_e = \frac{D_1}{P_0} + g$$

Dividend growth rate:

$$9.23\,(1+g)^4 = 13.03$$
$$(1+g)^4 = 1.412$$
$$1+g = 1.09$$
$$g = 9\%$$
$$D_1 = 13.03\,(1 + 0.09) = 14.20 \text{ cents}$$
$$k_e = \frac{14.20}{138} + 0.09 = 0.193 \text{ (i.e. 19.3\%)}.$$

$$k_e = k_e^{\,i} + (1 - T)\,(k_e^{\,i} - k_d)\,\frac{V_d}{V_e}$$

$$19.3 = k_e \text{ ungeared} + (1 - 0.35)\,(k_e \text{ ungeared} - 13)\,\frac{4{,}400}{9{,}936}$$

k_e ungeared = 17.9%

Wemere

$$k_e \text{ geared} = 17.9 + (1 - 0.35)\,(17.9 - 13)\,\frac{2{,}400}{10{,}600} = 18.6\%$$

$$\text{WACC} = 18.6\% \times \frac{10{,}600}{10{,}600 + 2{,}400} + 13(1 - 0.35) \times \frac{2{,}400}{10{,}600 + 2{,}400} = 16.7\%$$

ADVANCED FINANCIAL MANAGEMENT (P4) – STUDY QUESTION BANK

(b) Which estimate should be used as discount rate

Both methods result in a discount rate of approximately 17%. They are both based on estimates from another company which has, for example, a different level of gearing. The cost of equity derived using the dividend valuation model is based on Folten's dividend policy and share price and not that of Wemere. The dividend policy of Wemere (e.g. the dividend growth rate) is likely to be different.

CAPM involves estimating the systematic risk of Wemere using Folten. The beta of Folten is likely to be a reasonable estimate, subject to gearing, of the beta of Wemere.

CAPM is therefore likely to produce the better estimate of the discount rate to use. However, this will be incorrect if the projects being appraised have a different level of systematic risk to the average systematic risk of Folten's existing projects or if the finance used for the project significantly changes the capital structure of Wemere.

(c) Use of discounted cash flow techniques in small unlisted companies

Discounted cash flow techniques allow for the time value of money and should therefore be used for all investment appraisal including that carried out by small unlisted companies. It is important for all managers to recognise that money received now is worth more than money received in the future. Discounting enables future cash flows to be expressed in terms of present value and for net present value to be calculated. A positive net present value indicates that the return provided by the project is greater than the discount rate.

One non-discounting method – accounting rate of return – is used because it employs data consistent with financial accounts, but it is not theoretically sound and is not recommended as a final decision arbiter. Nevertheless it registers appreciation of the impact of a new project on the financial statements and thus likely impact on users of these statements.

Discounted payback measures how long it takes to recover the initial investment after taking account of the time value of money. It is a useful initial screening method but should not be used alone since it ignores cash flows outside the payback period. A problem for all companies, not only small unlisted companies, is estimation of the discount rate. This can be partly overcome by calculating the IRR (i.e. the discount rate at which the NPV is zero). This provides a "break-even" cost of capital (i.e. a yield which is then acceptable provided the capital cost of the business "could not be lower").

Answer 11 CRESTLEE

(a) Appropriate discount rate

The discount rate should reflect the systematic risk of the individual project being undertaken. Unless the risk of the textile expansion and the diversification into the packaging industry are the same, their cash flows should not be discounted at the same.

The discount rate to be used should not be the cost of the actual source of funds for a project, but a weighted average of the costs of debt and equity which is weighted by the market values of debt and equity. It is possible to estimate an existing weighted average cost of capital for Crestlee, but the rate cannot be applied to new projects unless the following assumptions are complied with:

(i) The project is marginal (i.e. it is small relative to the size of the company). Taken together the two projects are not marginal, but this is not a crucial assumption as long as the costs of debt or equity do not alter because of the size of the financing required.

(ii) All cash flows of the project are level perpetuities. This is unrealistic for "real world" projects, but again makes little difference to the validity of the estimated weighted average cost of capital.

The remaining two assumptions are more important:

(iii) The project should be financed in a way that does not alter the company's existing capital structure. The net present value investment appraisal method cannot handle a significant change in capital structure; if such a change occurs the adjusted present value method (APV) should be used.

Crestlee's existing capital structure using market values is:

	$m	%
30 million ordinary shares at 380 cents	114.00	66
$56 million bonds at $104	58.24	34
	172.24	

If the two investments are considered as a "package":

	$m	%
New finance being raised	9.275 equity	66
$56 million bonds at $104	4.725 debt	34
	14.000 m	

The company's capital structure does not change as a result of these two investments.

(iv) The project should have the same level of systematic risk as the company's existing operations. As the textile investment is an existing operations it is reasonable to assume that it has the same systematic risk. The diversification into packaging could have very different risk characteristics. The company's existing weighted average cost of capital should not be used as a discount rate for the diversification.

Textile expansion

The discount rate may be based upon the company's weighted average cost of capital (given that assumptions (iii) and (iv) are not violated).

$$WACC = K_e \frac{E}{E+D} + K_d (1-t) \frac{D}{E+D}$$

Using the capital asset pricing model k_e may be estimated by

$k_e = 6\% + 1.2 (14\% - 6\%) = 15.6\%$

k_d is taken as the current cost of loan stock, 11% (alternatively a rate could have been estimated using the redemption yield of the bond).

$WACC = 15.6\% \times {}^{66}/_{100} + 11\% (1 - 0.33) \, {}^{34}/_{100} = 12.8\%$

This is the suggested discounted rate for the expansion.

Packaging diversification

The systematic risk of diversifying into the packaging industry may be estimated by referring to the systematic risk of companies within that industry. However, the equity beta is influenced by the level of financial risk (gearing). Unless the market weighted gearing of Canall and Sealalot is the same as Crestlee, it is necessary to "ungear" the equity beta of these companies (to remove the effect of financial risk) and regear to take account of Crestlee's financial risk.

Gearing	Canall ($m)	%	Sealalot ($m)	%
Equity	72.0	81	138	91
Debt	16.8	19	13	9
	88.8		151	

These are both significantly different from Crestlee.

Ungearing Canall (assuming debt is risk free and $\beta_d = 0$):

$$\beta_a = \left[\frac{V_e}{(V_e + V_d(1-T))}\beta_e\right] = \frac{72}{72 + 16.8(1-0.33)} \times 1.3 = 1.124$$

Ungearing Sealalot:

$$\beta_a = \frac{138}{138 + 13(1-0.33)} \times 1.2 = 1.129$$

These are very similar. The ungeared equity beta of the packaging industry will be assumed to be 1.125.

Regearing for Crestlee's capital structure:

$$\beta_e = \beta_a \times \frac{V_e + V_d(1-t)}{V_e} = 1.125 \times \frac{114 + 58.24(1-0.33)}{114} = 1.51$$

k_e is estimated to be:

$6\% + 1.51(14\% - 6\%) = 18.08\%$

WACC = $18.08\% \times {}^{66}/_{100} + 11\% (1 - 0.33) \, {}^{34}/_{100} = 14.4\%$

15% is not an appropriate discount rate for either of these projects. The less risky textile expansion has an estimated discount rate of 12.8%, and the diversification 14.4%.

(b) **Validity of the directors' views**

The marketing director might be correct. If there is initially a high level of systematic risk in the packaging investment before it is certain whether the investment will succeed or fail, it is logical to discount cash flows for this high risk period at a rate reflecting this risk. Once it has been determined whether the project will be successful, risk may return to a "more normal" level, and the discount rate reduced commensurate with the lower risk.

The other board member is incorrect. If the same discount rate is used throughout a project's life the discount factor becomes smaller and effectively allows a greater deduction for risk for more distant cash flows. The *total* risk adjustment is greater the further into the future cash flows are considered. It is not necessary to discount more distant cash flows at a higher rate.

Answer 12 HOTALOT

(a) **Explanation of terms**

The equity beta measures the systematic risk of a company's shares. A beta of 0.95 suggests that Hotalot is slightly less risky than the market as a whole.

The alpha value measures the abnormal return on a share. Hotalot's shares are currently earning 1.5% more than would be expected from the firm's beta. The average alpha for the market is zero. An investor should buy Hotalot's shares until the price rises and the alpha falls to zero. The alpha of 1.5% will only be temporary.

(b) **Estimation of discount rate**

Hotalot's diversification into freezer production will change the company's risk profile. The systematic risk of freezer production can be estimated from the betas of the firms already producing freezers. As all the companies listed have a similar market value, the weighted average equity beta is:

$$\frac{1.1 + 1.25 + 1.30 + 1.05}{4} = 1.175$$

The equity beta reflects the financial gearing of the companies in the industry. It is therefore necessary to degear the equity beta of the freezer industry, and re-gear to take account of Hotalot's gearing.

Gearing of freezer industry (MV): Equity $192m Debt $40.1m

To de-gear industry beta:

$$\beta_u = \frac{E}{E + D(1-T)} \beta_e$$

$$= \frac{192}{192 + 40.1(0.65)} \times 1.175 = \frac{192}{218} \times 1.175 = 1.035$$

Gearing of Hotalot (MV)   Equity $33.92m   Debt $17.4m

To re-gear for Hotalot;

$$\beta_e = \beta_u \left(1 + (1-t)\frac{D}{E}\right) = 1.035 \left(1 + \frac{74(0.65)}{33.92}\right) = 1.38$$

Required return = $R_f + \beta(R_m - R_f)$ = 9% + 1.38(16% – 9%)

= 9% + 1.38(7%) = 9% + 9.66% = 18.66%

This is the required rate of return for Hotalot's equity investment in freezers.

The WACC required is therefore $k_e \dfrac{E}{E+D} + k_d(1-t)\dfrac{D}{E+D}$

$18.66\% \dfrac{33.92}{51.32} + 9.5\%(1-0.35)\dfrac{17.4}{51.32} = 12.33 + 2.09 = 14.43\%$

Hotalot should use a discount rate of 14.43% for the appraisal of its diversification into freezer production.

(c)   Risk associated with corporate debt

It is not realistic to assume that corporate debt is risk-free. Companies may default on both the interest payments and the principal repayments. If corporate debt is not entirely risk-free, then ungeared betas will be underestimated, and geared betas will be overestimated.

Research by the Bond Investors Association says the default rate in "junk bonds" during the 1980s was running at 11.2%. Between 1980 and 1989, 631 corporate bond issues worth $30.1 billion defaulted.

As Hotalot only pays 9.5% compared with a risk-free rate of 9% Hotalot debt can be assumed to have a beta value of 0.06, say.

The asset beta (ungeared) is determined by:

$\beta_u = \beta_e \dfrac{E}{E + D(1-t)} + \beta_d \dfrac{D(1-t)}{E + D(1-t)}$

$\beta_u = 1.175 \times \dfrac{192}{192 + 40(1-0.35)} + 0.06 \times \dfrac{40(1-0.35)}{192 + 40(1-0.35)}$

Re-gear: solve for β_e using Hotalot's gearing:

$\beta_u = \beta_e \dfrac{E}{E + D(1-t)} + \beta_d \dfrac{D(1-t)}{E + D(1-t)}$

$1.04 = \beta_e \dfrac{33.92}{33.92 + 17.4(1-0.35)} + 0.06 \dfrac{17.4(1-0.35)}{33.92 + 17.4(1-0.35)}$

$1.04 = \beta_e (0.75) + 0.015$

$\beta_e = 1.367$

$k_e = 9\% + (16\% - 9\%)\,1.367 = 18.57\%$

$\text{WACC} = 18.57\% \dfrac{33.92}{51.32} + 9.5\%(1-0.35)\dfrac{17.4}{51.32}$

= 12.27 + 2.09 = 14.36%

STUDY QUESTION BANK – ADVANCED FINANCIAL MANAGEMENT (P4)

This compares with the previous WACC of 14.43%, which as stated above was overestimated.

(d) **Systematic and unsystematic risk**

The Capital Asset Pricing Model assumes that shareholders are well diversified, and therefore only concerned with systematic risk. However, Hotalot's shareholders may not all be well diversified, and may be concerned with the specific risk applicable to Hotalot.

Even well diversified shareholders should not completely ignore unsystematic risk. The total risk of a company, both systematic and unsystematic risk, determines the probability of bankruptcy, which can incur significant costs for equity investors.

Answer 13 AMBLE

(a) **IRR**

Relevant cash flows ($000s)

Year	0	1	2	3	4	
Direct labour		354	552	608	669	
Material Z		102	161	174	188	
Components P & Q & variable costs		275	421	454	490	
Management salaries		67	72	77	82	
Depreciation		–	–	–	–	
Selling expenses		166	174	183	192	
Head office costs		–	–	–	–	
Rental		120	126	132	139	
Interest	–	–	–	–	–	
Other overhead		50	53	55	58	
		1,134	1,559	1,683	1,818	
Sales		1,320	2,021	2,183	2,356	
Net cash flows		186	462	500	538	
Tax-allowable depreciation		213	213	213	213	
Taxable profit		(27)	249	287	325	
Tax payable		(9)	87	100	114	

Cash flows for calculation of IRR

	0	1	2	3	4	NPV
Net cash flow (above)		186	462	500	538	
Taxation		9	(87)	(100)	(114)	
New machinery	(864)					
Salvage value					12	
Cash flows	(864)	195	375	400	436	
Calculate IRR by trial and error						NPV
0%	(864)	195	375	400	436	542
20% factor	1.0	0.833	0.694	0.579	0.482	
	(864)	162	260	232	210	0

Therefore IRR is 20%

Notes:

		Year 1	Year 2	Year 3	Year 4
(i)	Sales price	110	115.5	121.27	127.34
	Units	12,000	17,500	18,000	18,500
	$000	1,320	2,021	2,183	2,356
(ii)	Direct labour cost	29.5	31.56	33.77	36.14
	Units	12,000	17,500	18,000	18,500
	$000	354	552	608	669

(iii) Material Z, 72,000 kilos are required in the first year. The relevant cost is 70,000 kilos in inventory, opportunity cost $99,000 plus 2,000 kilos at $1.46 giving a total cost of $101,920.

(iv) Only incremental management salaries are relevant, the two new managers plus the replacement deputy manager.

(v) The opportunity rental of $120,000 is the relevant cost.

(vi) Other fixed overhead – the apportionment of rates is not a relevant cost.

	Year 1 $000	Year 2 $000	Year 3 $000	Year 4 $000
Tax:				
Sales less cash costs	186	462	500	538
Tax-allowable depreciation	213	213	213	213
Taxable	(27)	249	287	325
Tax (35%)	(9)	87	100	114

Year 1 assumes the company has other profits.

When calculating IRR by trial and error, the use of 0% is a simple calculation, which gives some idea of the next percentage figure to try. As interpolation is usually more accurate than extrapolation the highest available percentage was tried. It was good fortune that this proved precisely correct.)

(b) Asset beta

An asset beta is the weighted average of the beta of equity and the beta of debt. It reflects the company's business risk. The difference between the company's asset beta and its equity beta reflects the company's financial risk. Only systematic risk is considered in an asset beta.

Using the CAPM, the required return is $R_f + \beta(R_m - R_f)$.

$8\% + 1.2(15\% - 8\%) = 16.4\%$

Since the product returns 20%, which is considerably more than the required return of 16.4%, the product should be introduced.

However:

- There may be non-financial factors which affect this decision.

- The new product may have a higher systematic risk than the company as a whole.

- Systematic risk is an appropriate measure only if either the company or the shareholder is well diversified.

- The CAPM is subject to criticism, both at the theoretical level, and regarding the practical problems of data collection. The figure of 16.4% calculated, may therefore not be the appropriate rate.

(c) **NPV using 17% discount rate**

Year	$000	17%	NPV $000
0	(864)	1.000	(864)
1	195	0.855	167
2	375	0.731	274
3	400	0.624	250
4	436	0.534	233
			60

The product will cease to be viable when the PV of the tax paid increases by $60,000.

	PV of tax at 35%			PV of tax at 50%		
Year	$000	17%	PV($000)	$000	17%	PV($000)
1	(9)	0.855	(8)	(13)	0.855	(11)
2	87	0.731	64	125	0.731	91
3	100	0.624	62	143	0.624	89
4	114	0.534	61	162	0.534	87
			179			256

The increase in the tax rate from 35% to 50% increases the PV of tax paid by 256 − 179 = $77,000. By interpolation it can be calculated that the PV of tax will increase by $60,000 at a tax rate of just under 47%. If tax rates rose to 47%, the project would not be viable.

Answer 14 PROGROW

(a) **Report on new machine purchase or expansion of garden tool production**

From a financial perspective the alternative investments may be compared by using the expected net present values of their incremental cash flows. On this basis expansion of garden tool production would be the favoured alternative as its expected NPV is $277,200, compared with $38,100 from introducing the new jack production process. The two investments have been discounted at different rates as they are of different risk.

Before making a decision we would draw your attention to a number of factors. Investment decisions should not be made purely on financial grounds. In this case the new process will involve making 50 workers redundant which could adversely affect the working relationships and motivation within your company.

Your concern about the possible effect on your share of the jack market may be well founded. If your competitors adopt the new process and are able to cut their prices you could lose market share unless you are able to cut your prices, which will reduce profitability and cash flow. Information is needed on your likely price of jacks if you do not introduce the new process.

The likely future developments in the garden tool markets and jack markets should be considered. If one market is likely to have better future opportunities then this should influence your decision. The likely cash flows after the initial five-year period will be important.

The expected NPVs are subject to a margin of error. As long as the technical specification and reliability of the new jack production process is well proven, the projections for the jack process are likely to be more accurate as you are not expanding sales. The garden tool projections assume that you can sell the extra 70,000 units at the same price, which may not be possible.

A major concern is the lack of any data about the need for extra working capital to accompany the increase in production, or information about whether any additional management or supervisory staff will be required, or if there are incremental overheads associated with the production process. The existing data might under-estimate the cash outflows associated with the expansion.

As both investments produce positive expected net present values might it not be possible to construct an extension to your existing premises to create enough space to undertake both? Obviously the cost of this would need to be taken into account, but it might also give the company the flexibility to take advantage of future opportunities.

Appendix

Incremental cash flows from the introduction of the new jack process

$000

Year	0	1	2	3	4	5	6
Direct labour saved		271.6	287.9	305.2	323.5	342.9	
Redundancy costs	(354)						
Retraining	(15)						
Maintenance		(46.8)	(48.7)	(50.6)	(52.6)	(54.7)	
Incremental taxable income	(369)	224.8	239.2	254.6	270.9	288.2	
Incremental tax		92.2	(56.2)	(59.8)	(63.6)	(67.7)	(72.0)
Taxed saved from the depreciation allowance		66.9	16.7	12.5	9.4	7.1	11.2
Cost of machines	(535)						
Sale of machines		125.0				40	
Net incremental cash flows	(904)	508.9	199.7	207.3	216.7	267.6	(60.8)
Discount factors (16%)	1	0.862	0.743	0.641	0.552	0.476	0.410
Present values	(904)	438.7	148.4	132.9	119.6	127.4	(24.9)

The expected NPV of incremental cash flows from the introduction of the new jack production process is: $38,100

Expansion of garden tool production

Incremental cash flows:

					$000			
Year		*0*	*1*	*2*	*3*	*4*	*5*	*6*
Sales			573.3	602.0	632.1	663.7	696.8	
Less:	Labour		244.9	259.6	275.1	291.6	309.1	
	Materials		178.1	188.8	200.1	212.1	224.8	
Incremental contribution			150.3	153.6	156.9	160.0	162.9	
Tax				(37.6)	(38.4)	(39.2)	(40.0)	(40.7)
Tax saved from the depreciation allowance			25.0	6.2	4.7	3.5	2.6	4.4
Capital equipment		(200)					14	
Net cash flows		(200)	175.3	122.2	123.2	124.3	139.5	(36.3)
Discount factors (12.39%)		1	0.890	0.792	0.704	0.627	0.558	0.496
Present values		(200)	156.0	96.8	86.7	77.9	77.8	(18.0)

Expected net present value is: $277,200

Notes

- It is assumed that the company has sufficient profits to fully benefit from the tax-allowable depreciation.

- Depreciation allowances:

    As investment is in the current tax year (year 0) it is assumed that tax saving from the depreciation allowances commences in year 1.

    Jack manufacture

		Allowance	*Tax saved*
Year 1	535.0	267.5	66.9
Year 2	267.5	66.9	16.7
Year 3	200.6	50.2	12.5
Year 4	150.5	37.6	9.4
Year 5	112.9	28.2	7.1

    Tax book value at date of disposal = 112.9−28.2 = 84.7

    Balancing allowance:

    84.7 − 40 = 44.7 × 25% = 11.2, tax saved in year 6

    Garden tool manufacture

	Allowance		*Tax saved*
Year 1	200.0	100.0	25.0
Year 2	100.0	25.0	6.2
Year 3	75.0	18.7	4.7
Year 4	56.2	14.1	3.5
Year 5	42.2	10.5	2.6

End balance 31.7 Balancing allowance:

31.7 − 14 = 17.7 × 25% = 4.4, tax saved in year 6

- The company's current weighted average cost of capital should not be used. The discount rate should allow for the different systematic risk of jack production and garden tool manufacture.

The discount rates may be estimated as follows:

Assuming the systematic risk of garden tool production is accurately reflected by the beta equity of other producers, this risk may be estimated by *ungearing* the beta of the other companies, and *regearing* it to take into account the different gearing level of Progrow.

As corporate debt is assumed to be risk free, the debt beta = 0

$$\beta \text{ asset} = \beta \text{ equity} \times \frac{E}{E + D(1-t)} = 1.4 \times \frac{50}{50 + 50(1-0.25)} = 0.8$$

Regearing for Progrow's capital structure, market value of equity $4.536 million and of debt $1.650 million.

$$\beta \text{ equity} = 0.8 \times \frac{4.536 + 1.65(1 - 0.25)}{4.536} = 1.018$$

Using CAPM, $k_e = R_f + \beta(R_m - R_f)$
$k_e = 7\% + 1.018(14\% - 7\%) = 14.13\%$

The post-tax cost of debt may be estimated by finding the post-tax IRR of the bond, although this may differ from the cost of the term loan.

Tutorial note: *The cost of debt cannot be assumed to be at the risk free rate; the examiner only allows this assumption when de-gearing/re-gearing betas as above.*

After tax interest = $15 (1 − 0.25) = $11.25

At 7% interest

	$
Discounted value of $11.25 for 10 years 11.25 × 7.024	79.02
Present value of $100 in 10 years' time 100 × 0.508	50.80
Market price	(125.00)
Net present value	4.82

At 8% interest

	$
Discounted value of $11.25 for 10 years 11.25 × 6.710	75.49
Present value of $100 in 10 years' time 100 × 0.463	46.30
Market price	(125.00)
Net present value	(3.21)

By interpolation the cost of debt is approximately:

$$7\% + \frac{4.82}{4.82 + 3.21} = 7.6\%$$

Using this estimate the weighted average cost of capital for garden tool production is:

$$\text{WACC} = 14.13\% \times \frac{4,536}{6,186} + 7.6\% \times \frac{1,650}{6,186} = 12.39\%$$

This will be used as the discount rate.

For jack manufacture

If the overall beta equity of Progrow is 1.3, and the beta equity of garden tools is 1.018, with garden tools representing 60% of the value of the company, the beta equity of jacks is estimated by:

$$1.3 = 1.018 \times 0.6 + \beta \text{ equity jacks} \times 0.4$$

$$\beta \text{equity jacks} = 1.723$$

Using CAPM, $k_e = R_f + \beta(R_m - R_f)$
$k_e = 7\% + 1.723(14\% - 7\%) = 19.06\%$

$$\text{WACC} = 19.06\% \times \frac{4,536}{6,186} + 7.6\% \times \frac{1,650}{6,186} = 16\%$$

- Apportioned salaries and head office overhead are irrelevant.

- Interest costs are not a relevant cash flow as the costs of any financing are encompassed within the discount rate.

(b) **Validity of comments**

(i) NPV

The managing director's daughter is correct that NPV does not take into account any future options arising from investment decisions. Such options could lead to additional NPVs and could influence the decision process. The valuation of options from capital investments that might occur in several years' time is, however, extremely difficult and is known as *real options pricing theory* For most companies it is enough to have an awareness of the nature of the possible options that might exist, and to use this qualitative information in the decision process.

NPV is not a perfect method of investment appraisal, but in a reasonably efficient market where the results of the investment decisions of managers (i.e. the expected NPVs) are quickly and accurately reflected in changes in a company's share price it is a valid technique to use as *part* of the strategic investment decision process. Non-financial factors are also important.

(ii)   Betas

The capital asset pricing model does have theoretical and practical weaknesses. These include:

- The basic model is single period whereas most investment decisions are multi-period.

- It is based upon perfect capital market assumptions.

- The use of historic data to estimate beta assumes that the future beta will be the same as the past which may not be the case.

- The required data may be difficult to obtain. What is the appropriate risk free rate? How can the risk and return of the market as a whole be established?

- Evidence suggests that CAPM does not provide a satisfactory measure of risk against return for small companies, low P/E ratio companies, very high or low beta securities, and the returns in certain months of the year and days of the week.

- The model considers the level of return required by shareholders but ignores any preference that they might have for income in the form of dividends and capital gains, which may be subject to different tax treatment.

- It assumes that shareholders are well diversified and are only interested in systematic risk.

Other factors besides systematic risk are likely to influence the required returns of shareholders. The *arbitrage pricing theory* does not suffer from many of the theoretical weaknesses of CAPM, and suggests that the required return is a function of a number of factors, such as interest rates, inflation rates and growth in industrial production. Unfortunately identifying the nature or number of relevant factors is extremely difficult, and the model has not been developed in a form that can be easily applied to aid practical capital investment decisions.

Despite its limitations, CAPM provides a simple and reasonably accurate way of expressing the relationship between risk and return, and offers a practical means of estimating the discount rate to be used in the appraisal of capital investments.

Answer 15 TAMPEM

(a)   NPV and IRR

The tax saving from tax-allowable depreciation are:

Year	Written down value	Allowance (25%)	Tax saving (30%)
1	4,400	1,100	330
2	3,300	825	248
3	2,475	619	186
4	1,856	464	139

NPV

Year	0	1	2	3	4
	$000	$000	$000	$000	$000
Operating cash flows		1,250	1,400	1,600	1,800
Taxation (30%)		(375)	(420)	(480)	(540)
Tax saving		330	248	186	139
Investment cost	(5,400)				
Realisable value					1,500
Net cash flows	(5,400)	1,205	1,228	1,306	2,899
Discount factors (10%)		0·909	0·826	0·751	0·683
Present values	(5,400)	1,095	1,014	981	1,980

The expected NPV is $(330,000)

The investment does not appear to be financially viable.

The weighted average cost of capital using CAPM is:

$k_e = 4\% + 1·5 (10\% - 4\%) = 13\%$

$$\text{WACC} = k_e \frac{E}{E+D} + k_d(1-t) \frac{D}{E+D} = 13\% (0·6) + 8\%(1 - 0·3)(0·4) = 10·04\%$$

APV

The relevant cash flows for APV are the same as for the NPV, except for the issue costs which are treated separately as a financing side effect.

Year	0	1	2	3	4
	$000	$000	$000	$000	$000
Net cash flows	(5,000)	1,205	1,228	1,306	2,899
Discount factors (9%)		0·917	0·842	0·772	0·708
Present values	(5,000)	1,105	1,034	1,008	2,052

Expected base case NPV is $199,000

Tutorial note: *The discount rate for the base case NPV is the ungeared cost of equity. Assuming corporate debt to be risk free (which is unlikely at 8%).*

$$\beta a = \left[\frac{V_e}{(V_e + V_d(1-T))}\beta_e\right] = \frac{2,700}{2,700 + 2,700(1-0.3)} \; 1·5 = 0·882$$

$K_{eu} = 4\% + (10\% - 4\%) \; 0·882 = 9·29\%$

Financing side effects:

Annual tax saving on interest payments on $2·7 million debt

$2,700,000 \times 8\% \times 0·3 = \$64,800$

ADVANCED FINANCIAL MANAGEMENT (P4) – STUDY QUESTION BANK

The present value of tax saving over four years discounted at the cost of debt is:

$64,800 × 3·312 = $214,618

	$
The estimated APV is:	
Base case NPV	199,000
Tax savings	214,618
Issue costs	(400,000)
	13,618

The investment appears to be marginally viable based upon the APV method.

(b) Validity of managers' views

Manager A advocates the use of NPV which is used by many companies worldwide. In an efficient market a positive NPV, in theory, should lead to a commensurate increase in the value of the company and share price. However, the use of the weighted average cost of capital (WACC) in NPV is only appropriate if there is no significant change in gearing as a result of the investment, the investment is marginal in size, and the operating risk of the company does not change. If WACC is estimated using the capital asset pricing model, it also relies upon the accuracy of this model which has many unrealistic assumptions.

The adjusted present value model, advocated by manager B, treats the investment as being initially all equity financed and then directly adjusts for the present value of any cash flow effects associated with financing. As gearing is expected to change as a result of the investment, APV might be better suited to the evaluation of this investment. However, it is not always easy to identify all of the relevant financing side effects, or the discount rate that used be used on each of the financing side effects. APV also relies upon unrealistic assumptions with respect to ungearing beta and the existence of perpetual risk free debt.

Both NPV and APV do not consider the potential value of real options (e.g. the abandonment option and the option to undertake further investments) that might exist as a result of undertaking the initial investment.

Answer 16 PROJECT REVIEW

(a) Corrected project evaluation and sensitivity analysis

The project cash flow contains a number of errors of principle which should be corrected. As the project cash flows are shown after tax, the corrections should be made net of tax by either adding back or deducting the change required.

- Interest has been deducted and should be added back as this finance charge is properly charged through the application of the discount rate.

- Financial accounting depreciation should be added back as this is not a cash flow.

- The indirect cost charge should be added back as this does not appear to be a decision relevant cost.

- Infrastructure costs should be deducted as these have not been included in the original projection.

- Site clearance and reinstatement costs of $5 million have been included net of tax.

■ The unclaimed balancing allowance (BA) is calculated as follows:

	0	1	2	3	4	5	6
Capital investment	150·00	50·00					
Deduct FYA at 50%	−75·00	−25·00					
Deduct allowances at 25% of residual		−18·75	−20·31	−15·23	−11·43	−8·57	−6·43
Pool	75·00	81·25	60·94	45·71	34·28	25·71	19·28
Proceeds of sale							7·00
Unclaimed BA							12·28

This will generate a positive tax benefit in year six of $3·68 million at the tax rate of 30%.

Tutorial notes: *The examiner appears to be making several assumptions (i) that the capital expenditure occurs at the end of a tax year, leading to an instant claim of the first year allowance (FYA); (ii) that the draft appraisal had claimed tax-allowable depreciation in the year of disposal (which would technically be incorrect); (iii) that the $7m disposal proceeds had been included pre-tax in the draft appraisal.*

The initial CAPEX is 150, initial allowance of 50% takes the tax book value down to 75. However after one year there is another 50 CAPEX, giving 25 initial allowance, plus 25% reducing balance allowance on the tax book value of the initial CAPEX (75 × 25% = 18.75). At the end of the first year the total tax book value = 150 -75 – 18.75 + 50 – 25 = 81.25 which is then used to find further allowances at 25% reducing balance. At the end of the last year the remaining tax book value is compared to sale proceeds and a balancing allowance claimed due to the loss on disposal.

The adjusted project cash flow and net present value calculation for this project are:

	0	1	2	3	4	5	6
Project after tax cash flow	−127·50	−36·88	44·00	68·00	60·00	35·00	20·00
Add back net interest			2·80	2·80	2·80	2·80	2·80
Add back depreciation (net of tax)			2·80	2·80	2·80	2·80	2·80
Add back ABC charge (net of tax)			5·60	5·60	5·60	5·60	5·60
Less corporate infrastructure costs			−2·80	−2·80	−2·80	−2·80	−2·80
Estimate for site clearance							−3·50
Tax benefit of unrecovered balancing allowances							3·68
Adjusted cash flow	−127·50	−36·88	52·40	76·40	68·40	43·40	28·58
Discount factor	1·0000	0·9091	0·8264	0·7513	0·6830	0·6209	0·5645
Discounted cash flow at 10%	−127·50	−33·52	43·31	57·40	46·72	26·95	16·14
Net present value	29·48						

The sensitivity of the project to a 1% increase in capital expenditure is as follows:

Sensitivity to a $1 million increase in CAPEX at year 0	0	1	2	3	4	5	6
Equipment purchase/ tax book value	1	0·50	0·37	0·28	0·21	0·16	0·12
First year allowance	−0·5						
Reducing balance		−0·13	−0·09	−0·07	−0·05	−0·04	−0·03
Tax book value	0·5	0·37	0·28	0·21	0·16	0·12	0·09
Impact upon CAPEX	−1						
Tax savings on allowances	0·15	0·039	0·028	0·021	0·015	0·012	0·009
Unrecovered allowance							0·027
Net impact	−0·85	0·039	0·028	0·021	0·015	0·012	0·036
Discount factor	1·0000	0·9091	0·8264	0·7513	0·6830	0·6209	0·5645
Discounted cash flow	−0·85	0·0355	0·0223	0·0158	0·0102	0·0075	0·0203
Net present value	−0·63						

Thus an increase in CAPEX by $1 million results in a loss of NPV of $0·63 million due to the benefit of the tax-allowable depreciation available discounted over the life of the project.

(b) **Discounted payback and duration**

	0	1	2	3	4	5	6
Discounted cash flows from project	−127·50	−33·52	43·31	57·40	46·72	26·95	16·14
Cumulative discounted cash flow	−127·50	−161·02	−117·72	−60·32	−13·60	13·35	29·48
Payback (discounted)	4·50						

The duration of a project is the average number of years required to recover the present value of the project.

Duration	0	1	2	3	4	5	6
Discounted cash flow at 10%			43·31	57·40	46·72	26·95	16·14
Present value of return phase	190·52						
Proportion of present value in each year			0·2273	0·3013	0·2452	0·1415	0·0847
Weighted years			0·4546	0·9039	0·9809	0·7073	0·5082
Duration (= sum of the weighted years)	3·55						

Payback, discounted payback and duration are three techniques that measure the return to liquidity offered by a capital project. In theory, a firm that has ready access to the capital markets should not be concerned about the time taken to recapture the investment in a project. However, in practice managers prefer projects to appear to be successful as quickly as possible. Payback as a technique fails to take into account the time value of money and any cash flows beyond the project date. It is used by many firms as a coarse filter of projects and it has been suggested to be a proxy for the redeployment real option. Discounted payback does surmount the first difficulty but not the second in that it is still possible for projects with highly negative terminal cash flows to appear attractive because of their initial favourable cash flows. Conversely, discounted payback may lead a project to be discarded that has highly favourable cash flows after the payback date.

Duration measures either the average time to recover the initial investment (if discounted at the project's internal rate of return) of a project, or to recover the present value of the project if discounted at the cost of capital as is the case in this question. Duration captures both the time value of money and the whole of the cash flows of a project. It is also a measure which can be used across projects to indicate when the bulk of the project value will be captured.

Its disadvantage is that it is more difficult to conceptualise than payback and may not be employed for that reason.

(c) **Report on project appraisal**

Report to Management
Prepared by: D Obbin, ACCA

I have reviewed the proposed capital investment and after making a number of adjustments have estimated that the project will increase the value of the firm by approximately $29·48 million. The project is highly sensitive to changes in the level of capital investment. Increases in immediate capital spending on this project will lead to a concomitant loss in the overall project value less the tax saving resulting from the increased tax-allowable depreciation. However, given the size of the net present value of the project, it is unlikely that an adverse movement in this variable would lead to a significant reduction in the value of the firm.

The analysis of the payback on this project using discounted cash flows suggests that the value of the capital invested will be wholly recovered within four years of commencement. The bulk of the cash flow recovery occurs early within the life cycle of the project with an average recovery of the total present value occurring 3·55 years from commencement.

On the basis of the figures presented and the sensitivity analysis conducted, I recommend the Board approves this project for investment.

For many years the Board has used payback as one technique for evaluating investment projects. The Board has noted concerns that (i) the method chosen does not reflect the cost of finance either in the cash flows or in the discount rate applied and (ii) it fails to reflect cash flows beyond the payback date. Discounted payback surmounts the first but not the second difficulty. I would recommend that the Board considers the use of "duration" which measures the time to recover either half the value invested in a project or, by alternative measurement, half the project net present value. Because this measure captures both the full value and the time value of a project it is recommended as a superior measure to either payback or discounted payback when comparing the time taken by different projects to recover the investment involved.

As part of its review process the Board has asked for sensitivities of the project to key variables. Sensitivity analysis demonstrates the likely gain or loss of project value as a result of small changes in the value of the variables chosen. Unfortunately, some variables (e.g. price changes and the cost of finance) are highly correlated with one another and focusing upon the movement in a single variable may well ignore significant changes in another variable. To deal with this and given our background information about the volatility of input variables and their correlation, I would recommend that a simulation is conducted taking these component risks into account. Simulation works by randomly drawing a possible value for each variable on a repeated basis until a distribution of net present value outcomes can be established and the priority of each variable in determining the overall net present value obtained. Furthermore, the Board will be in a position to review the potential "value at risk" in a given project.

I recommend that the Board reviews a simulation of project net present values in future and that this forms part of its continuing review process.

Answer 17 DARON

(a) **Report for the managers of Daron**

Any recommendation regarding the sale of the company to a competitor for $20 million should be made in the best interests of the shareholders. An offer of $20 million is an 8.7% premium over the current share price.

Estimates of the present values of future cash flows suggest that if party A wins the election the company's equity value will be $16.3 million and only $7 million if party B wins. In this light the offer of $20 million appears very attractive. .

However, these estimates are by no means precise. Inaccuracy could exist due to:

- Incorrect inflation estimates.
- Errors in sales volume and cost projections.
- Inaccurate discount rate estimates.
- The assumption of a constant 30% corporate tax rate.

Sensitivity analysis is recommended to analyse the significance of changes in key variables. The cash flow estimates do not incorporate any value for options relating to opportunities that might exist between now and 20X6 if operations continue. Nor is there data on the expected realisable value of the company at year 20X6. Even if further investment was not undertaken at that time, the present value of the realisable value of land, buildings and cash flow released from working capital needs to be considered. This would increase the above present value estimates.

Appendix 2 shows the financial estimates of the hotel purchase. An APV of $0.56 million suggests that the hotel investment is financially viable. However, this estimate is also subject to many of the possible inaccuracies noted above. The base case NPV is heavily influenced by the realisable value of $10 million in 20X1. Future hotel values could vary substantially from this estimate.

Investment in the hotel industry is a strategic departure from the company's core competence. If the objective is primarily to diversify activities to reduce risk this may not be in the shareholders' best interest as they can easily achieve diversification of their investment portfolios, through unit trusts or similar investments. As the company is in a declining industry, in the long term diversification may be essential for survival. A medium to long term strategic plan should be formulated examining alternative strategies, and alternative investments which may offer better financial returns than the hotel investment, and/or be closer to the company's existing core competence.

(i) **Appendix 1**

Present value estimates

$million
Political party A wins the election

	20X7	20X8	20X9	20Y0	20Y1	after 20Y1
Sales	28.0	29.0	26.0	22.0	19.0	19.0
Variable cost	17.0	18.0	16.0	14.0	12.0	12.0
Fixed costs	3.0	3.0	3.0	3.0	3.0	3.0
Depreciation	4.0	3.0	3.0	2.0	1.0	–
Taxable	4.0	5.0	4.0	3.0	3.0	4.0
Taxation (30%)	1.2	1.5	1.2	0.9	0.9	1.2
	2.8	3.5	2.8	2.1	2.1	2.8
Add back depreciation	4.0	3.0	3.0	2.0	1.0	–
Working capital		1.0	2.0	3.0	3.0	–
Net cash flow	6.8	7.5	7.8	7.1	6.1	2.8
Discount factors (13%)	0.885	0.783	0.693	0.613	0.543	3.517 × 0.543
Present values	6.0	5.9	5.4	4.4	3.3	5.3

Expected total present value, up to year 20X6 = $30.3 million. We have discounted 'free cash flow to the firm' (i.e. cash available to both equity *and* debt investors) at the average required return of equity and debt investors (i.e. WACC). This gives the theoretical *total* value of the company to its investors (i.e. market value of equity + market value of debt). We need an *equity* valuation to compare to the $20 million offered for the company's shares

Equity value = total value – market value of debt = 30.3–14 = $16.3 million

**$million
Political party B wins the election**

	20X7	20X8	20X9	20Y0	20Y1	after 20Y1
Sales	30.0	26.0	24.0	20.0	16.0	16.0
Variable costs	18.0	16.0	15.0	12:0	11.0	11.0
Fixed costs	3.0	3.0	4.0	4.0	4.0	4.0
Depreciation	4 0	3.0	3.0	2.0	1.0	–
Taxable	5.0	4.0	2.0	2.0	0	1.0
Taxation (30%)	1.5	1.2	0.6	0.6	–	0.3
	3.5	2.8	1.4	1.4	0	0.7
Add back depreciation	4.0	3.0	3.0	2.0	1.0	–
Working capital	(1.0)	2.0	2.0	3.0	3.0	–
Net cash flow	6.5	7.8	6.4	6.4	4.0	0.7
Discount factors (18%)	0.847	0.718	0.609	0.516	0.437	3.127 × 0.437
Present values	5.5	5.6	3.9	3.3	1.7	1.0

Expected total present value, up to year 20X6 = $21 million

Equity valuation = 21 – 14 = $7m

Notes:

Discount rates

- Political party A wins

	$m
Market value of equity 20 million shares at 92c=	18.4
Debt	14.0
	32.4

The risk free rate *including* inflation is (1.04) (1.05) =1.092 or 9.2%
The market return *including* inflation is (1.10) (1.05) = 1.155 or 15.5%
Using CAPM, $K_e = R_F + (R_m - R_F) \beta_e$
$K_e = 9.2\% + (15.5\% - 9.2\%) 1.25 = 17.075\%$

$$WACC = 17.075\% \times \frac{18.4}{32.4} + 10\% (1 - 0.3) \frac{14}{32.4} = 12.72\% \text{ or approximately } 13\%.$$

- Political party B wins

The risk free rate including inflation is (1.04) (1.10) = 1.144 or 14.4%
The market return including inflation is (1.10) (1.10) = 1.21 or 21%
$K_e = 14.4\% + (21\% - 14.4\%) 1.25 = 22.65\%$

$$WACC = 22.65\% \times \frac{18.4}{32.4} + 15.5\% (1 - 0.3) \frac{14}{32.4} = 17.6\% \text{ or approximately } 18\%.$$

Tutorial note: *This is only a rough estimate as the share price is likely to fall with higher inflation, leading to higher gearing.*

Both K_e and K_d could alter because of these factors.

The use of the current share price in both WACC estimates is problematic. In an efficient market this price will reflect the present uncertainty about the forthcoming election. Once this uncertainty is resolved the share price is likely to change, leading to new market weighted gearing levels. Fortunately the investment decision is not highly sensitive to marginal changes in the discount rate.

Expected values

The use of expected values is not recommended as it does not reflect a situation that is likely to occur in reality.

(ii)   **Appendix 2**

$million
Cash flows, possible hotel purchase

	20X7	*20X8*	*20X9*	*20Y0*	*20Y1*
Revenue	9.0	10.0	11.0	12.0	13.0
Variable costs	6.0	6.0	7.0	7.0	8.0
Fixed costs	2.0	2.0	2.0	2.0	2.0
Taxable	1.0	2.0	2.0	3.0	3.0
Taxation (30%)	0.3	0.6	0.6	0.9	0.9
	0.7	1.4	1.4	2.1	2.1
Working capital	(1.0)	–	–	(1.0)	–
Realisable value					10.0
Net cash flows	(0.3)	1.4	1.4	1.1	12.1
Discount factors (14%)	0.877	0.769	0.675	0.592	0.519
Present values	(0.3)	1.1	0.9	0.7	6.3

Base case NPV = ($9.0) m + $8.7m = ($0.3) m

Tutorial note: *For APV the base case NPV is required, which is estimated from the ungeared cost of equity.*

Assuming corporate debt is risk free

$$\beta_e \text{ ungeared} = \beta_e \text{ geared} \frac{E}{E + D(1-t)}$$

$$= 1.25 \times \frac{18.4}{18.4 + 14(1-0.3)} = 0.82$$

K_e ungeared = 9.2% + (15.5% – 9.2%) 0.82 = 14.4% or approximately 14%

Financing side effects for the five year period:

Including issue costs, the gross sum required will be $\dfrac{9m}{0.98}$ = $9,184,000.

$9.18m × 10% × 30% per year tax saving = $275,520 per year

Discounted at 10% over 5 years gives a present value of 3.791 × $275,520 = $1,044,000

Tutorial note: *This assumes that an extra $9.184 million debt capacity is created by the hotel investment. If less debt capacity is created the present value of the tax shield attributable to the investment will be reduced.*

The 10% coupon is assumed to correctly reflect the risk of the convertible, and is used as the discount rate for the tax savings.

The estimated APV is the base case NPV plus the financing side effects:

	$m
Base case NPV	(0.30)
Issue costs	(0.18)
PV of tax saving	1.04
APV	0.56

(b) Implications of financing with convertible bonds

Daron's current gearing, measured by the book value of medium and long term loans to equity is: $\dfrac{14}{22}$ or 63.6%

No information is provided about short-term loans which would increase this figure further. A $9 million convertible bond issue would initially increase gearing to

$\dfrac{23}{22}$ or 104.5%

a level that involves "high" financial risk especially for a company in a declining industry. The coupon rate of 10%, or $918,400 interest per year would have to be paid for five years or more. Convertible bonds normally carry lower coupon rates than straight debt. Daron can borrow long term from its bank at 10% per year, and the 10% coupon on the convertible appears to be expensive. However, this could be explained by the market seeking a relatively high return because of the size of the loan.

If conversion takes place the gearing level will fall, but this is not possible for at least five years. At the $100 issue price the effective conversion price is $\dfrac{\$100}{60}$ or 167 centos per share

This represents an average share price increase of 12.7% per year over five years, which is possible if market prices in general increase, but is by no means guaranteed.

The existence of the call and put options has potentially significant implications for Daron. The call option allows the company to limit the potential gains made by bond holders. If the share price reaches 200 centos between 1 January 20X2 and 31 December 20X4 the company can force the bond holders to convert, giving maximum capital gains on conversion of 33 centos per share (relative to the $100 issue price). This is a small gain and may not be popular with investors. If the share price falls below 100 centos between the same dates, the bond holders can ask the company to redeem the bonds at par, forcing the company to find $9 million for repayment of the bonds. If the market price of the shares has only moved by a maximum of eight centos over five years, the company might experience difficulty refinancing the $9 million, leading to severe problems in finding the cash for redemption.

Answer 18 MERCURY TRAINING

(a) **Cost of equity and weighted average cost of capital**

Tutorial note: the key is to build-up Mercury's asset beta as a weighted average of the asset beta of training (using Jupiter as a proxy) and the asset beta of the financial services sector. Theoretically the weighting should be according to the relative value of Mercury's training and financial services assets but, as we don't know this, we use the fact that financial services accounts for one-third and Mercury's revenues and hence training two thirds.

De-gear Jupiter's equity beta:

$$\beta a = \left[\frac{V_e}{(V_e + V_d(1-T))}\beta_e\right] + \left[\frac{V_d(1-T)}{(V_e + V_d(1-T))}\beta_d\right]$$

$$\beta a = \left[\frac{88}{(88 + 12(1-0.4))}1.50\right] = 1.39$$

De-gear the equity beta of financial services sector:

$$\beta a = \left[\frac{75}{(75 + 25(1-0.4))}0.90\right] = 0.75$$

Mercury's combined asset beta = $(1.39 \times {}^2/_3) + (0.75 \times {}^1/_3) = 1.18$

Re-gear to Mercury's equity beta:

$$1.18 = \left[\frac{70}{(70 + 30(1-0.4))}\beta e\right]$$

βe = 1.48

Cost of equity geared = 4.5% + (1.48 × 3.5%) = 9.68%

WACC = (9.68% × 0.7) + ((4.5% + 2.5%) × (1 − 0.4) × 0.3)) = 8%

The equity cost of capital is used for valuing flows to equity investors (such as dividends or Free Cash Flow to Equity).

The weighted average cost of capital is for valuing flows attributable to the entity i.e. to all classes of long-term capital (such as project cash flows or Free Cash Flow to the Firm).

(b) Likely range of issue prices

At the low end the firm's net assets at fair value would be the realisable value of the equity between a willing buyer and seller. This is 650c per share which would represent the lower end of any negotiating range.

Using the dividend valuation model we estimate the share price at the upper end using the latest DPS of 25c per share and the cost of equity capital of 9·68%. Three potential growth rates present themselves: the historic earnings growth which at 12% is greater than the firm's equity cost of capital and is therefore not sustainable over the very long run, the anticipated growth rate of the two sectors weighted according to the firm's revenue from each (0·67 × 6% + 0·33 × 4% = 5·33%) and the rate implied from the firm's reinvestment:

$$g = br_e = \frac{(100 - 25)}{100} \times 0.0968 = 7.26\%$$

Value of the firm using the growth model and the higher of the two feasible growth rates:

$$P_0 = \frac{D_0(1+g)}{r_e + g}$$

$$P_0 = \frac{25 \times (1.0726)}{(0.0968 - 0.0726)} = \$11.08 \text{ per share}$$

In addition, the share price gives a spot estimate of the value of a dividend stream in the hands of a minority investor. If the option to float is taken then a share price of $11·08 could be achieved especially if a portion of the equity and effective control are retained. However, if a sale is made to a private equity investor then it may be appropriate to value the firm taking into account the benefits of control which can be substantial if the purchaser is able to generate significant synergistic benefits either in terms of revenue enhancement, cost efficiency or more favourable access to the capital market. Control premiums can be as much as 30–50% of the spot price of the equity. In this case an opening negotiation may start with a share price of $16·62.

(c) Public listing versus private equity finance

The two principal sources of large-scale equity finance are either through a public listing on a recognised stock exchange or through the private equity market. The former represents the traditional approach for firms who have grown beyond a certain size and where the owners wish to release, in whole or in part, their equity stake within the firm, or where they wish to gain access to new, large scale equity finance. The procedure for gaining a public listing is lengthy and invariably requires professional sponsorship from a company that specialises in this type of work. Depending upon the jurisdiction there are three stages that may have to be fulfilled before a firm can raise capital on a stock exchange:

(1) Formalise the company's status as a public limited company with rights to issue its shares to the public. In some jurisdictions this requires re-registration and in others it is implicit in the conferment of limited liability.

(2) Seek regulatory approval for admission to a public list of companies who have met the basic criteria required for entry to a stock exchange (in the UK this process is under the jurisdiction of the Financial Services Authority).

(3) Fulfil the requirements of the exchange concerned which may entail the publication of a prospectus which is an audited document containing, among other things, projections of future earnings and profitability.

The disadvantage of public listing is that a company will be exposed to stake building by other companies, regulatory oversight by the stock exchange and greater public scrutiny. Stock exchanges require that quoted companies comply with company law as a matter of course but also that they adhere to various codes of practice associated with good governance and takeovers. They must also comply with stock exchange rules with respect to the provision of information and dealing with shareholders.

Private equity finance is the name given to finance raised from investors organised through a venture capital company or a private equity business. As the name suggests these investors do not operate through the formal equity market but they operate within the context of the wider capital market for high risk finance. Because of its position, PEF does not impose the same regulatory regime as the public market. Transaction costs tend to be lower and there is evidence to suggest that private equity finance offers companies the ability to restructure and take long term decisions which have adverse short term consequences. In some jurisdictions there are favourable tax advantages to private equity investors.

Answer 19 BIGUN

(a) **Report on acquisitions**

To The Directors, Klein Co
From Anna Liszt
Date Today

Subject Cost of acquisitions to Klein Co

Contents

1 Terms of reference
2 Summary
3 Klein Co
4 PTT Co
5 Conclusions
6 Appendix

1 Terms of reference

The following report estimates the values of Klein Co and PTT Co.

2 Summary

The following table gives some estimates of the possible value of the two companies.

Valuation basis	Klein Co	PTT Co
P/E ratio	$10.15m	$10.28m
Dividend valuation	$16m	$12.96m
Net asset value	$6.3m	$6.5m

Because these valuations are based on estimates they must be seen as a guide only. Details of these calculations are given in the appendix.

3 Klein Co

The P/E ratio approach for Klein is the best estimate available; being based on actual earnings and the observed P/E ratio it gives the actual market value at March 20Y3. Note, however, that the situation of Klein might have changed significantly since that date. The dividend valuation approach gives a higher valuation for Klein, but the assumption that investors expect past growth to continue into the future is questionable.

The asset valuation is of little worth, no indication being given of current values, goodwill, etc.

4 PTT Co

PTT is not a quoted company and therefore any estimate of its value will be somewhat arbitrary.

The dividend valuation of $12.96m is probably the best estimate but, once again, caution must be exercised due to the difficulty in estimating growth.

The P/E ratio approach is suspect as the multiple of Klein (a quoted company) has been used. It is usually considered that non-quoted firms should have much lower P/E ratios and a reduction of up to 50% on this valuation is possible.

For similar reasons as those given for Klein the asset value of PTT is of limited use.

5 Conclusions

All of the above figures should be seen as educated guesses. The final price paid will depend upon how much each party wishes to sell and how strongly Bigun wishes to buy. The estimates of $10.15m and $12.96m for Klein and PTT respectively are probably the best guide but premiums of up to 25% on opening market price are not uncommon, rising to 50% plus if the bid is contested.

6 Appendix

Klein

(1) P/E ratio approach

EPS × P/E ratio = Market value per share

Current EPS = $\dfrac{(\$1.5m - (\$6m \times 11\%)) \times 0.65}{5m \text{ shares}}$

= $0.1092 per share

P/E ratio = 18.6 : 1 (given)

Market price per share on historic EPS = $0.1092 × 18.6 = $2.03

Total value of Klein equity = $2.03 × 5m shares

= $10.15m

(2) Dividend valuation

D_0 = EPS × Proportion paid out as dividend

   = $0.1092 × 40%   = $0.04368

$$P_0 = \frac{D_0(1+g)}{k_e - g} = \frac{0.04368 \times 1.105}{0.12 - 0.105} = \$3.22 \text{ per share}$$

Therefore, total value: = $3.22 × 5m   = $16.1m

PTT

(3) Dividend valuation

$$D_0 = \frac{(\$1.4m - (\$5.5m \times 10\%)) \times 0.65 \times 0.75}{2.8m \text{ shares}}$$

= $0.14799 per share

$$P_0 = \frac{D_0(1+g)}{k_e - g}$$

$$= \frac{0.14799 \times 1.095}{0.13 - 0.095}$$

= $4.63 per share

Total value of PTT equity

   = $4.63 × 2.8m

   = $12.96m

(4) P/E valuation – using P/E ratio for Klein

EPS   = $0.19732

(i.e. $D_0 \times \frac{1}{0.75} = 0.14799 \times \frac{1}{0.75} = 0.19732$)

$0.19732 × 18.6   = $3.67 per share

Total value of equity of PTT

   = $3.67 × 2.8m

   = $10.28m

(b) **Packages to be offered by Bigun**

The packages that may be offered partly depend upon the sum of money involved. Let us assume that both companies are bid for at a total cost of $10.2m + $13.0m + a premium, say, $26 million.

The following packages could be used.

A cash offer

This has the advantage that all parties are assured of the sum received. However, it could put the shareholders in the victim companies in a capital gains tax paying position. Further, Bigun has only $5m of cash, and borrowing or an equity issue would be required to raise the remainder of the cash.

A loan stock for share exchange

Bigun could offer to exchange loan stock in return for the shares of the victim companies. This would give the victim shareholders a fairly safe income stream and not expose them to immediate capital gains tax. It would, however, prevent them from participating in future profit growth and this might not be popular.

From the viewpoint of Bigun it would cause a significant increase in gearing which might be of concern to existing investors.

A share-for-share exchange

Bigun could offer to exchange new shares for the existing shares in Klein and PTT. At a current market price of $2.98 (EPS 16.21 cents × P/E ratio 18.4), and a bid of $26m, this would require the issue of approximately 8.7m shares. The current EPS of Bigun is 16.21 cents, whereas the incremental EPS on the new shares is only

$$\frac{\text{Current equity of Klein and PTT}}{8.7\text{m shares}} = \frac{\$1{,}098{,}500}{8{,}700{,}000} = 12.6 \text{ cents}$$

This would result in a reduction in EPS (and possibly market value) of Bigun shares.

Overall each of the various packages presents problems. Bigun shareholders might not be happy with a cash offer because of liquidity problems, whereas the use of loan stock could drive gearing to an unacceptable level. An equity issue could result in a reduction in EPS though much would depend upon the combined earnings of the three companies. A compromise solution often adopted would be to use a mixture of the above packages, for example a cash and equity offer.

Answer 20 DEMAST

(a) **Advantages and disadvantages of growth by acquisition**

Growth by acquisition is said to allow companies to expand much more rapidly than by organic growth. Rapid increases in size may offer:

- Economies of scale in production, marketing, R & D and finance. A reduction in the company's risk, and cost of capital.

- Greater market share and market power. In some markets to operate effectively requires the achievement of a "critical mass" size.

Additionally acquisitions may allow:

- Improvements in gearing.

- Purchase of patents, brands or skilled management.

- Synergistic effects.

- Entry into a new market quickly.

- Acquisition of undervalued assets or companies, as is the stated strategy of BZO International. This may encompass the removal of relatively inefficient management.

However, there is evidence that many acquisitions are financially unsuccessful. There is often some abnormal return for the shareholders of the target company (in the form of high prices received for their shares), but very little for the bidding company's shareholders. Acquisitions often experience difficulties in integrating the operations of the companies concerned (unless asset-stripping is the motive for the acquisition).

(b) **Financial prudence of bids**

Demast is an unlisted company, with no market price. Ideally the valuation of the company should be based upon the expected net present value of future cash flows, but accurate estimates of this value will rarely be available in an acquisition situation. Valuation could in practice be based upon either assets or earnings. For Nadion, which is likely to be purchasing Demast as a going concern, an earnings valuation is appropriate. BZO International has a strategy of acquiring what are perceived to be undervalued companies. If the intention is to quickly dispose of all or part of the company, the realisable value of Demast's assets would provide a useful guide, but if asset stripping is not to occur an earnings-based valuation would once again be recommended.

Asset valuations

No precise estimate of the realisable value of assets is possible. Net asset value, adjusted for a 10% decrease in the value of inventory, is $5,950,000 or 149 cents per share. This, however, ignores important factors including:

(i) Land and buildings have not been revalued since 20X0. In the light of the subsequent recession and fall in commercial property prices, the realisable value could be less than the book value of $4 million.

(ii) No information is provided regarding the difference between book and realisable values of other tangible assets.

(iii) The patents are not valued in the statement of financial position. These could have substantial value if they have a number of years to run.

Earnings valuations

Two common methods of "earnings" based valuations are the P/E ratio and the dividend valuation model.

P/E – As Demast is not listed a P/E valuation must be based upon the P/E of a similar company. The only available information for a company in the same industry is for Nadioli, a much larger company.

The EPS of Demast is 80.5 cents

EPS of Nadion is 58 cents

P/E of Nadion is $\dfrac{320}{58} = 5.52$

If this is used for Demast the estimated value per share is

5.52 × 80.5 cents = 444 cents

Although Nadion is listed and much larger than Demast, the much higher growth rates of Demast might justify the use of the similar P/E to Nadion.

Dividend valuation model

$$P = \dfrac{D_1}{K_e - g}$$

Current DPS of Demast is $\dfrac{1,500}{4,000} = 37.5$ cents

At 9% growth the expected net dividend is 37.5 (1.09) = 40.875 cents

$P = \dfrac{40.875}{0.16 - 0.09} = 584$ cents per share

All of these estimates are subject to considerable margins of error.

Value of the bids

7 September – BZO bids 7 1 0 × $^2/_3$ = 473 cents per share

2 October – Nadion bids 170 cents plus effectively $4 per share ($100 bond at par for $6.25 nominal value or 25 ordinary shares), total 570 cents per share plus the conversion opportunity.

The conversion is currently at an implied price of $\dfrac{\$100}{26} = 385$ cents per share.

This is only 14.9% above the current share price of Nadion (335 cents), and the opportunity for substantial capital gains on conversion exists as there are up to five years before the final conversion date. A rise in stock market price could mean that Nadion issues new shares on conversion at well under market price to Demast's old shareholders.

19 October – BZO cash offer of 600 cents per share.

Commentary

Although all offers are significantly above the estimated asset valuation, the final successful bid is only 16 cents above the dividend valuation model figure. If this is accurate, the bid would seem to be financially prudent. However, BZO's strategy is to acquire undervalued companies. Unless BZO has knowledge of how to significantly increase the value of Demast (e.g. by disposing of part of the operations, or land) the acquisition of Demast does not appear to be in line with this strategy. Additionally financing the 600 cents cash offer with a $24 million term loan increases the book value of BZO's gearing (measured by loans and overdraft to shareholders' funds) from its already high level of $\frac{30+35}{69}$ = 94%.

If the stock market is efficient the significant fails in BZO's share price on the occasions of both of the company's bids illustrate that the acquisition is not regarded as financially beneficial by the company's shareholders.

(c) Problems of corporate governance

Knowledge is required of the nature of corporate governance, and discussion of possible conflicts between the objectives of directors and shareholders of both the acquiring and acquired company using specific information on an acquisition.

Corporate governance is the system by which companies are run. The board of directors should act on behalf of the shareholders of the company, taking note of other interest groups such as the government, creditors, customers and employees.

In an acquisition situation the actions of directors are constrained by the City Code on Takeovers and Mergers, a set of self-regulatory rules administered and enforced by the Panel on Takeovers and Mergers. The directors of both the bidding and bid for companies should disregard their own personal interests when advising shareholders.

It is questionable whether BZO's directors' actions are in the best interests of the company's shareholders, given the market reaction to the bid and the likely adverse effects on the company's gearing and interest cover. The company appears short of liquidity (current ratio 0.79:1), and may be trying to maintain its high growth in revenue through acquisitions.

The directors of Demast advised shareholders to reject the bid of Nadion worth 570 cents plus a likely capital gain on conversion, and accept the bid from BZO of 600 cents, which also offered them seats on subsidiary boards within BZO. It could be argued that the directors were acting in their own interests to retain well-paid employment, and not in the interests of the owners of the 75% of the shares not controlled by the directors and their families, although the value of the conversion option is difficult to quantify. Acceptance of the bid by BZO might also affect the operations and employment levels of Demast, if part of the operation were to be sold, or the patents sold. Continuity of current operations would be more likely under the ownership of Nadion, a company in the same industry, although some cost-saving rationalisation might occur, with loss of employment.

Answer 21 LACETO

(a) Offer price

Laceto will wish to pay the minimum price that will attract the majority of Omnigen's shareholders to sell. The current market price of 410 cents per share, or a total market value of $123 million, is likely to be the lowest that shareholders of Omnigen would accept, and unless there is an expectation that Omnigen's shares will fall further in value in the near future, a premium over the current market price will normally be payable.

If industry P/E ratios are used to value Omnigen, the range of values would be $182 million to $210 million. (Omnigen's total earnings after tax of $14 million, multiplied by the PEs of 13:1 and 15:1.) However, Omnigen's current P/E ratio is 8·78:1, given a value of $123 million. Even if the share price had not fallen it would only have been just over 13:1, or a value of $184 million. Unless there is an expectation that Omnigen's share price will soon return to a higher level the use of a forecast PE/ or comparative P/Es of companies which might have very different characteristics to Omnigen is not recommended.

The realisable value of assets, $82 million, is substantially below the estimates based on P/E ratios, probably because Omnigen is a profitable company which is planned to continue trading after the potential acquisition. The realisable value of assets is not the recommended valuation method unless it produces a value higher than the value as a going concern.

A better method of estimating the value of Omnigen is to use the cash flow projections to find the present value of Omnigen to Laceto. This will be based upon the free cash flow after replacement expenditure and expenditure required to achieve the forecast growth levels.

Financial year	*20X2*	*20X3*	*20X4*	*20X5*	*After 20X5*
	$m	$m	$m	$m	$m
Net sales	230	261	281	298	
Cost of goods sold (50%)	115	131	141	149	
Selling and administrative expenses	32	34	36	38	
Tax-allowable depreciation	40	42	42	42	
	187	207	219	229	
Taxable	43	54	62	69	
Taxation (30%)	12·9	16·2	18·6	20·7	
	30·1	37·8	43·4	48·3	
Add tax-allowable depreciation	40	42	42	42	
Less cash flow needed for asset replacement and forecast growth	(50)	(52)	(55)	(58)	
Net cash flow	20·1	27·8	30·4	32·3	
Discount factors (14%) **Note**	0·877	0·769	0·675	0·592	
Present values	17·6	21·4	20·5	19·1	$19 \cdot 1 \frac{19 \cdot 1(1 \cdot 03)}{0 \cdot 14 - 0 \cdot 03} = 178 \cdot 8$

Total present value is $257·4 million (the sum of the present values for each year). This value is the value of the entire entity (i.e. equity plus debt). The value of debt will depend upon the final gearing, and will vary between approximately $46 million and $59 million (18%–23% gearing), giving a value of equity between $198 million and $211 million. If growth is 5% the present value of the entity would be $301·4 million, and the value of equity between $232 million and $247 million.

These estimates use a present value to infinity estimate beyond 20X5. If a shorter time horizon was used (e.g. 10 years) the estimates would be considerably reduced.

Assuming these cash flow projections are reasonably accurate, which itself must be subject to serious doubt (e.g. can the imbalance after year five between tax-allowable depreciation and replacement capital expenditure continue indefinitely), it is clearly worth Laceto offering a premium over the current market price for the shares of Omnigen. In theory, using present values to infinity, it could afford to offer a premium of more than 50% above the current market price, but to increase its own value it would offer the lowest price that would attract more than 50% of the shareholders of Omnigen. It is not possible to know what this price would be. An initial bid might offer a 25–30% premium above the current price, or between $154 million and $160 million. If that bid was refused then there is scope for increasing it up to a maximum of the estimated equity present values discussed above.

It must be stressed that all of the above estimates are subject to significant margins of error, and that valuation for takeovers is not a precise science.

Note:

Omnigen's cost of equity after the acquisition is used as this is likely to reflect the systematic risk of the activities of Omnigen within Laceto. As the range of expected gearing levels is quite small (18–23%), and gearing is relatively low, it is assumed that the cost of equity will not significantly change over this range of gearing, other than the change already reflected in the increase in the equity beta by 0·1.

$k_e = 6\% + 1·3(14\% – 6\%) = 16·4\%$

The cost of debt is not given but may be estimated from the data regarding Laceto's bond. As Omnigen currently has a lower gearing than Laceto, it is assumed increasing Omnigen's gearing should not have a significant effect on Laceto's cost of debt, even if the overall gearing increases to 23%.

The cost of debt, by trial and error is:

At 6% interest	
$12(1 – 0·3) \times 2·673 =$	22·45
$100 \times 0·840 =$	84·00
	106·45
At 5% interest	
$12(1 – 0·3) \times 2·723 =$	22·87
$100 \times 0·864 =$	86·40
	109·27

Market price of bond = 108.8. Therefore the post-tax cost of debt is close to 5%

By interpolation $5\% + \dfrac{0.47}{0.47 + 2.35} \times 1\% = 5·17\%$

The weighted average cost of capital may be estimated for the full range of expected gearing:

At 18% gearing:
The weighted average cost of capital is $16·4 \times 0·82 + 5·17\% \times 0·18 = 14·38\%$

At 23% gearing:
The weighted average cost of capital is 16·4 × 0·77 + 5·17% × 0·23 = 13·82%

The estimated WACC does not change dramatically over the possible range in gearing.

14% will be used as the discount rate.

(b) Report on possible defences against a bid by Agressa.com

Defences against a bid will differ according to whether or not the bid has yet been made.

If no bid has been made Laceto can attempt to make itself unattractive to any potential bidder. Laceto might establish "poison pills" such as granting the right to alternative shareholders to purchase its shares at a deep discount, or dispose of some of its key activities ("crown jewels") to make it less attractive to Agressa. The company might also introduce "golden parachutes" for key staff, expensive severance contracts which come into effect if executive jobs are lost as a result of an acquisition. The articles of association could be amended to require a high percentage of shareholders to approve a merger or acquisition, for example 75% plus. Strategic acquisitions are also possible, whereby companies are acquired by Laceto which would be unattractive to a bidder, but are developed to be an integral part of Laceto's activities.

Laceto should also ensure that the financial press and the company's shareholders are kept fully informed about the company's financial strengths and future strategy, with particular focus on key institutional shareholders which are likely to determine the success or failure of any bid. Assets should be regularly revalued to ensure that shareholders are aware of "current" values.

If Laceto has significant free cash flow it might consider the repurchase of shares in the expectation that the share price will increase and make a takeover more expensive to a potential bidder such as Agressa.

Financial summaries of the two companies are:

	Agressa.com	Laceto
	$m	$m
Revenue	190	420
Profit before tax	8	41
Taxation	2	12
Market capitalisation of shares	397·5	304
Price/earnings ratio	66:1	10·5:1

Despite its smaller revenue and net assets Agressa.com has a higher market capitalisation, which is manifested in the P/E ratio of 66:1. This probably reflects its position as a "dot.com" company rather than a traditional retailer.

Once a bid has been made, probably the most important defence against the bid is to persuade shareholders that Agressa.com is currently overvalued. It has relatively small earnings, but a P/E of 66:1 suggests that the market expects the company to experience rapid future growth.

In the limited period of their existence "dot.com" companies have experienced great volatility in their share price, many have yet to exhibit sustained growth, and some have failed. Laceto might highlight the history of dot.com companies and their relative risk. It could also criticise the logic behind the acquisition, and the strategic fit of the two companies, although the latter might be difficult as there is an overlap in existing activities.

It might also be argued that the shares of Laceto are undervalued. The company is earning more than $40 million before tax and its P/E ratio at 10·5:1 is lower than other companies in the electrical sector. Unless the P/E and prospects of the company are being strongly pulled down by the clothing activities, Laceto should release forecasts (with supporting assumptions) of future earnings and dividends to support the argument that it is undervalued.

Laceto might consider making a counter bid for Agressa.com, although this could be contrary to the strategic plans of the company, and might be difficult to achieve given the P/E difference of the companies.

If the combined market share of the two companies is large enough the bid might be referred to regulatory authorities such as the Competition Commission in the UK. Given the size of the companies this is not likely in this case.

A further possibility is to approach a "white knight", a preferred alternative bidder for the company, but this, if successful, would also result in the company being taken over.

(c) Payment method

Payment may be made in ordinary shares, preference shares, some form of debt, often with a conversion or warrant option attached, cash, or some combination of these. From an investor's perspective cash provides a known, precise sum, and might be favoured for this reason. However, in some countries payment in cash might lead to an immediate capital gains tax liability for the investor. Preference shares and debt are rarely favoured by investors as they alter the characteristic and risk of the investment. Payment with ordinary shares offers a continuation in ownership of the entity, albeit as part of the successful bidder. However, relative share prices will change during the period of the bid, and the owner of shares in the potential victim company will not know the precise post-acquisition value of the bid.

Neither of the potential bids in (a) or (b) could be financed entirely in cash without significant new external borrowing, with its resultant impact on gearing. In part (b) the volatility of dot.com shares might make payment in shares unattractive to investors. Sometimes investors are given a choice in the method of payment, with the logic that different forms of payment might be attractive to different types of investor. This could influence the success or failure of both bids, but is problematic for the bidder in that the cash needs and number of shares to be issued are not known, and the company's capital structure may alter in an unplanned manner. Ideally a bidder would like to tailor the form of the bid to that favoured by major investors in the potential victim company.

Answer 22 MINPRICE & SAVEALOT

(a) Analysis of bid

The bid will only be accepted by shareholders of Savealot if the value of the bid is at a premium over the current share price. The premium required for acceptance will differ between shareholders.

At current market prices the bid of four Minprice shares for three Savealot shares values Savealot shares at 309 cents, a premium of 14 cents or 4·7% above the current market price. This is only a relatively small premium, and unless acceptance of the bid is recommended by Savealot's directors, is unlikely to be attractive to many of Savealot's shareholders.

Factors that might influence the decision include:

- Savealot currently has higher growth in dividends and earnings per share than Minprice. Similarly, the Price/Earnings ratio of Savealot is 14·75, and of Minprice 13·9 indicating market expectations of Savealot continuing to have slightly better prospects.

- Using the dividend growth model $P = \dfrac{D_1}{k_e - g}$, the intrinsic value of Savealot's shares may be estimated at $\dfrac{12.5(1.08)}{0.13 - 0.08} = 270$ cents, where 12·5 cents is the current dividend per share.

    This would suggest that Savealot shares are currently overvalued, and might encourage shareholders to sell. Such a conclusion would imply that the market is inefficient, and is not correctly pricing Savealot's shares.

- If the shareholders are considering keeping Minprice's shares after the acquisition they may be concerned that Minprice is much more highly geared than Savealot.

    Measured by long term loans to shareholders funds, gearing levels are:

	Book value	Market value
Minprice	$\dfrac{314}{222} = 141\%$	$\dfrac{364}{696} = 52\%$
Savealot	$\dfrac{17.5}{54.5} = 32\%$	$\dfrac{17.5}{118} = 14\cdot8\%$

    Savealot's shareholders may be reluctant to accept the extra financial risk. Naturally, they would have the opportunity to sell Minprice shares if they accepted the offer, but this would involve transactions costs and would be at an uncertain price.

- The difference in dividend policy may be important to some shareholders. Dividend yield for Minprice is 3·4%, for Savealot it is 4·2%, and dividend cover for Minprice is 2·1 times, for Savealot 1·6 times.

    Minprice's shareholders are likely to welcome the bid if it increases the value of their shares. The estimated effect on share price of the bid is:

	$million
Total earnings available to shareholders 50 + 8 =	58
Number of shares 300 million + 53.333 million	353·33 million
Expected earnings per share	16·42 cents
Expected P/E ratio (market weighted average of Minprice and Savealot P/E ratios)	14·02
Estimated price (P/E × EPS)	230 cents

    This is a slight fall in share price.

    However, when the effects of the rationalisation are announced the impact on expected NPV will be at least $6·8m − $9·0m + $2·70m × 3·605 = $7·53m.

This will add approximately $\frac{\$7 \cdot 53m}{353 \cdot 33m}$ = 2·1 cents to the value of Minprice's shares, restoring the value to approximately 232 cents.

In terms of the effect on share value Minprice's shareholders are likely to be neutral. If, however, there are other synergies or growth opportunities as a result of the acquisition then Minprice's shareholders are likely to welcome the bid. For example if employing some of Savealot's more able managers can improve the cash flows and growth of Minprice.

Wage savings are likely to be for a longer period than five years, adding a further benefit to share price.

(b) **Possible effects of amended offer terms**

The financial attraction of the zero coupon bond can be assessed by estimating the redemption yield and/or likely immediate capital gain. At the current price of 295 cents, a zero coupon bond is being offered for the equivalent to 295 cents × 10 = $29.50.

This is redeemable at $100 in 10 years' time.

The gross redemption yield on the bond may be estimated by solving $\$29 \cdot 50 = \frac{\$100}{(1+r)^{10}}$

The required discount factor is 0·295 in ten years. This is found from present value tables to give an interest rate of 13%. A redemption yield of 13% is significantly higher than the current 10% yield on new ten year loan stock, and might be attractive to Savealot's shareholders.

Assuming the zero coupon bond and new ten year loan stock have the same risk, the expected market price of the zero coupon bond upon issue may be estimated as:

Price = $\frac{\$100}{(1+0.1)^{10}}$ = $38·55

This is an expected premium, per Savealot share, of $\frac{\$38 \cdot 55 - \$29 \cdot 50}{10}$ = $0·905

or almost 31%.

As this would be available as an immediate capital gain it might be attractive to Savealot's shareholders.

In practice, risk is likely to differ slightly as the securities have a different duration.

Tutorial note: *duration is a measure of the relative volatility of bonds caused by/due to changes in prevailing interest rates. It differs from the maturity of the bond by considering the impact of cash flows within the life of the bond. The greater the impact of cash flows within the life of the bond then the shorter is the duration and the less volatile is the bond. Only in the case of a zero coupon bond is the duration equal to the maturity.*

Although the bonds would increase Minprice's relatively high level of gearing, there would be no immediate adverse cash flow effects, unless a sinking fund was created to meet the redemption payment in 10 years' time. A cash offer of 325 cents per share is a 10% premium above the current market price, which is better than the initial share offer but significantly worse than the expected premium with the zero coupon bond. Savealot's shareholders will know exactly how much they will receive, which is not the case if they are paid in securities, but might be liable to taxation on capital gains that they have made since purchasing the share. No immediate capital gains tax liability would exist if payment was made in shares or bonds.

(c) **Advice on defences**

Any defences against a bid must be legal, and fall within the City Code on Takeovers and Mergers. Some of the directors' suggestions would not be permitted.

After a bid had been made Savealot would be prohibited from altering its Articles of Association to require a 75% of shareholders to approve the acquisition.

Section 151 of the Companies Act, 1985 prohibits a third party, for a fee, purchasing the company's shares. This suggestion is likely to be viewed as the company effectively purchasing its own shares and would be illegal.

It is possible to announce that profits are likely to double next year, but the assumptions underlying such a statement would need to be clearly specified so that shareholders could make their own judgement as to its validity.

Savealot could mount an advertising campaign criticising the management of Minprice, but any statements about performance must be supported by relevant data.

Tangible assets could be revalued by an independent external valuer. Whether or not this has any effect on the perceived market value of Savealot would depend upon market efficiency. If the market is efficient the current value of tangible assets would already be known and would form part of the existing market price. In such circumstances a professional revaluation would not result in shareholders placing a higher value on the company.

Answer 23 DRICOM

Report for the board of directors of Dricom Co on the proposed reconstruction

The scheme of reconstruction is likely to be successful if:

- It leaves all providers of finance in at least as good a position as they would have been had the reconstruction not taken place.

- It treats all parties fairly.

- Adequate finance is provided for the company's needs.

- As a result of the reconstruction the company is expected to be financially viable.

If the reconstruction does not take place it is possible that the company will be forced into receivership during the next year or soon afterwards as losses are likely to continue without the new investment. Even if the company survives 20X8, the $1 million repayment of the convertible bond in 20X9 is likely to pose a major cash flow problem.

The following analysis assumes 30 September 20X7 values, but the situation could have deteriorated since that time.

If the company was to go into receivership, the expected realisable value of assets would be:

	$000
Land and buildings	1,200
Plant and machinery	1,600
Inventory	670
Receivables	1,090
Cash	35
	4,595

Existing creditors are:	
Secured	
9% bond 500	
8% convertible bond	1,000
Bank term loan	800
	2,300
Redundancy payments	1,000
Unsecured	
10% loan stock	500
Overdraft	620
Other creditors	940
	2,060

The secured creditors are likely to be fully repaid, and the redundancy payments made, but the unsecured creditors will only receive approximately 63 cents in the dollar ((4,595 – 2,300 – 1,000)/2,060), assuming all rank equally.

Ordinary shareholders would receive nothing.

The cash flows associated with the reconstruction are:

Outflows:	$000
Purchase of new machinery and equipment	2,250
Redundancy payments	500
Payment to ordinary shareholders	280
	3,030

Inflows:	
Venture capital company	1,000
BXT bank	1,200 (incremental loan)
Directors and employees	750
Sale of surplus machinery	300
	3,250

There is also $35,000 of existing cash. The financing provision looks adequate (assuming the overdraft remains unchanged), but no allowance has been made for possible incremental working capital that will be required in conjunction with a likely increase in sales. It is assumed that the cash resources will be adequate to finance this, but a more detailed evaluation of working capital requirements is recommended.

The estimated realisable value of assets immediately after the reconstruction, before any significant change in working capital requirements is forecast to be:

	$000
Land and buildings	1,200
Old plant and machinery	1,300
New machinery and equipment*	2,250
Inventory	670
Receivables	1,090
Cash (3250–3030+35)	255
	6,765

*The realisable value of new machinery and equipment is likely to be less than the purchase price of $2.25 million.

New creditors would be:		
Secured		*Annual interest*
9% bond	500	45
Bank term loan	2,000	260
Overdraft	620	62
	3,120	367
Unsecured		
10% loan stock	500	50
Other creditors	940	–
	1,440	50
Total creditors	4,560	417

As long as the realisable value of the new machinery and equipment is not significantly less than its book value, the position of creditors has improved, and, on the basis of this data, full repayment should be made in the event of liquidation.

The reaction of the various providers of finance is likely to be:

Ordinary shareholders

The offer of 28 cents per share is a premium of almost 22% over the current share price and unless the shareholders believe that there is some other way that the company can be returned to profitability it is likely to be accepted. However, some shareholders might wish to continue to own shares in the company, and might prefer an offer of new shares to a cash redemption. The company might consider this alternative, which would also reduce the need for financing.

BXT bank

If the company fails BXT bank will receive full repayment of the $800,000 term loan and an expected 63% repayment of the overdraft.

Dricom would request an extra $1.2 million term loan at an additional 1% interest rate, and would offer security on the overdraft.

New secured creditors would be:

		$000
9% bond 500		
Bank term loan		2,000
Overdraft		620
		3,120

Unless the realisable value of the new machinery and equipment is less than $620,000, there now appears to be ample security for all of the bank's loans.

Interest cover from 20X8-X9 is forecast to be:

$$\frac{\text{Profit before tax and interest}}{\text{Interest}} \quad \frac{\$750,000 +}{\$417,000} = 1.8:1$$

This is relatively low interest cover and might not be satisfactory to the bank. The attitude of the bank to a larger term loan is likely to depend upon convincing the bank that a minimum of the forecast profit figure can be achieved.

Straight bond holders

The position of the bond holders remains unchanged. In either situation they are likely to receive full repayment. They may require some form of incentive (e.g. the addition of warrants to the bond) to agree to the reconstruction.

Loan stock holders

The loan stock holders, who are unsecured, stand a much better chance of full repayment of their loan after the reconstruction and are likely to agree to the reconstruction.

Convertible bond holders

This is potentially the most difficult group of creditors. As secured creditors they are likely to receive full repayment in a liquidation. They are being asked to exchange certain repayment for new, risky ordinary shares at an effective price of $94/60, or 157 cents per share. The directors and employees are being offered shares at 150 cents per share, and the venture capital organisation at $1 million/700,000 or 143 cents per share. Even if the convertible bond holders were willing to exchange their bonds for ordinary shares, which is unlikely due to the risk, they would not be willing to pay more for the shares than other groups.

The validity of a new share price of around 150 cents per share must be questioned. Without full information on expected future cash flows detailed analysis cannot be undertaken. However, the expected P/E ratio of Dricom may be compared with the industry average.

Dricom

	No tax $000	With tax $000
Earnings before interest and tax	750 +	750+
Interest	417	417
Taxable income	333	333
Taxation	–	110
	333	223
Earnings per share	$\frac{333}{1,800} = 18.5$ cents	$\frac{223}{1,800} = 12.4$ cents
Expected P/E ratio (based on 150 cents per share)	8:1	12:1

The with-tax scenario represents the normal situation, giving a P/E ratio of approximately the industry average. Given the company's relatively poor interest cover, and recent history it is doubtful whether investors would be willing to pay 150 cents for new shares as part of the reconstruction. It may be necessary to issue a larger number of shares at a lower share price to make the offer attractive, and to raise the required amount of finance.

To secure the agreement of the convertible bond holders Dricom may have to offer them redemption of the bonds, with the associated impact on financing requirements.

The venture capital organisation

The venture capital provider would bear a major risk, as it would hold only equity. The price of 143 cents per share might be regarded as too high by a venture capital provider. Under the proposed reconstruction a total of 1.8 million new 25 cents par value shares would be issued, of which the venture capital organisation would own 700,000 or almost 39% (directors and employees 28%, convertible bond holders 33%), probably giving it effective control of the company. Almost certainly a venture capital company would require significant board representation. It might also require fixed price options on future share issues or other 'sweeteners' which would provide potential capital gains. Many venture capital organisations would not be willing to take such a high equity stake in a company.

Other creditors

Other creditors are in a similar position to the unsecured loan stock holders, and would stand a much better chance of full repayment of their loan after the reconstruction. Other creditors are likely to agree to the reconstruction.

Directors and employees

Although the company's directors have presumably agreed to participate in the purchase of the shares the attitude of the company's employees is unknown. They may not wish to, or be able to, subscribe to the amount of shares on offer. The success of the proposed reconstruction will partly depend upon finance being agreed by the company's employees.

Conclusion

The reconstruction as currently proposed is unlikely to succeed. The company should consider altering the proposed terms that are to be offered, especially to the existing ordinary shareholders, the convertible bond holders and to the venture capital provider. The price at which new ordinary shares are to be offered should be reviewed and a lower price may be necessary.

Answer 24 ASTER

Tutorial note: *the calculations of gearing required in (a) are extremely time consuming but would carry relatively few marks (4–6 marks). Candidates who spent too much time on the calculations would fail the question. The recommended approach is to do the calculations for years 1 and 2 and then assume that gearing will be above 100% after 4 years. As long as comments made are consistent with assumed numbers full credit will be awarded. Such marks are much easier and faster to obtain than calculations.*

(a) **Report on the financing mix for the proposed management buy-out**

Assuming the airport can be purchased for $35 million, the financing mix is likely to be:

$4 million 50 cents ordinary shares, managers/employees
$1 million 50 cents ordinary shares, ASTER
$20 million floating rate loan at LIBOR + 3%, EPP Bank
$10 million mezzanine debt with warrants, Allvent.

It is possible for up to $5 million of the EPP Bank loan to be replaced by mezzanine finance, but as the cost of mezzanine finance is 18% in comparison with an initial 13% for the bank loan, and the existence of warrants with the mezzanine finance could dilute the future percentage ownership of the managers/employees, it is likely that only $10 million mezzanine finance would be used.

The main advantage of the financing package is that it would allow the buy-out to go ahead, and the managers/employees to have control of the organisation with ownership of 80% of the equity, whilst only contributing 11% of the required capital.

The effectiveness of control, however, depends upon managers and employees remaining a cohesive voting group. If less than 50% of shares are to be held by the key senior management group control is less secure.

A disadvantage of achieving control with a small percentage of the required capital is that capital gearing will be extremely high. Even in comparison to other management buy-outs an initial debt to equity ratio of 600% ($30 million debt to $5 million equity) is unusually high. It is understandable that EPP Bank, as the major risk bearer of debt, has imposed a covenant that seeks to reduce capital gearing.

Allvent is offering unsecured mezzanine finance. This is very high risk debt and a premium of 5% over secured debt is not unusual. $2 million of the debt is repayable each year during the five-year period, which may result in cash flow problems for Airgo, or necessitate the company seeking further finance. If the warrants are exercised, up to 1 million new shares would be issued raising $1 million in new capital.

The ownership structure following the exercise of all the warrants would be approximately 73% managers/employees, 18% ASTER and 9% Allvent, which still maintains control for managers/employees.

The projected statements of profit or loss are detailed in Appendix 1. Assuming no further borrowing, share issues or revaluation of assets during the next four years, the book value of gearing is expected to move to approximately:

Year	1	2	3	4
Debt	28	26	24	22
Equity	7.15	9.79	12.94	16.61
%	392	266	185	132

If the warrants are exercised this will result in an extra $1 million equity capital, but this will still leave expected gearing significantly above 100%. This estimate is based upon the assumption that no dividends are paid for four years, which may not be acceptable to all managers/employees in the buy-out.

The covenant restriction is likely to be a problem in four years' time.

The covenant gives EPP Bank the right to recall the loan but there is no certainty that it will do so. If interest payments and any other conditions of the loan are being met, the bank may not exercise its call option on the loan, especially as the loan is secured against the land and buildings of the airport. If the covenant is believed to be a significant problem, action that Airgo might take includes:

- Investigate the possibility of obtaining alternative finance in four years' time if the loan is recalled. This could include a stock market quotation.

- Renegotiate the covenant to allow a longer period (e.g. six years) for the 100% gearing to be achieved, or for a higher gearing ratio to be permitted.

- If further expansion is planned during the next four years, attempt to finance such expansion with equity. This might include a runway extension to allow long-haul flights which could significantly increase airport revenue.

- Improve profitability and hence increase shareholders' equity through increased retentions. Cost savings might be possible in comparison with current performance (e.g. Airgo might be able to provide central services at a lower cost than would be charged by ASTER).

Appendix 1 – Projected statements of profit or loss for the next four years

Year	1	2	3	4
Landing fees	14,700	15,435	16,207	17,017
Other revenue	9,030	9,482	9,956	10,453
	23,730	24,917	26,163	27,470
Labour	5,460	5,733	6,020	6,321
Consumables	3,990	4,190	4,399	4,619
Central services	3,000	3,150	3,308	3,473
Other expenses	3,675	3,859	4,052	4,254
Interest	4,400	4,040	3,680	3,320
	20,525	20,972	21,459	21,987
Taxable profit	3,205	3,945	4,704	5,483
Taxation	1,058	1,302	1,552	1,809
Dividend	0	0	0	0
Retained earnings	2,147	2,643	3,152	3,674

Notes and assumptions

- Landing fees, other revenue, labour, consumables and other expenses continue as at the last statement of profit or loss by 5% per year:

- It is assumed that the central services of ASTER continue to be used. ASTER is a major shareholder and has a vested interest in providing efficient service and marketing.

- No dividend is assumed to be paid during the first four years.

- The data is based upon a projected funding requirement of $35 million. This does not allow for working capital requirements, which could increase gearing and interest costs significantly.

- If the interest cap is purchased, this will require immediate finance of $800,000 which gives protection against interest rates of 15% or higher. Whether the cap is used depends upon expectations of future interest rate levels.

- The interest rate on the floating rate loan is assumed not to change.

(b) **Further information required from MBO team**

There is very little information provided that would allow an assessment of the viability of the proposed management buy-out. Information that would be necessary includes:

- Detailed cash flow projections for Airgo, preferably providing alternative scenarios using different economic assumptions. An NPV analysis might also be included.

- The medium and long-term strategic plans of Airgo.

- Full details of all directors and key employees, to ensure that the company personnel have the necessary expertise and experience.

- Is the company prepared to offer warrants or other terms that would make a $10 million loan attractive to the lender? Is any security available, including personal security from directors?

- Would Airgo be prepared to accept one or more representatives of your venture capital company on its board of directors?

Answer 25 MBO

(a) **Advice to buy-out team**

Assuming the forecasts provided in the question are correct, estimates of gearing over the next four years are:

		$000		
Year	1	2	3	4
Earnings before interest and tax	1,100	1,144	1,190	1,237
Interest	460	395·4	324·3	246
Taxable	640	748·6	865·7	991
Taxation (30%)	192	224·6	259·7	297·3
Retained	448	524·0	606·0	693·7

	$000				
Year	*0*	*1*	*2*	*3*	*4*
Book value of equity	2,000	2,448	2,972	3,578	4,271·7
Book value of debt	5,000	4,353·6	3,642·6	2,860·5	2,000
Gearing	250%	178%	123%	80%	47%

The book value gearing after four years is estimated to be 47%, if the venture capitalist has not exercised the warrants. If the warrants have been exercised equity would increase by $1 million, and the gearing would fall to 38%, below the suggested figure for a successful AIM issue.

Tutorial note: *warrants are share options "attached" to an issue of new shares (in this case) or to an issue of new debt. The reason to attach warrants is to make the new share/debt issue "sweeter" for potential investors. If the warrants are later exercised then the firm will receive another injection of cash (the strike price of the options) and its value of equity rises and hence gearing falls.*
Note that if warrants are attached to debt then the debt itself is not convertible debt; it is straight debt which must be repaid even if the warrants are exercised.

Notes:

(i) Equity at the time of the buy-out is $2,000,000

(ii) Interest:

On debt taken over $2 million × 8% = $160,000 per year;

On new debt: Equal annual payments to redeem $3 million in 4 years will require

$$\frac{3,000,000}{3.170} = \$946,372$$

		$000		
Year	Start of year	Interest	Repayment	Owed at year end
1	3,000	300	646·4	2,353·6
2	2,353·6	235·4	711·0	1,642·6
3	1,642·6	164·3	782·1	860·5
4	860·5	86·0	860·4	0

(b) **Minimum price per share**

The AIM issue is expected to be successful with a gearing of less than 40%, which requires the exercise of the warrants, increasing the expected value of equity to $5·272 million. The book value of equity divided by the number of shares provides an estimate of the minimum price per share:

$$\frac{\$5\cdot272m}{3m \text{ shares}} = 176 \text{ cents}$$

Unless the listing places a value of at least this much on equity, the existing shareholders would be unlikely to undertake the listing. The actual share price at listing is likely to be much higher than this, and to reflect future cash flow expectations rather than book values.

Answer 26 EQUITY AND DEBT ISSUES

(a) Methods for raising new equity finance – unlisted company

A company is required by law to offer an issue of new equity finance on a pro-rata basis to its existing shareholders. This ensures that the existing pattern of ownership and control will not be affected if all shareholders take up the new shares offered. Because the right to be offered new equity is a legal one, such an issue is called a rights issue.

If an unlisted company decides that it needs to raise a large amount of equity finance and provided existing shareholders have agreed, it can offer ordinary shares to new investors (the public at large) via an offer for sale. Such an offer is usually part of the process of seeking a stock exchange listing, as it leads to the wider spread of ownership that is needed to meet stock exchange listing regulations. An offer for sale may be either at fixed price, where the offer price is set in advance by the issuing company, or by tender, where investors are invited to submit bids for shares. An offer for sale will result in a significant change to the shareholder structure of the company, for example by bringing in institutional investors. To ensure that the required amount of finance is raised offers for sale are underwritten by institutional investors who guarantee to buy any unwanted shares.

A placing is cheaper than an offer for sale. In a placing, large blocks of shares are placed with institutional investors, so that the spread of new ownership is not as wide as with an offer for sale. While a placing may be part of seeking a listing on a stock exchange (for example, it is very popular with companies wanting to float on markets for smaller companies such as the Alternative Investment Market in the UK), it can also provide equity finance for a company that wishes to remain unlisted.

New shares can also be sold by an unlisted company to individual investors by private negotiation. While the amount of equity finance raised by this method is small, it has been supported in recent years by government initiatives such as the Enterprise Investment Scheme and Venture Capital Trusts in the UK.

(b) Factors to be considered

The factors that should be considered by a company when choosing between an issue of debt and issue of equity finance could include the following:

Risk and return

Raising debt finance will increase the gearing and the financial risk of the company, while raising equity finance will lower gearing and financial risk.

Financial risk arises since raising debt brings a commitment to meet regular interest payments, whether fixed or variable. Failure to meet these interest payments gives debt holders the right to appoint a receiver to recover their investment. In contrast, there is no right to receive dividends on ordinary shares, only a right to participate in any dividend (share of profit) declared by the directors of a company. If profits are low, then dividends can be passed, but interest must be paid regardless of the level of profits. Furthermore, increasing the level of interest payments will increase the volatility of returns to shareholders, since only returns in excess of the cost of debt accrue to shareholders.

ADVANCED FINANCIAL MANAGEMENT (P4) – STUDY QUESTION BANK

Cost

Debt is cheaper than equity because debt is less risky from an investor point of view. This is because it is often secured by either a fixed or floating charge on company assets and ranks above equity on liquidation, and because of the statutory requirement to pay interest. Debt is also cheaper than equity because interest is an allowable deduction in calculating taxable profit. This is referred to as the tax efficiency of debt.

Ownership and control

Issuing equity can have ownership implications for a company, particularly if the finance is raised by a placing or offer for sale. Shareholders also have the right to appoint directors and auditors, and the right to attend general meetings of the company. While issuing debt has no such ownership implications, an issue of debt can place restrictions on the activities of a company by means of restrictive covenants included in issue documents such as bond trust deeds. For example, a restrictive covenant may specify a maximum level of gearing or a minimum level of interest cover, or may forbid the securing of further debt on particular assets.

Redemption

Equity finance is permanent capital that does not need to be redeemed, while debt finance will need to be redeemed at some future date. Redeeming a large amount of debt can place a severe strain on the cash flow of a company, although this can be addressed by refinancing or by using convertible debt.

Flexibility

Debt finance is more flexible than equity, in that various amounts can be borrowed, at a fixed or floating interest rate and for a range of maturities, to suit the financing need of a company. If debt finance is no longer required, it can more easily be repaid (depending on the issue terms).

Availability

A new issue of equity finance may not be readily available to a listed company or may be available on terms that are unacceptable with regards to issue price or issue quantity, if the stock market is depressed (a bear market). Current shareholders may be unwilling to subscribe to a rights issue, for example if they have made other investment plans or if they have urgent calls on their existing finances. A new issue of debt finance may not be available to a listed company, or available at a cost considered to be unacceptable, if it has a poor credit rating, or if it faces trading difficulties.

Answer 27 IXT

(a) Why cost of debt is normally less than cost of equity

In an efficient market the return to an investor should reflect the risk taken by the investor. For an individual company the providers of debt finance experience less risk than the providers of equity finance because:

- Interest on debt is payable before any dividends are paid to shareholders, and must be paid at the due date.

- In the case of liquidation, debt finance is repaid in full before any payment is made to shareholders.

The return required from debt is, therefore, less than that required from equity finance (return is measured by the interest or dividend yield *plus* any capital gain or loss). The cost of debt and equity to the company is the return required by investors in each of these forms of finance (ignoring personal tax effects). Cost of debt is, therefore, normally less than the cost of equity.

(b) Appraisal of suggested strategy

Using only debt finance to raise £5 million per year for the next five years appears to be an unusual strategy. Whether or not it is feasible depends upon the effect of this financing strategy on the company's financial gearing (and hence financial risk), interest cover and cash flow, and the market's reaction to such a strategy.

It is difficult to accurately predict how these factors will alter during the next five years, but the data allow approximate estimates to be made.

To illustrate the possible effects of issuing £5 million debt for each of the next five years it is assumed that all of the new debt is in the form of 13% bonds and that the cost and quantity of existing debt does not change. Other types of new debt at different interest rates would naturally result in different estimates.

Year	Now	1	2	3	4	5
	£000	£000	£000	£000	£000	£000
EBIT (20% per year growth)	13,750	16,500	19,800	23,760	28,512	34,214
Interest (650 increase per year)	3,000	3,650	4,300	4,950	5,600	6,250
Taxable profit	10,750	12,850	15,500	18,810	22,912	27,964
Tax at 35%	3,762	4,497	5,425	6,583	8,019	9,787
Earnings available to shareholders	6,988	8,353	10,075	12,227	14,893	18,177
Dividend (40% payout)	2,795	3,341	4,030	4,891	5,957	7,271
Retained earnings	4,193	5,012	6,045	7,336	8,936	10,906
Interest cover (EBIT/interest payable)	4.6	4.5	4.6	4.8	5.1	5.5
Gearing (Total loans/ shareholders' funds)	24,000	29,000	34,000	39,000	44,000	49,000
	24,600	29,612	35,657	42,993	51,929	62,835
	98%	98%	95%	91%	85%	78%
Earnings per share (pence)	43.7	52.2	63.0	76.4	93.1	113.6

Interest cover is expected to increase during the five year period. Interest cover shows the extent to which earnings can decline before the company might be unable to meet its interest charges. Although no comparative data for other companies in IXT's industry are available, IXT's cover appears to be adequate.

Financial gearing is expected to fall, because the expected retained earnings are larger than the increased debt financing. Investors are not likely to object to a gradual reduction in gearing and financial risk, unless the current level of gearing is considered to be optimal.

Earnings per share are expected to more than double which should be regarded favourably by shareholders and lead to an increase in IXT's share price.

On the basis of this data Mr Axelot's suggested strategy is feasible and likely to be acceptable to both shareholders and lenders to the company. It does not appear to be too risky.

(c) **Finance for current expansion**

The effect of the 13% bond has been estimated in answer to part (b), with gearing in year one remaining at 98%, interest cover falling slightly, and earnings per share increasing by 19%. If the warrants are exercised in five years' time, there could be some dilution in earnings per share depending upon the return IXT could earn from the additional funds provided by exercising the warrants. IXT's share price would have to increase by approximately 12.5% per year to make it worthwhile exercising the warrants at 450 pence per share. Given the company's expected growth in profits, a 12.5% per year growth in share price is quite likely.

The Swiss franc bond would initially have the same effect on gearing as the 13% bond. The 8% per year interest rate might look attractive. However, if the exchange rate between the pound sterling and the Swiss franc alters the pound sterling interest cost and the cost of the principal repayment will alter. From the purchasing power parity theorem, with inflation at 8% per year in the UK and 2% per year in Switzerland, the value of the pound is expected to fall relative to the Swiss franc by:

$$\frac{0.02 - 0.08}{1.08} = 5.56\% \text{ per year.}$$

The expected end of year exchange rate is CHF 2.3091 – 2.3139 per £.

In year one, assuming interest to be payable at the year end, interest payable is:

$$\frac{12.25 \times 8\%}{2.3091} = £424,408 \text{ or } 8.49\% \text{ of £5m.}$$

The £ principal to be repaid if the £ fell by 5.56% per year for 10 years would be £8.87 million, an additional £3.87 million. The relative cost of the Swiss franc loan and the 13% bond depends upon how the exchange rates move. Because of foreign exchange risk, although initially cheaper, the Swiss franc loan could, in present value terms, be the more expensive alternative.

The placing will require $\frac{£5m}{£2.45} = 2,040,816$ new shares (ignoring issue costs).

The effect of this in year one will be:

	Now	Year 1
EBIT	13,750	16,500
Interest	3,000	3,000
Taxable	10,750	13,500
Taxation	3,762	4,725
	6,988	8,775
EPS (pence)	43.7	48.6

Year 1 gearing is expected to be $\frac{24,000}{29,865 + 5,000}$ = 68.8% and interest cover 5.5 times.

If IXT wishes to reduce financial gearing and increase interest cover this can be achieved by the placing. Expected EPS is lower than if debt finance is used, but is still an increase of 11% on the current level. The use of a placing, probably with institutional investors, is likely to alter the ownership of the company's ordinary shares. This might be unpopular with existing shareholders, especially Mr Axelot who currently has the controlling interest.

STUDY QUESTION BANK – ADVANCED FINANCIAL MANAGEMENT (P4)

As long as 98% gearing is not considered to be a problem, debt finance is likely to have the most favourable impact on earnings per share, and potentially on share price.

(d) Mezzanine financing

Mezzanine financing is considered to be part-way between debt and equity financing. Formally it is high yield debt, often at an interest rate of 4 – 5% above LIBOR (London interbank offered rate), and normally has equity warrants attached. Mezzanine ranks (in liquidation) below all other forms of debt and is much more risky than secured debt. However, the expected returns are much higher, both because of the higher interest rate and because of possible gains from exercising equity warrants.

Mezzanine financing might be useful to IXT as it provides an additional type of finance which might allow more finance to be raised than is possible using only "senior" debt and equity. Examples of where mezzanine financing has been used include leveraged takeovers, management buy-outs and corporate restructuring.

Answer 28 NEW DEBT ISSUE

(a) Coupon rate on the new debt

Yield on four year treasuries	5.1%
Estimated credit spread	0.9%
Required coupon	6%

If the firm's bankers have overestimated the credit risk then a coupon of 6% will result in the debt being issued at a premium in the market.

If they have set the spread too low then the debt will not be fully taken up and the bank will have to issue it at a discount – creating a shortfall in the $400 million required.

The investment bank suggests that a yield of 6% would guarantee that the issue would be taken up by its institutional clients. The firm may wish to ask for an underwriting agreement to that effect although there would inevitably be a charge for this.

(b) Impact of the new debt issue

Current market value of existing debt = $1,200 \times \dfrac{25}{75}$ = $400m

Yield on three year treasuries	3.5%
Current credit spread	0.5%
Required yield	4%
Average coupon	4%

Therefore current market value = par value.

Following the increase in credit risk the required yield on the existing debt will rise to 3.5% + 0.9% = 4.4%.

Revised market value (per $100 par value):

	$	4.4% DF	PV
t1-3	4	2.754	11.02
t3	100	0.879	87.9
			98.92

Working – 3 year annuity factor at 4.4% = $\dfrac{1-(1+0.044)^{-3}}{0.044}$

Revised market value of existing debt = $400m × $\dfrac{98.92}{100}$ = $396m

Value of new issue $400m

Total value of debt $796m

The firm's effective cost of debt capital is calculated by weighting the yields of the two components of debt and then adjusting for tax:

$$= \left[\frac{400}{400+396} \times 6\% + \frac{396}{400+396} \times 4.4\%\right] \times 0.7$$

$$= 3.64\%$$

Current cost of debt capital is 4% × (1 – 0·3) = 2·8% so the increase in gearing will raise the firm's cost of debt capital (after tax) by 84 basis points. However, this increase is in part due to the longer term to maturity on the new borrowing rather than the increase in the credit spread.

(c) **Advantages and disadvantages of this mode of capital financing**

Debt finance is a relatively low cost method of raising long term finance. Under static trade off theory we would expect higher gearing to generate improvements in the firm's cost of capital given the benefit of the tax shield. However, the cost of debt capital consists of three components: the pure risk free rate, the term premium and the credit spread. In this case we are proposing to alter our capital structure by taking on longer term debt and thus the advantages of higher gearing are to a certain extent obscured. Pecking order theory suggests that debt finance should be preferred to new equity finance and is normally taken by the market as a signal that management believe that the company is undervalued. In the context of an efficient market this is doubtful but it is certainly the case that there are strong agency effects through debt. Debt will exert a greater discipline over our action than equity finance and tends to suppress opportunistic investment and over consumption of perks.

From a transactions costs perspective, debt tends to be preferred for the acquisition of general assets with high marketability and equity for intangibles and highly specific assets. In the airline business finance of this level is normally for aeroplane acquisitions which do have a reasonably active second hand market.

Answer 29 PAVLON

(a) Dividend policy

(i) Nature and suitability

Pavlon has pursued a consistent policy prior to its listing of paying a constant percentage of its earnings as a dividend, as seen from the following table:

Years prior to listing	Dividend per share cents	No of shares 000s	Total dividend $000s	Profits after tax $000	Payout ratio %
5	3.60	21,333	768	1,800	43
4	4.80	21,333	1,024	2,400	43
3	6.16	26,667	1,643	3,850	43
2	6.56	26,667	1,749	4,100	43
1	7.12	26,667	1,899	4,450	43

The effect of maintaining a constant payout ratio is that dividends fluctuate with earnings. The fact that Pavlon's dividends per share have increased over the last five years follows simply from the fact that earnings have been rising over the relevant period. Whether Pavlon's policy is suitable for a company listed on the Stock Exchange depends on what view is taken of dividend policy. There is a school of thought, characterised by the dividend irrelevancy hypothesis, which suggests that share values are the present value of future dividends discounted at a rate which reflects the risk associated with the underlying earnings.

Since dividend policy does not affect the risk of the earnings stream, the pattern of dividend payments cannot affect the value of the shares (i.e. dividend policy is irrelevant). The leading advocates of the dividend irrelevancy hypothesis are Modigliani and Miller (M&M). Their position is at variance with the traditional view which argues that the pattern of dividend payments can have an effect on share values. M&M have demonstrated beyond doubt that dividend policy is irrelevant in a perfect capital market and, since dividend policy does not affect values, the policy pursued by Pavlon will be as good as any other in a perfect capital market. However, since in the real world the capital market is not perfect, most of the arguments are about the effect of dividend policies on share values in an imperfect (i.e. real) capital market. This is discussed below:

(ii) Proposed final dividend

A final dividend of 2.34 cents per share will mean a total dividend for the year of 5.5 cents. The total number of shares issued is now 40,000,000; therefore the total dividend for the year will be $2.2 million. This represents 40% of the earnings for the year and is a small reduction in the payout ratio used by the company in the preceding five years. As noted above, whether or not this constitutes a suitable or appropriate dividend for the two categories of shareholder identified depends on which view of dividend policy is taken.

If the dividend irrelevancy hypothesis is true, a dividend of 5.5 cents per share is likely to be as good as any other. However, if the dividend irrelevancy hypothesis does not hold in an imperfect market, different policies could materially affect share prices and hence shareholder wealth.

Most of the discussion on the effects of dividend policy centres on two market imperfections. Firstly, the effect of distorting taxes. If a company pays a dividend, the shareholder receives the dividend. If the company retains the profits, the shareholder should get a corresponding capital gain. In a perfect market all shareholders will be indifferent as between dividends and capital gain because there are not distorting taxes and capital gains can instantly, effortlessly and without cost be converted into cash. In fact, dividends and capital gains are taxed differently, since dividends are accompanied by a tax credit at the basic rate and capital gains are subject to the annual exemption. The latter exemption may not be significant for wealthy private individuals and therefore they would show a preference for dividends. However, an additional point to consider is that capital gains facilitate tax and cash flow planning since the tax is only paid as the gain is realised. Therefore it is not clear whether such individuals would favour the reduced payout ratio.

The attitude of institutional investors will again depend on their tax position. Many institutions require a steady cash flow to meet their outgoings. While it is theoretically possible to convert capital gains into cash, the transaction costs of so doing usually mean that major institutional investors prefer a steady stream of dividends.

The second imperfection is the "information content of dividends". In a perfect capital market all investors have knowledge of the underlying earnings stream and value the company accordingly. In the real world the market is starved of up-to-date information about the company and may pay substantial attention to company dividend declarations.

Failure to maintain dividend growth or a payout ratio may be interpreted as a sign of weakness and have disastrous effects on share prices, at least in the short run.

It can also be argued that companies attract a clientele of shareholders that are satisfied with the policy that the company pursues. A company with such a constant policy as Pavlon is likely to have gathered around itself a group of investors who are satisfied with that policy. In such circumstances any change in policy is likely to be unpopular, irrespective of whether the majority of shares are owned by wealthy private individuals or institutional investors.

(b) **Dividend valuation model**

(i)   Calculations

The basic form of the dividend valuation model is as follows:

$$P_0 = \frac{d_0(1+g)}{k_e - g}$$

However, this can only be used where $k_e > g$. In the first three years, since growth is greater than k_s, the model cannot be used in this form. The dividends over the next three years are as follows:

Year	1	2	3
Dividend per share (cents)	6.33	7.27	8.36

The present value of these dividends at 12% is

$6.33 \times 0.893 + 7.27 \times 0.797 + 8.36 \times 0.712 = 17.40$ cents

From year 4 onwards dividends grow at 8% and therefore the basic model may be used to obtain value t₃. This must then be discounted back to t₀, i.e.

$$\frac{8.36 \times 1.08}{0.12 - 0.08} \times 0.712 = 160.71 \text{ cents}$$

According to the dividend model, shares in Pavlon should be worth 178.11 cents ex-dividend. The current cum-dividend value is $1.95 cum dividend ($78m ÷ 40m). The ex-dividend price (less the final dividend) is 192.66 cents. Therefore Pavlon's shares are currently over-valued.

(ii)   Weaknesses of the dividend valuation model

(1)   The dividend valuation model assumes that the share price is the discounted present value of future dividends. If the market uses some other model to value shares (e.g. one based on reported profits and a P/E ratio or which reflects the value of the underlying assets), the results of the model will be unreliable.

(2)   The model as used here assumes constant growth in perpetuity, which is at best unrealistic.

(3)   The results produced by the use of the model are only as good as the data input. It is obviously difficult to estimate k_S and to predict future dividend growth accurately.

Answer 30 TYR

(a)   Current dividend policy

Estimates of earnings and dividend per share, and their growth rates are shown below:

	Post-tax earnings per share (cents)	Growth (%)	Dividend per share (cents)	Growth (%)	Inflation (%)
20X7	47·9	–	19·2	–	
20X8	51·3	7·1	20·1	4·7	5
20X9	55·2	7·6	20·9	4·0	4
20Y0	55·9	1·3	21·5	2·9	3
20Y1	61·9	10·7	22·2	3·3	3
Overall compound growth		6·6		3·7	

From the above data TYR appears to be following a policy of paying a constant dividend per share, adjusted for the current year's level of inflation.

The only possible indication from the data of whether or not the dividend policy has been successful is the relative performance of TYR's share price in comparison to the market index. This, however, would rely upon the assumption that the choice of dividend policy influences the share price.

	S&P 500 index	Growth (%)	Share price (cents)	Growth (%)
20X7	2895	–	360	–
20X8	3300	14·0	410	13·9
20X9	2845	(13·8)	345	(15·9)
20Y0	2610	(8·3)	459	33·0
20Y1	2305	(11·7)	448	(2·4)
Overall compound growth		(5·5)		5·6

TYR's share price has increased over the four-year period by an annual compound rate of 5·6%, much better than the annual fall of 5.5% suffered by the S&P 500 index. This does not prove that the dividend policy has been successful. The share price might be influenced by many other factors, especially the potential long-term cash flow expectations of the shareholders. Additionally comparison with the S&P 500 index does not measure the performance of TYR relative to companies in its own industry/sector.

(b) Additional information required

- Direct feedback from shareholders, especially institutional shareholders, stating whether or not they are happy with the current dividend policy.

- Full details of the registered shareholders, and size of holdings. TYR might have a desired spread of shareholders, which could be influenced by the dividend policy adopted.

- Knowledge of the impact of taxation of dividends on shareholders' attitudes, and specifically on their preferences between dividends and capital gains.

- The amount of capital investment the company wishes to undertake. The use of retained earnings and other internally generated funds avoids issue costs and the information asymmetry problems of external financing. The level of dividends paid affects the amount of internal funds that are available for investment.

- The impact of dividend payments on corporate liquidity.

- The signals provided by dividend payments about the future financial health of the company. For example, would the fact the dividend growth is lagging behind earnings growth be considered a positive or negative signal?

(c) Evaluation of 20Y1 share price

Using the Dividend Growth Model market price = $\dfrac{D_1}{k_e - g}$

where D_1 is the expected next dividend, k_e is the cost of capital and g the growth rate in dividends. Using the average compound growth of 3·7%:

$$\dfrac{D_1}{k_e - g} = \dfrac{22 \cdot 2(1 \cdot 037)}{0 \cdot 11 - 0 \cdot 037} = 315 \text{ cents}$$

The actual share price at the end of 20X1 appears to be overvalued relative to the dividend growth model.

This does not prove that the actual market price was overvalued. The dividend growth model relies upon restrictive assumptions, such as constant growth in dividends per share, which is unlikely to occur. There are also several factors that influence share prices that are not included within the model. Growth in earnings per share has increased more than growth in dividend per share, and it might be better to use the earnings growth rate in the model as this might more accurately reflect the financial health of the company.

Answer 31 UNIGLOW

(a) Meaning and importance of terms

Delta measures the change in the option price (premium) as the value of the underlying share moves by 1%.

$$\text{Delta} = \frac{\text{change in the price of the option}}{\text{change in the price of the underlying share}}$$

It is measured by N(d1) in the Black-Scholes option pricing model.

As the share price falls delta falls towards zero. Delta may be used to construct a risk free hedge position, whereby overall wealth will not change with small changes in share price.

Theta measures the change in the option price as the time to expiry increases. The longer the time to expiry of an option; the greater its value. Theta may be used to estimate by how much the value of an option will fall as time to maturity reduces.

Vega measures the change in option price as a result of a 1% change in the share price volatility or variance. As volatility increases, the value of both call and put options increases.

All three are of use to treasury managers when hedging their investments. As their values approach zero the hedged position will become unaffected by changes in these variables.

(b) Delta hedge

(i) Devising the hedge

N(d1) is required to determine the delta hedge.

$$d_1 = \frac{\ln(P_a/P_e) + (r + 0.5s^2)t}{s\sqrt{t}}$$

$$d_1 = \frac{\ln(200/220) + (0.06 + (0.5 \times 0.5^2))0.25}{0.5\sqrt{0.25}}$$

$= -0.19624$

From normal distribution tables:

$N(d_1) = 0.5 - 0.0778 = 0.4222$

Delta = 0.4222

To protect against a fall in Sunglow's share price, the easiest hedge would be to write (sell) call options on Sunglow's shares. A delta of 0.4222 means that the relevant hedge

ratio is $\frac{1}{0.4222} = 2.368$

To hedge 100,000 shares:

$$\frac{100{,}000 \times 2\cdot 368}{1{,}000} = 237 \text{ call options on Uniglow's shares need to be written.}$$

(ii) Comment

A hedge such is this is only valid for a small change in the underlying share price. As the share price alters the option delta will alter and the hedge will need to be periodically rebalanced.

Answer 32 BIOPLASM

Using the Black-Scholes model for European options:

P_a is estimated to be either $350e^{(-0.067)(15)}$ or $500e^{(-0.067)(15)} = 128.11$ or 183.02

The exercise price, $P_e = 400$

The interest rate, $r = 0\cdot 05$

Time, $t = 15$

Volatility, $s = 0\cdot 430$

Using call price = $c = P_a N(d_1) - P_e N(d_2)e^{-rt}$

Where:

$$d_1 = \frac{\ln(P_a/P_e) + (r + 0.5s^2)t}{s\sqrt{t}}$$

If P_a is $128\cdot 11$

$$d_1 = \frac{\ln(128.11/400) + (0.05 + (0.50 \times 0.43^2))15}{0.43\sqrt{15}} = 0\cdot 600$$

$= d_2 = d_1 - s\sqrt{t}$

$= 0\cdot 600 - 1\cdot 665 = -1\cdot 065$

From normal distribution tables:

$N(d_1) = 0\cdot 5 + 0\cdot 226 = 0\cdot 726$
$N(d_2) = 0\cdot 5 - 0\cdot 357 = 0\cdot 143$
Inputting data into call price = $P_a N(d_1) - P_e N(d_2)e^{-rt}$

Call price = $(128.11 \times 0\cdot 726) - (400 \times 0.143 \times e^{-0.75})$

$= 93\cdot 01 - 27\cdot 02 = \$65\cdot 99$ million

If P_a is 183·02

$d_1 = 0·814$
$d_2 = -0.851$

From normal distribution tables:

$N(d_1) = 0·5 + 0·292 = 0·792$
$N(d_2) = 0·5 - 0·303 = 0·197$
Call price = $107·73 million

Under both scenarios the call option has a value in excess of the static NPV estimates. With a $350 million present value from sales the expected NPV is ($50 million), but the value of the call option is $66 million. With a $500 million present value from sales the expected NPV is $100 million, whilst the call option value is $108 million. If the data are correct then the option pricing model would suggest that the company should develop the patent no matter which present value occurs.

However, valuing a long-term option such as this is subject to restrictive assumptions and will be subject to a considerable margin of error. Possible problems include:

- The accuracy of the present value forecasts, and the use of the correct discount rate to assess their risk.

- The accuracy of the estimated development cost of the drug for commercial use. This estimate could be subject to substantial error as it relates to a new product and probably to new technology.

- Accuracy of the estimated variance. As this is a new drug the variance of returns from other Biotech companies might not be relevant, and the Black-Scholes model is quite sensitive to this variable. The model also assumes that this volatility will be constant for the 15 year period which is very unlikely.

- The Black-Scholes model was developed for European options. As development of the drug could take place at any time during the 15 year period the option is an American option rather than a European option.

- What will happen after 15 years? Although competition will probably eliminate most abnormal returns the company is likely to have built up a strong brand image and could still generate positive NPVs after this time which have not been included in the above calculations.

- How likely is it that a competitor might develop a superior drug? If this occurs the projections will be very adversely affected.

Because of the potential margin of error, Bioplasm should be cautious about accepting the values produced by the option pricing model, although they might be used as part of the overall decision process. This should also include the NPV estimates and strategic considerations. The company would also be advised to investigate possible cash flows after the patent period has expired.

ADVANCED FINANCIAL MANAGEMENT (P4) – STUDY QUESTION BANK

Answer 33 FORUN

(a) Hedging strategies

(i) Managing director's proposed strategy

The economic data presented by the managing director gives some indication of the likely future economic strength of the four countries, and could form part of a strategic evaluation.

According to the purchasing power parity theory all of the foreign currencies are expected to depreciate in value relative to the pound sterling with the smallest depreciation in countries 1 and 4, Although PPP may hold quite well in the long run, there may be significant deviations from PPP in the short run. The impact of the other variables may be summarised in many ways. The table below is a simple assessment with a + for the two best countries, and a – for the two worst.

	1	2	3	4	Comment
Inflation	+	–	–	+	
GDP growth		+	+	+	
Balance of payments	+		+		(related to population)
Base rate	+		+	+	
Unemployment	+		+	–	
Population	+	+		–	(+ for larger markets)
Currency reserves	+		+	–	(related to population)
IMF loans	+	+		–	(related to population)

Country 1 scores highly, except for inflation, economic growth and interest rates country 4 scores poorly, and is heavily indebted to the IMF relative to its small population size. Other data such as per capita GNP and international indebtedness other than to the IMF would be useful to the analysis. The managing director's major concern is economic exposure, the impact of foreign exchange rate changes on the sterling expected NPV of overseas operations.

Strategic decisions should *not* be made on the basis of the above information alone.

The information provides a macro-economic analysis. Even with a relatively weak economy at the micro level a subsidiary within a particular industry may perform well. Examining macro-economic data fails to give a complete picture.

Additionally it is possible that a depreciation in the value of a foreign currency might have a beneficial effect rather than a detrimental effect on economic exposure of Forun. If the price elasticity of demand is such that export sales from the foreign subsidiary increase substantially because of the relatively cheaper prices in a depreciated currency, the overall effect in sterling NPV terms might be an increase, not a decrease. If the managing director is concerned about economic exposure one way to reduce such exposure is by diversifying international operations, and financing, among many different countries. Concentrating activities in two foreign countries might lead to greater economic exposure risk, not less. The manager's strategy to concentrate on countries 1 and 4 is based upon incomplete information and is not recommended.

(ii) Benefit of non-executive director's suggestion

The non-executive director is concerned about the effects of translation exposure, specifically on expected foreign exchange loss of £1 5 million.

If a foreign currency is expected to depreciate relative to sterling, translation exposure may be reduced by reducing net exposed assets.

Early collection by foreign subsidiaries of foreign currency receivables will not reduce net exposure (unless the foreign currency is expected to depreciate by more than the currency of the foreign subsidiary). A better tactic would be to delay collection of foreign currency receivables until after significant depreciation of the subsidiary's currency had occurred, the receivables will then yield a higher amount of the subsidiary's currency. From a group viewpoint early collection could increase translation exposure rather than reduce it.

Early repayment of foreign currency loans could be beneficial, if the loans are in relatively hard currencies, and if the subsidiary has the funds available to make such a repayment without detrimental effects on its operations.

Reducing inventory levels in foreign countries will reduce net asset exposure. However, before this, or any other balance sheet hedging techniques are used, the effect on the efficient operation of the company must be considered. There is little point in reducing inventory levels if this causes production bottlenecks or failure to satisfy customer demand, and potentially a loss of orders.

The non-executive director is concerned about a loss on translation of £15 million. Translation losses are not realised economic losses. Part of such a loss may be from translating the historic cost of overseas tangible assets; in reality the sterling economic value of such assets may be little changed if inflation in the foreign country increases the *market* value of such assets. Hedging against translation losses might result in reducing rather than increasing sterling NPV as such hedges may be opposite in direction to hedges that would be undertaken to protect against transaction exposure.

Will the reported £15 million loss have an adverse effect on Forun's share price? If the stock exchange is efficient the company's share price will react to relevant changes in the company's expected cash flows, not reported translation losses. The reported loss could have little or no effect on share price. Hedging is normally undertaken to protect against the risk of transaction exposure, not translation exposure.

(b) **Intragroup transactions**

(i) *Multilateral netting*

Multilateral netting is an effective means of reducing the transactions costs associated with foreign exchange transactions that are payable to banks. The netting of Forun's intra-company US dollar exposures gives the following net payments and receipts.

			$000				
	UK	1	2	3	4	Total receivable	Net receipts (payments)
UK	–	300	450	210	270	1,230	(470)
1	700	–	420	–	180	1,300	220
2	140	340	–	410	700	1,590	380
3	300	140	230	–	350	1,020	(110)
4	560	300	110	510	–	1,480	(20)
Total payments	1,700	1,080	1,210	1,130	1,500	6,620	–

Some dollar payments will still need to be made from the UK, country 3 and country 4 to countries 1 and 2. However, such payments will total a maximum of $600,000 against the total trade value of $6,620,000, saving transactions and other costs on more than $6,000,000.

(ii)   Alternative hedging strategies

As Forun is risk averse with respect to short-term foreign exchange risk, the company is recommended to hedge against any transaction exposure risk. To reduce foreign exchange transaction risk, hedging should take place after establishing the net exposure position in all currencies. The net group dollar exposure on the intra-company trade is of course zero, as dollar receipts equal dollar payments. Hedging will be undertaken on the net transaction exposure of third party trade.

Exposure

Tutorial note: *Sterling transactions are not exposed.*

	Receipts	Payments	Net
Australia	$3 million	$3 million	
US	$12 million		$12 million
New Zealand		$13 million	($13 million)

These net figures are the only ones that require hedging.

Hedging may be undertaken on the forward foreign exchange market, currency futures market, or currency option markets.

Forward market

The relevant outright rates are:

	3 months	6 months
US$ per £	1.4720 – 1.4770	1.4550 – 1.4600
NZ$ per £	2.4140 – 2.4180	2.3830 – 2.3870

US$ receipts $\dfrac{\$12m}{1.46} = £8{,}219{,}178$ NZ$ payments $\dfrac{NZ\$13M}{2.383} = £5{,}455{,}308$

Currency futures

Currency futures may be used to hedge the US dollar and NZ dollar exposures. Futures attempt to "lock in" the current rate through any losses on the spot market when the currency is actually purchased or sold being offset by gains on the futures market. Forun could, for example, try to lock in the current spot price of $1.4990. This is, however, unlikely as it can fix the price at the better rate of $1.46 to £ on the forward market. Futures contracts involve margin payments (a form of security deposit) and expiration of basis (i.e. futures market price will move by a different amount to the spot market price).

If the spot in six months is $1.46 and assuming the futures price moves by the same amount as the spot price, $US receipts, using December contracts:

$\dfrac{12m}{1.480} = £8{,}108{,}108$ requires hedging or 129.73 contracts

Thus *buy* 130 sterling December contracts at 1.4800.

In six months sell 130 December sterling contracts at 1.441 (3.9 cents less than 1.4800, to reflect the 3.9 cents fall in the spot rate).

Spot market gain is: $\dfrac{\$12\,m}{1.499} - \dfrac{\$12\,m}{1.46} = £213,841$

Future market loss is 390 ticks × $6.25 × 130 contracts = $\dfrac{\$316,875}{1.46} = £217,038$

(The value of a tick is 0.0001 × £62,500 expressed in $ or $6.25.)

The total expected receipts using futures is:

$\dfrac{\$12,000,000}{1.4990} = £8,005,337 - £217,038 + £213,841 = £8,002,140$

NZ$ payments – NZ$ are required, therefore sell £ contracts using December contracts:

$\dfrac{NZ\$13m}{2.4480} = £5,310,457$

This requires 84.97 or 85 contracts.

Sell 85 sterling December at 2.4480.

If the spot in six months is 2.383 NZ$ per £ and assuming the futures price moves by the same amount as the spot price, in six months buy 85 sterling December contracts at 2.375.

Spot market loss is: $\dfrac{13m}{2.456} - \dfrac{13m}{2.383} = £162,149$

Futures market gain is 730 ticks × NZ$6.25 × 85 = $\dfrac{NZ\$387,813}{2.387} = £162,469$

Total expected cost using futures is:

$\dfrac{NZ\$13,000,000m}{2.4560} = £5,293,160 + £162,149 - £162,469 = £5,292,840$

This is significantly less than the cost of forward cover calculated above, but ignores change in the level of basis and the need to provide a margin deposit for futures transactions. Any differences in the tax treatments of the two alternatives are also ignored.

Currency options

$/£ options are available. Forun has a $12 million receivable in six months' time and wishes to protect against exchange risk. However, options, whilst protecting against downside risk, also allow companies to benefit from favourable exchange rate movements. Forun is likely to select December options as these cover the entire period of the currency exposure.

Call options are required as sterling is to be purchased with US dollars.

The exercise price selected will depend upon how much currency risk protection Forun requires. A $1.50 per £ exercise price will protect the current spot rate ($1.499 per £) at a relatively low premium cost. Both this and the $1.525 per £ exercise price are out-of-money options offering relatively low cost protection. To provide better protection than from a forward contract at $1.46 per £, an exercise price of $1.45 per £ is necessary, with a much higher premium cost.

ADVANCED FINANCIAL MANAGEMENT (P4) – STUDY QUESTION BANK

Possible costs are:

At 1.450 exercise price, buy $\dfrac{\$12m}{1.450} = \dfrac{£8,275,862}{£31,250} =$ 265 December contracts

Premium cost £8,281,250 × 5.75 cents – $476,172 or £318,297 (at spot of $1.4960 per £)

At 1.4750 exercise price $\dfrac{\$12m}{1.4750} = \dfrac{£8,135,593}{£31,250}$ = 261 contracts

Premium cost = £8,156,250 × 3.42 cents = $278,944 or £186,460

At 1.50 exercise price $\dfrac{\$12m}{1.50} = \dfrac{£8m}{£31,250} = 256$ contracts

Premium cost = £8m × 1.95 cents = $156,000 or £104,278

The choice of hedging strategy for dollars will depend upon expectations of future exchange rates, always bearing in mind the objective of protecting against exchange risk.

The outcome of the following spot exchange rates would be:

		£ million receipts in 6 months			
Exchange rates ($ per £)		1.35	1.40	1.45	1.50
Forward contracts		8.219	8.219	8.219	8.219
Futures (expected)		8.002	8.002	8.002	8.002
Currency options					
Exercise price	1.450	8.571	8.253	7.958	7.958
	1.475	8.702	8.385	8.089	7.949
	1.500	8.785	8.467	8.172	7.896

Tutorial note: *The 1.45 and 1.475 option contracts involve slightly more than the $12 million receipts, being $12,007,813 and $12,030,469 respectively. If the options are exercised Forun would have to purchase the extra dollars at spot to fulfil the full contract size, and would experience a foreign exchange loss or gain on the amounts purchased.*

Unless the company expects the dollar to strengthen to around $1.40 per £ in six months' time, forward contracts are the recommended dollar hedge.

Answer 34 STORACE

(a) **Sterling receipts**

  (i) *Price in sterling* = £100,000

  (ii) *Invoice price in dollars*

   = 100,000 × 1.11 = 111,000

Exchange rate in three months' time (spot rate) = 1.20 – 1.09

Therefore, £ received is between £92,500 and £101,835

(iii)   Invoice in dollars $111,000

Forward rates

Spot	1.1100 – 1.1100
Three months pm	(0.0120) – (0.0115)
Three months forward	1.0980 – 1.0985

Sell dollars forward at $1.0985 to £1

Receive £101,047

(b)   Report comparing methods of invoicing

> **To**   Storace Co
> **From**   Gluck & Co, Chartered Accountants
> **Date**   3 January 20X0
>
> **Re   Methods of invoicing export order**

You have asked us to advise on the best method of invoicing one of your foreign clients, Jacquin Inc. Three methods are under consideration:

(1)   Invoice in sterling.

(2)   Convert the sterling price into dollars at the current spot rate, invoice in dollars and convert the dollars into sterling at the spot rate prevailing on receipt of the dollars three months hence.

(3)   Invoice in dollars and sell the dollars forward at the three month forward exchange rate.

Our calculations in Appendix 1 show the expected sterling receipts resulting from each of the three options. In summary they are as follows:

(1)   £100,000
(2)   Between £92,500 and £101,835
(3)   £101,047

In general, the objective in deciding on the method of invoicing foreign clients should be to minimise exchange rate risk (i.e. the potential losses suffered by the company as a result of movements in the exchange rate between the date of invoice and the date of payment). Stated simply, if your company wishes to speculate on the foreign currency exchanges, there are easier ways of doing it than exporting goods to foreign customers.

Given this objective the obvious answer is to invoice in sterling which completely eliminates any exchange rate risk from the view point of the selling company. By invoicing in sterling and thereby guaranteeing the sterling receipt three months hence, Storace will pass on the exchange risk to the foreign customer, Jacquin Inc. The management of Jacquin Inc will then have to decide whether to buy the £100,000 needed to meet the invoice in the forward market or wait until the payment date and buy in the spot market. However, it may not be prepared to accept the risk. Therefore it is possible that your client may not be prepared to accept a sterling invoice. If you wish to keep the business you may have to invoice in the currency of your foreign client. In these circumstances the choice is between options (2) and (3).

Option (3), to cover your position in the forward market, is also riskless provided your client pays on the due date. Indeed, since the dollar is trading at a premium in the forward market (i.e. the market expects the value of the dollar to rise) it is possible for your client to make a "profit" of £1,047 by using this method of invoicing as compared with invoicing in sterling. However, if your client defaults on payment for whatever reason, you will still have to honour your contract to deliver $111,000 three months hence.

Another option is to invoice in dollars and convert the dollars at the spot rate prevailing in three months' time. Depending on the strength of the dollar at that time, you could receive between £92,500 and £101,835. Compared with option (3) this gives a potential gain of £788 if the exchange rate moves to $1.09, and a potential loss of £8,547 if the rate moves to $1.20. These figures assume that management expectations of the future spot rate are correct.

Conclusions

Ultimately the choice must depend on the commercial considerations affecting your company. Although invoicing in sterling is the simplest solution, it is unlikely to lead to a sale. The choice is therefore between options (2) and (3). Under option (2) there is a chance that only £92,500 will be received, which could mean that a loss is made on the sale of the machine. Therefore, you will probably prefer the certain £101,047 given by a forward contract. To protect yourself against the possibility of a delay in payment by Jacquin Inc, I would suggest that you consider using an option date forward contract where delivery can take place between two dates rather than on a single date. You will receive less than £101,047 because the contract rate will be less favourable from your point of view, but the difference will not be great.

(c)   **Implications of a major export drive**

If the company decides to engage in a major exports sales drive, there are four decisions to be made in which corporate financial management will have a major role to play.

(i)   *Choice of organisation*

A company can sell its product in a variety of ways abroad (e.g. direct to customers or agents, via a branch or department established in that country or via a subsidiary company established in that country).

(ii)   *Financing branches/subsidiaries*

Overseas branches/subsidiaries will require financing. Financial managers will need to consider both the cost of funds and exchange risk (e.g. whether a loan to finance a subsidiary should be taken in sterling or a foreign currency).

(iii)   *Protecting against exchange risk on receipts*

This is the subject of part (a) of the question and can be covered by dealing in the forward markets as explained in part (b).

(iv)   *Assessing creditworthiness of overseas customers*

A company may experience more problems in assessing the creditworthiness of overseas customers than of domestic customers. The risk of default by an overseas customer can be insured against via the Export Credits Guarantee Department. The ECGD also gives banks guarantees on cash advanced against such insurance policies, thus providing a company with the means to finance increased working capital requirements resulting from overseas sales.

Answer 35 PARTICIPATING OPTION

The outcome of any currency option hedge will depend upon what spot rate exists in 6 months' time. However, it is possible to assess the outcomes at different rates.

The participating option has no premium cost and gives a worst case rate of $1·65 per £. At exchange rates between $1·61 per £ and $1·65 per £ the company would suffer a fall in pound receipts when compared to the current spot rate. At rates of less than $1·61 per £ the option would not be exercised and any gain against current spot that the company made when selling the dollars at spot would be shared with the seller of the participating option.

At the current spot rate receipts would be $\dfrac{1,800,000}{1.61} = £1,118,012$

Exchange rate:	£ receipts from $1·8m	Change relative to current spot (£)
1·70 Option exercised	1,090,909	– 27,103
1·65 Option exercised	1,090,909	– 27,103
1·60 Option not exercised, rate 1·605	1,121,495	3,483
1·55 Option not exercised, rate 1·58	1,139,241	21,229

Traded options

June call options are required as other contracts expire before payment is due.

If the company does not wish to pay more than £10,000 in premium, then only the 1·65 and 1·70 options are available. The 1·70 option offers poor protection against a weakening of the dollar.

The 1·65 option will require $\dfrac{1,800,000}{1.65 \times 31,250} = 34\cdot91$ or 35 contracts

The premium cost is $35 \times 31,250 \times 1\cdot1$ cents $= \dfrac{\$12,031}{1.6055} = £7,494$

If exercised these contracts require $31,250 \times 35 \times 1\cdot65 = \$1,804,687$

The receipts are only $1·8 million and an additional $4,687 will need to be bought at spot to fulfil the contract.

Exchange rate:	£receipt		Premium	Change £
1·70 Option exercised	1,093,750	– 2,757	–7,494	– 34,513
1·65 Option exercised	1,093,750	– 2,841	–7,494	– 34,597
1·60 Option not exercised	1,125,000		–7,494	–506
1·55 Option not exercised	1,161,290		–7,494	35,784

Unless the dollar is expected to strengthen significantly the participating option looks the better alternative.

However, the company might also consider an option collar whereby a call option was purchased and a put option sold to reduce the net premium payable. Possibilities include buy June 1·65 calls at 1·1 cents and sell June 1·55 puts at 0·9 cents resulting in a net premium of 0·2 cents. This would result in a worst case (ignoring inexact contract sizes) position of $1·652 per £ and a best case position of $1·552 per £. However, this still involves significant exchange rate risk. A better collar would be to buy 1·60 calls at 5·3 cents and sell 1·60 puts at 4·0 cents, resulting in a net premium of 1·3 cents. This would lock-in the exchange rate at $1·613 per £ including premium cost, which is almost identical to the current spot rate exchange rate of $1·61 per £.

Answer 36 MJY CO

From a group perspective a sensible hedging strategy would be to net off as many offsetting currency receipts and payments as possible, and to only hedge the relevant net amounts.

As MJY is a UK based multinational, the payments and receipts in pounds are not exposed to currency risk and should be ignored.

All $ and € receipts and payments within the group and with third party companies are relevant when estimating the group currency exposure. In the case of intragroup trade, a receipt for one company is a payment for another.

From a group view, relevant $ receipts are: 90 + 50 + 40 + 20 + 30 = 230
$ payments are: 170 + 120 + 50 = 340
$110,000 net payments need to be hedged
€ receipts are: 75 + 85 + 72 + 20 + 52 + 35 = 339
€ payments are: 72 + 35+ 50 + 20 + 65 = 242
€97,000 net receipts need to be hedged

Forward market hedges

Buy $ 3 months forward: $\dfrac{\$110,000}{1\cdot7835} = £61,676$

Sell € 3 months forward: $\dfrac{97,000}{1\cdot4390} = £67,408$

Currency options

It is now 31 December. The time of the transactions is 31 March. As the February options will have expired, May options should be used. Pounds need to be sold to purchase dollars, therefore MJY will need to purchase put options. The dollar payment is $110,000, which is the equivalent of approximately one £62,500 option contract.

Option hedge

Strike price	$ if exercised	Premium ($)	Premium £ (at spot 1·7982)	Overhedge ($)	Overhedge (£) (at forward 1·7861)
1·80	112,500	3,338	1,856	2,500	1,400
1·78	111,250	2,625	1,460	1,250	700

Worse case outcomes using currency options:
1·80: 62,500 + 1,856 – 1,400 = £62,956
1·78: 62,500 + 1,460 – 700 = £63,260

These are both much worse than the forward hedge, but if the dollar was to weaken to more than the relevant strike price, the option could be lapsed, and the necessary $110,000 purchased in the spot market at a more favourable exchange rate.

For a relatively small hedge of this nature a multinational company would probably use a forward contract as it involves less administrative time and costs, and fixes the payment of £61,676.

Answer 37 OMNIOWN

(a) **Interest rate hedging**

(i)   A forward rate agreement (FRA)

This involves fixing the future interest rate now for the £5m. It involves an agreement tailor-made to the company's requirement in terms of amount and dates. Once an FRA has been entered into Omniown must pay interest at the agreed rate. The rate offered will depend on the market's current perception of future interest rates. The FRA is based on a notional principal (i.e. it is independent from the underlying loan which should be arranged separately). It would protect the firm from rate increases but if the actual rate fell below the forward rate the company would not benefit from this decrease (i.e. it would still have to pay the rate per the forward rate agreement).

The mechanics of an FRA are that if actual rates are in excess of the rate per the FRA, the bank will compensate the company by the amount of the excess. Similarly, if actual rates are below the agreed rate the company pays the difference to the bank.

There is no initial premium payable on an FRA. FRAs can normally be arranged for up to two years into the future.

(ii)   Interest rate futures

These are contracts of standard amounts and for standard periods of time running from a limited number of dates. They are therefore less flexible than an FRA but are similarly binding on both parties. For Omniown protection against interest rate increases could be achieved by selling futures contracts now. As interest rates rise the value of futures contracts will fall. Hence Omniown can buy back the contracts at a lower price and make a profit. This profit should compensate the company for the increase in interest rates though this profit is unlikely to match perfectly the additional interest costs incurred. Interest rate futures involve payment of a small initial margin.

(iii)   An interest rate cap

This is an option which enables the treasurer to fix a maximum interest rate for a period in the future but if the rate falls the treasurer can choose not to use the option and take advantage of the lower rate. Because of this additional benefit – of taking advantage of lower rates – options tend to be more expensive: they involve payment of a premium in advance at the time the contract is entered into.

(b) **Effect of using futures market**

Cost of a 2% increase in interest	=	$5,000,000 \times 1/100 \times 6/12 = £50,000$
Effect of a 1 tick move in price on one contract	=	$500,000 \times 0.0001 \times 3/12 = £12.50$
So 2% (i.e. 200 ticks) would cause a profit of	=	£2,500 per contract = £12.50 × 200

Therefore, need $\dfrac{50,000}{2,500} = 20$ contracts

			£
	(i)	Extra interest	(50,000)
		Effect on futures price: (sell now at 86.25; buy in 3 months at 84.25) 2% = 200 ticks; this decrease in price of futures will result in a gain of 12.50 × 200 × 20	50,000
		Overall effect	0

100% hedge efficiency

			£
	(ii)	Extra interest	(50,000)
		Effect on futures price: (sell now at 86.25; buy in 3 months at 84.75) Gain 1.5% = 150 ticks × 12.50 × 20	37,500
		Net loss	(12,500)

$$\text{Hedging efficiency} = \frac{37{,}500}{50{,}000} \times 100 = 75\%$$

			£
	(iii)	Reduction in interest 5,000,000 × $^1/_{100}$ × $^6/_{12}$	25,000
		Effect on futures: (sell now at 86.25; buy in 3 months at 87) Loss 0.75% = 75 ticks × 12.50 × 20	(18,750)
		Net gain	6,250

$$\text{Hedging efficiency} = \frac{25{,}000}{18{,}750} \times 100 = 133\%$$

(c)   Evaluation of interest rate cap

			£	£
	(i)	Cost using futures hedge 5,000,000 × $^{14}/_{100}$ × $^6/_{12}$		350,000
		Cost using interest rate cap: Premium 5,000,000 × 0.002	10,000	
		Interest rates rise by 2%, therefore will use cap to pay 14%	350,000	
		Total cost	360,000	

Therefore, futures hedge is cheaper.

(ii)	Cost using futures hedge – per (i) above		350,000
	Add: Net increase		12,500
			362,500

Cost using interest rate cap:
Interest rates rise, therefore will again use
cap to pay 14% and premium –
per (i) above 360,000

Therefore, interest rate cap is cheaper.

(iii) Cost using futures hedge 350,000
Less: Net gain – per (ii) above 6,250

Net cost 343,750

Cost using interest rate cap:
Interest rates fall, therefore will not use
the cap. Instead take advantage
of lower actual rates:
Cost: Interest $5,000,000 \times (0.14 - 0.01) \times {}^{6}/_{12}$ ... 325,000
Add: Premium 10,000

335,000

Therefore, interest rate cap is cheaper.

Answer 38 MANLING

(a) Disintermediation and securitisation

Disintermediation refers to removal of intermediaries or "cutting out the middle man". It occurs in the case of large public limited companies which wish to raise finance or to lend funds. Rather than dealing with a bank which serves the function of matching funds from depositors with loans required by companies, the companies deal directly between themselves (i.e. they avoid using the bank, or other financial intermediaries).

Securitisation refers to the process of creating new financial instruments (or "paper") which are tradable and issued to support fresh corporate debt. Bonds, floating rate notes (FRNs) and bonds are all examples of securitised paper.

Disintermediation and securitisation can help the financial manager in the following ways:

■ Disintermediation makes it possible to raise funds more cheaply than by borrowing from the bank – this assumes that the company has a suitable credit rating to be able to participate in borrowing from other non-financial corporates.

■ Certain types of bank loan have conditions attached to them (e.g. provision of security). These conditions may be avoided by borrowing from others.

■ Securitisation offers more flexibility in terms of the type of borrowing obtained; for example, financial managers can tailor the maturity date to the exact financing needs of the company.

- Securitisation raises the profile of corporate issuers, whose names are seen more prominently in the financial markets.

- Securitisation makes debt easily marketable, producing finer interest rates for the borrowers and flexibility for lenders.

- It avoids the queuing system which exists for some debt issues.

- Alternative sources of finance and ways of investing surplus funds are made available to financial managers.

(b)(i) Evaluation of interest rate swap to Manling

(1) LIBOR remains at 10% for the whole year

Existing commitment: Fixed rate of		12%

Commitment after the swap:

(A)	Cost of fixed rate loan	12%
(B)	Floating rate paid to the other company $10 + 1\frac{1}{2}$	$11\frac{1}{2}\%$
(C)	Rate received from the other company	$(11\frac{5}{8}\%)$
	Net rate incurred	$11\frac{7}{8}\%$

	£
Saving in interest £14m × (12% − $11\frac{7}{8}\%$)	17,500
Arrangement fee	(20,000)
Increase in cost	2,500

Therefore, swap would not be beneficial, although the final cost, after tax, is mitigated to £2,500 (1 − t) = £2,500 (1 − 0.35) = £1,625

(2) LIBOR falls to 9% after six months

Commitment after the swap:

(A)	Cost of fixed rate loan	12%	12%
(B)	Floating rate paid to the other company $10 + 1\frac{1}{2}$	$11\frac{1}{2}\%$	
	$9 + 1\frac{1}{2}$		$10\frac{1}{2}\%$
(C)	Rate received from other company	$(11\frac{5}{8}\%)$	$(11\frac{5}{8}\%)$
		11.875%	10.875%

Saving in interest:

	£
First six months £14m × (0.12 − 0.11875) × $^6/_{12}$	8,750
Second six months £14m × (0.12 − 0.10875) × $^6/_{12}$	78,750
	87,500
Arrangement fee	(20,000)
Net benefit	67,500

Therefore, swap is beneficial. After tax, the benefit of the swap over the year will equal £67,500 (1 − 0.35) = £43,875

(ii) Evaluation of whether both companies can benefit

Cost to the other company

(1)	Cost of floating rate finance 10 + 1⅛	11⅛%
(2)	Fixed rate interest to Manling	11⅝%
(3)	Amount received from Manling floating rate of 10 + 1½	(11½%)
Net cost of fixed rate finance		11¼%

The other company would otherwise pay 11¾% for fixed rate finance, and is thus saving 11¾% − 11¼% = ½% under the swap.

Therefore, under the present swap agreement, with LIBOR = 10%, the savings being achieved are:

(1)	Manling	⅛%
(2)	Other company	½%
Total saving		⅝%

It is this saving which needs to be shared equally between the two firms.

Shared equally = ⅝ ÷ 2 = $^5/_{16}$% to each company.

At the moment, the other company obtains a ½% saving compared to the $^5/_{16}$% it would obtain if savings were shared equally. It must therefore give, by way of the interest rates applied to the swap, $^3/_{16}$% (½% − $^5/_{16}$%) of additional benefit to Manling. This would give Manling an equal ⅛% + $^3/_{16}$% = $^5/_{16}$% benefit in comparison to the finance it would otherwise obtain.

Thus, the other company should either pay $^5/_{16}$ more as a fixed interest charge to Manling (making that charge 11⅝% + $^5/_{16}$% = 11$^{13}/_{16}$%) or receive an interest rate of $^5/_{16}$% less from Manling by way of floating rate charge. That is, commit Manling to Paying LIBOR + 1½% less $^5/_{16}$% (i.e. LIBOR + 1$^5/_{16}$%; 11$^5/_{16}$% if LIBOR = 10%). In summary the overall finance costs for both companies under both options become either:

Fixed rate	12%	
Floating rate		11 1/8%
Floating rate swap	11 1/2%	(11 1/2%)
Fixed rate swap (bal fig)	(11 13/16%)	11 13/16%
Overall cost	11 11/16%	11 7/16%

or:

Fixed rate	12%	
Floating rate		11 1/8%
Floating rate swap	(11 5/8%)	11 5/8%
Fixed rate swap (bal fig)	11 5/16%	(11 5/16%)
Overall cost	11 11/16%	11 7/16%

Thus, the benefit to each company is:

	£
14m × 5/16%	43,750
Less: Arrangement fee	20,000
Net benefit before tax	23,750

Net benefit after tax 23,750 × (1 − 0.35) = £15,437

(c) Short-term investments available

- Short-term bank deposit in domestic or foreign currency.

- Treasury Bills – issued by the government and risk-free.

- Local authority debt – carrying slightly higher interest than Treasury Bills to reflect higher risk.

- Certificates of deposit issued by British or foreign banks.

- Bills of exchange and trade bills issued by companies.

- Deposits with building societies.

- Purchase of equity shares. This is likely to be undesirable because of the risk of capital loss and transaction costs.

- Placement in the money markets. Such placements are unsecured, but generally very low risk as borrowing counter parties will be prime organisations.

- Purchase of commercial paper (i.e. promissory notes issued by prime borrowers). Such investment is highly flexible – commercial paper being easily sold when needed to realise cash.

- Working capital. The company could look to see whether sales could be boosted to advantage by investing more in receivables or inventory.

  The company could also consider discount availability on early settlement of creditor balances.

The factors to take into account when comparing these alternatives are yield, risk of default and marketability. The yield will normally be higher as the risk increases.

Answer 39 MURWALD

(a) Futures and options hedges

The treasury team believe that interest rates are more likely to increase than to decrease, and any hedging strategy will be based upon this assumption. There is also a requirement that interest payments do not increase by more than £10,000 from current interest rates.

Current expectations

£12 million deficit, interest payments £12m × 7.5% × 0.5 = £450,000

Futures hedges (Either March or June contracts may be used – or both.)

Tutorial note: *The suggested solution uses June contracts.*

(i)   If interest rates rise

With an expected £12m deficit – using June contracts.

As a six months hedge is required the number of contracts will be

$$\frac{£12m}{£500,000} \times 2 = 48 \text{ contracts}$$

The tick value is £500,000 × 0.0001 × $^3/_{12}$ = £12.50

Cash market	Futures market
Current cost £450,000	December 1, sell three month sterling futures at 93.10
With 2% increase £12m × 9.5% × 0.5 = £570,000	After interest rate increase buy 48 three month sterling futures at 91.30
Extra cash market cost = £120,000	Futures gain 48 × 180 × £12.5 = £108,000

Net additional cost after hedging = £12,000

If Murwald expects basis risk to exist (i.e. the futures price moves by a different amount to the cash market interest rates), the number of contracts could be modified to reflect such risk. However, basis risk is difficult to predict.

(ii)   If interest rates fall

With an expected £12m deficit

Cash market	Futures market
Current cost £450,000	Sell 48 contracts at 93.10
With 1% decrease	Buy 48 contracts at 94.00

£12m × 6.5% × 0.5 = £390,000

Cash market saving	Futures market loss
£60,000	48 × 90 × £12.50 = £54,000

Overall net extra saving £6,000

Based upon these futures prices hedging in the futures market does not allow the company to guarantee that interest costs in the case of a deficit do not increase by more than £10,000.

Options hedges

The expectation is for interest rates to rise, therefore put options on futures will be purchased. (If interest rates rise the value of the put options will also increase.)

For example using the 9400 exercise price:

(i)   If interest rates rise

With an expected £12m deficit

Cash market	Options market
Current cost £450,000	Buy 48 options at 9400 strike price at 1.84
New cost £570,000	The option may be exercised to sell June futures at 94.0
Extra cash market cost is £120,000	June futures may be purchased on LIFFE at 91.30
	Profit from options is:
	94 − 91.30 − 1.84 = 86 ticks 86 × 48 × £12.5 = £51,600
Net extra cost is £68,400	

In reality the options are likely to be sold rather than exercised as being June contracts, they will still have time value which will be reflected in the option price. The gain from the options sale is therefore likely to be higher than the gain from exercising the options. However, no data is provided on option prices on 1 March.

(ii)   If interest rates fall

With an expected £12m deficit

Cash market	Options market
Current cost £450,000	Buy 48 options at 9400 strike price at 1.84
New cost £390,000	The futures price moves to 94.0 and the option would not be exercised
Cash market saving £60,000	The loss on options is the premium paid 48 × 184 × £12.50 = £110,400
Net extra cost £50,400	

Summary

	Futures	Options
2% interest rate increase £12m deficit	(12,000)	(68,400)
1% interest rate decrease £12m deficit	6,000	(50,400)

Different option outcomes will exist if different put option exercise prices are selected. The best exercise price to select if the put options are exercised will be the 9350 option.

This will give a gain if exercised of:

93.50 – 91.30 – 1.25 = 0.95 or 95 ticks
95 × 48 × £12.50 = £57,000

If the futures price moves to 94.0, the option will not be exercised, and the loss will be the premium paid of

125 × 48 × £12.5 = £75,000

Outcomes:

2% increase   9350 options
£12 million deficit   £(63,000)

1% decrease
£12 million deficit   *£(15,000)*

Neither futures nor options hedges can satisfy, with certainty, the requirement that the interest payment should not increase by more than £10,000.

However, one way to achieve this would be to use a collar option, whereby downside risk is protected, but potential gains are also limited. A collar effectively fixes a maximum and minimum interest rate.

If a company expects to be borrowing and is worried about interest rate increases, a suitable collar can be achieved by *buying* put options and *selling* call options, to reduce the cost of protection.

For example a collar could be achieved by buying 48 options at 9400 strike price at 1.84 and selling 9400 call options at 1.74, a net premium cost of 0.10 (other alternatives are possible).

Murwald does not want interest to move adversely by more than £10,000 for a six month period on a £12 million loan.

In annual terms this is a $\frac{£10,000}{£12m} \times 2 = 0.167\%$

A put option at the current interest rate (6%) and a total premium cost of less than 0.167% will satisfy the company's requirement. In the above example the total premium cost is 0.10%, and no matter what happens to interest rates Murwald can fix its borrowing cost at:

7.6% (100 – 94.00 + 0.10 net option premium plus the 1.5% risk premium)

This satisfies the requirement. (Interest payments would be £12m × 7.6% × 0.5 = £456,000 which is £6,000 worse than current interest rates.)

The use of a collar is the recommended hedging strategy, but the company should consider the implications of the collar if a cash surplus were to occur rather than a cash deficit.

(b) Alternative interest rate hedges

(i) A forward agreement (FRA) is a contract to agree to pay a fixed interest rate that is effective at a future date. As such Murwald could fix now a rate of interest of 6.1% (for example) to be effective in three months' time for a period of six months. If interest rates were to rise above 6.1% the counter-party, usually a bank, would compensate Murwald for the difference between the actual rates and 6.1%. if interest rates were to fall below 6.1% Murwald would compensate the counter-party for the difference between 6.1% and the actual rate.

(ii) OTC interest rate options (including interest rate caps). Instead of market traded interest rate options such as those that are available on LIFFE, Murwald might use OTC options through a major bank. This would allow options to be tailored to the company's exact size and maturity requirements. An OTC collar would be possible, and the cost of this should be compared with the cost of using LIFFE options.

(iii) Interest rate swaps. Murwald expects to borrow at a floating rate of interest. It might be possible for Murwald to swap its floating rate interest stream for a fixed rate stream, pegging interest rates to approximately current levels (the terms of the swap would have to be negotiated). Interest rate swaps are normally for longer periods than six months.

Answer 40 TURKEY

(a) Establishing the hedge

The company expects to have to borrow £3 million for 4 months from 1 February and is fearful that short-term money market interest rates (CDs) might rise from their current level of 8.8%.

At the current level of interest rates, the loan interest cost (the target cost) would be:

£3m × $^4/_{12}$ × 0.088 = £88,000

To hedge their interest rate on the loan, the company needs to sell futures contracts as follows:

- Number of contracts required: £3m/£0.5m × $^4/_3$ = 6 × $^4/_3$ = 8.
- Sell 8 £ March futures at a price of 91.44.

The number of contracts used hedges Turkey's full potential exposure to interest rate risk. If it is thought that there was a significant chance that substantially less than £3 million might be required, then a judgement would have to be made by the company's treasury department about how much risk exposure it would want to leave unhedged.

The March contracts would be the most suitable to use as they have the next expiry date after the loan would be drawn down.

The December contracts would obviously not be suitable as they would have expired before the loan was required. Although the June and September contracts could be used, it would be inadvisable to do so as they are likely to expose the company to a greater degree of basis risk.

The hedge is set up by selling futures because they represent selling interest on 3-month deposits at $100 - 91.44 = 8.56\%$. Thus if interest rates subsequently rise (which represents an adverse move as far as the company's loan is concerned), the company will have profited by locking into a sale at a lower interest rate.

Finally, 8 contracts are required (rather than 6) because of the "maturity mis-match". Three-month interest rate futures are being used to hedge a four month loan. As a result, the number of contracts required to hedge the interest liability over four months has to be adjusted by the factor of $^4/_3$.

(b) **Outcome of hedge**

On 1 February, Turkey will borrow £3 million at 11.2% interest:

	£
Actual interest cost (£3m × $^4/_{12}$ × 0.112)	112,000
Target interest cost	88,000
Loss on target	24,000

Company closes out its futures position by reversing the earlier deal:

Buy 8 £ March contracts at 89.34

Profit on futures:

Bought at	89.34
Sold at	91.44
Profit	2.1% = 210 ticks/contract

Total profit: $8 \times 210 \times £12.50 = £21,000$

Hedge efficiency $= \dfrac{\text{Profit}}{\text{Loss}} = \dfrac{£21,000}{£24,000} = 87.5\%$

The hedging strategy has been reasonably successful. However, Turkey did not achieve a perfect (100% efficient) hedge because the futures price did not move precisely in line with interest rates:

Change in futures price: $91.44 - 89.34 = 2.1\%$
Change in interest rates: $11.2\% - 8.8\% = 2.4\%$

The 0.3% difference represents the shortfall of the futures profit over the loss on target:

£3m × $^4/_{12}$ × 0.003 = £3,000

	£
Loss on target	24,000
Profit on futures	21,000
Shortfall	3,000

ADVANCED FINANCIAL MANAGEMENT (P4) – STUDY QUESTION BANK

Answer 41 GLOBAL DEBT

(a) Reasons for problem

The "global debt problem" has existed for some countries for nearly thirty years. It developed partly as a result of a massive increase in petrol and other commodity prices during the 1970's and 1980's. This together with widespread economic recession, reductions in the imports of many advanced countries from developing countries, and relatively high levels of international interest rates, meant that many countries were forced to borrow internationally to meet their import requirements of essential goods such as fuel and foodstuffs. Such countries often experienced large current account deficits, and could not get access to the necessary hard currency to pay for imports other than by borrowing. Many also suffered from capital flight, with funds leaving the country to find what was perceived to be a safer international home. Major international banks were very willing to lend to sovereign nations, as historically country default risk had been low. Arguably banks' risk assessment took too optimistic a view and vast amounts of sovereign loans were agreed, with countries such as Mexico and Brazil borrowing in excess of 100 billion dollars. Debt servicing payments in some countries exceeded 50% of total export earnings, and domestic savings were insufficient to provide the necessary funds to repay international debts. Continuing current account deficits made the situation even worse in many countries. Many countries had insufficient hard currency to meet the debt servicing conditions of their loans.

Financial contagion refers to the spread of economic and financial problems from one country to another. As barriers to trade, investment and capital flows are reduced or eliminated the resultant more "global" economy is more susceptible to contagion. As can be seen from the problems of the Thai baht in 1997, the problems of even a relatively small economy can easily have severe economic impacts on neighbouring countries and even upon larger countries such as Brazil and Russia. Financial contagion potentially worsens the impact of the international debt problem. If financial problems in one country directly lead to similar problems in several others it accentuates the debt servicing difficulties.

(b) Attempts to resolve the international debt problem

- Lending additional funds to the countries, sometimes to meet current interest payments and prevent default. Most lending has been accompanied by suggested or imposed economic reforms to try and address the fundamental causes of the problem. Such reforms are often based upon stringent conditions set by the IMF.

- Rescheduling the repayment of debt to extend the repayment period and reduce current cash outflows.

- Writing off some or all of the debt. Where lenders are institutions such as international banks this naturally requires their agreement, and has substantial cost for them.

- Sale of debt for less than face value.

- Swapping debt into some other form of commitment. This includes swaps from debt into the equity of local companies, or even promises to reduce pollution, provided enhanced education etc.

Financial problems are most often experienced in those countries that have fixed exchange rates and an overvalued currency; suffer from large short-term capital outflows; or have overheated parts of the economy (especially the property sector). Fixed exchange rate systems are also much more likely to be the subject of speculative attacks. Financial crises are also associated with weak economic fundamentals such as high unemployment, low growth in GDP, high short-term debt to currency reserves, balance of payments deficits and high real interest rates.

Governments might reduce the risk of financial problems and the potential associated contagion by altering the exchange rate system and trying to address these economic issues. For example, the government might adopt a floating rate regime (although this will impact upon other aspects of the economy), or possibly a currency board system. Governments should closely monitor important sectors of the economy to assess the risks within those sectors, and consider the use of taxation, monetary policy and/or exchange controls to prevent a crisis occurring.

Answer 42 BEELA ELECTRONICS

(a) Consultant's suggestion

The consultant's report should not be used as the only basis for the African investment decision, because:

- The decision should be taken after evaluating the risk/return trade-off; financial factors (e.g. the expected NPV from the investments); strategic factors; and other issues including political risk. Political risk is only one part of the decision process (although in extremely risky countries it might be the most important one).

- The scores for the three countries are:

    | Country 1 | 29 |
    | Country 2 | 24 |
    | Country 3 | 28 |

    Just because previous clients have not invested in countries with scores of less than 30 does not mean that Beela should not. The previous countries may not have been comparable with these in Africa. This decision rule also ignores return. If return is expected to be very high, a relatively low score might be acceptable to Beela.

- The factors considered by the consultant might not be the only relevant factors when assessing political risk. Others could include the extent of capital flight from the country, the legal infrastructure, availability of local finance and the existence of special taxes and regulations for multinational companies.

- The weightings of the factors might not be relevant to Beela.

- Scores such as these only focus on the macro risk of the country. The micro risk, the risk for the actual company investing in a country, is the vital factor. This differs between companies and between industries. A relatively hi-tech electronics company might be less susceptible to political actions than, for example, companies in extractive industries where the diminishing bargain concept may apply.

- There is no evidence of how the scores have been devised and how valid they are.

(b) Political risk management

Prior to investing Beela might negotiate an agreement with the local government covering areas of possible contention such as dividend remittance, transfer pricing, taxation, the use of local labour and capital, and exchange controls. The problem with such negotiations is that governments might change, and a new government might not honour the agreement.

The logistics of the investment may also influence political risk:

- If a key element of the process is left outside the country it may not be viable for the government to take actions against a company as it could not produce a complete product. This particularly applies when intellectual property or know-how is kept back.

- Financing locally might deter political action, as effectively the action will hurt the local providers of finance.

- Local sourcing of components and raw materials might reduce risk.

- It is sometimes argued that participating in joint ventures with a local partner reduces political risk, although evidence of this is not conclusive.

- Control of patents and processes by the multinational might reduce risk, although patents are not recognised in all countries.

Governments or commercial agencies in multinationals' home countries often offer insurance against political risk.

Answer 43 IMF

A large current account deficit means that the value of exports of goods, services, investment income and current transfers is much less than the value of imports of these items. If the government believes that the deficit is not a temporary phenomenon, which will be largely self-correcting, it may attempt to reduce the deficit by taking one or more of a selection of economic measures. However, a country with large foreign currency reserves may decide to finance the deficit by running down some of those reserves and may not take significant additional actions for some time.

Economic measures

(1) Monetary policy. A government will often take deflationary measures to reduce the money supply. This may be through increases in interest rates, or attempting to reduce the money supply through actions such as credit restrictions, wage and/or price controls and reductions in government expenditure. Increased interest rates will tend to reduce local borrowing and demand for imports, and attract overseas funds into the country to take advantage of the higher interest rates (until interest rate and exchange rates are in equilibrium once more)

(2) Fiscal policy. Governments often reduce consumer spending, including spending on imports, by increasing taxation.

(3) Devaluation. If the country is part of a fixed exchange rate system the currency may be devalued in order to make imports more expensive and exports more competitive.

(4) Exchange controls, tariffs, and quotas are all measures, which may be used to reduce imports, and to reduce a current account deficit. However, these may be contrary to World Trade Organisation (WTO) agreements.

(5) Export stimulation through government subsidies, although these too are often restricted by the WTO.

(6) Borrowing. The government may finance the deficit by borrowing from international commercial banks or international organisations such as the IMF. Such borrowing, however, may not tackle the underlying symptoms of the deficit.

The IMF may provide loans to help finance a balance of payments deficit. An important feature of most IMF loans is the conditions attached to the loans. Countries receiving IMF loans are required to take strong economic measures to try to improve or eliminate the economic problems that made the loans necessary, and to stimulate medium to long-term economic development. These conditions typically include currency devaluation, controls over inflation via the money supply, public expenditure cuts to reduce government budget deficits and local tax increases. Most loans are for a period of up to five years. The IMF also offers loans under the Extended Fund Facility in order to overcome severe structural balance of payments problems, and special supplementary borrowing facilities, often at concessionary rates of interest, to countries with severe problems.

The actions of the IMF help to reduce volatility in international exchange rates, and to facilitate world trade. This has beneficial effects on the trading activities of multinational companies. However, the strong influence of the IMF on the macroeconomic policies of developing nations often leads to short term deflation and to reductions in the size of markets for multinational companies' products. Conflicts may exist between multinationals, who wish to freely move capital internationally, and governments trying to control the money supply and inflation. Tax increases often accompany economic austerity measures, import tariff quotas may make operations more difficult and increases in interest rates raise the cost of finance. In the medium to long term the structural adjustments might stimulate economic growth and increase the size of markets for multinational companies, but IMF economic conditions may cause significant short to medium term difficulties for subsidiaries of multinationals in the countries concerned.

Most of the government policies discussed above tend to reduce domestic economic growth and increase unemployment, and are detrimental to a multinational company operating in the country concerned. For example, the impact of higher interest rates usually results in higher borrowing costs for a multinational company.

A possible beneficial effect is when the multinational exports a high proportion of its products, and the incremental demand stimulated by the devaluation/fall in value of the local currency results in an overall increase in the present value of cash flows to the multinational.

Answer 44 POLYCALC

(a) **Adjusted present value**

Base-case discount rate (£-terms)

$$\beta_{asset} = 1.40 \times \frac{4}{4 + 1(1 - 0.35)} = 1.20$$

Base Case discount rate = $9\% + (9.17\% \times 1.20) = 20\%$

A$ Project tax charge (A$m)

	Years 1 – 4
Revenue	18
– Operating costs	(5)
– Depreciation	(3.75)
= Taxable profit	9.25
Tax charge	4.625

A$ Project (A$m)

Year	0	1	2	3	4
Capital equipment	(15)				
Working capital	(5)				5
Revenues		18	18	18	18
Costs		(5)	(5)	(5)	(5)
Taxation		(4.625)	(4.625)	(4.625)	(4.625)
Net cash flow	(20)	8.375	8.375	8.375	13.375

£m Base Case Present Value calculation

Year	A$m		Exchange rate		£m		20% Discount rate		£m PV Cashflows
0	(20)	÷	2	=	(10)	×	1	=	(10)
1	8.375	÷	$2(1.10)^1$	=	3.807	×	0.833	=	3.171
2	8.375	÷	$2(1.10)^2$	=	3.461	×	0.694	=	2.402
3	8.375	÷	$2(1.10)^3$	=	3.146	×	0.579	=	1.821
4	13.375	÷	$2(1.10)^4$	=	4.568	×	0.482	=	2.202
Base Case PV								=	(0.404)

PV of tax shield

£5m × 0.10 = £500,000 = Annual interest
£500,000 × 0.35 = £175,000 = Annual tax relief

PV of tax relief: 175,000 × 3.170 = £554,750

PV of issue costs

£5m × 0.025 × (1 – 0.35) = £81,250

Adjusted present value

	£m
Base Case PV	(0.404)
PV tax shield	0.555
PV issue costs	(0.081)
Adjusted present value	£0.07m or +£70,000 approx
	Therefore accept

(b) Intended financing plans

The company's proposed financing plans for the Australian project can be criticised on the basis that they have not taken the opportunity to arrange them so as to help limit exposure to foreign exchange risk.

By having a long-lived Australian dollar (A$) asset the company is exposing itself to both foreign exchange translation and economic risk. This risk can be reduced by matching the A$ assets as closely as possible to an A$ liability.

(c) Limitations and difficulties

There are two main limitations to the use of CAPM for generating project discount rates. The first is that the model only generates a single-period rate of return (i.e. no discounting is involved) and so, strictly speaking, it should not be used to generate a discount rate for a multi-period analysis such as NPV. However, if it can reasonably be assumed that both the risk-free return and the excess market return will remain approximately constant over the life of the project then the limitation can be overcome.

The second limitation is that there is some evidence to suggest that the CAPM is an incomplete model in that there are other determinants of risk besides beta. However evidence on this point is somewhat mixed and even if beta is not the sole determinant of systematic risk, it would appear to be by far the most important determinant.

The difficulties met in attempting to use the CAPM to generate project appraisal discount rates are mainly caused by data identification difficulties of the three inputs: the risk-free return, the excess market return and the project beta.

With the risk-free return the problem is to identify a genuinely risk-free rate of return. Normally, the return on T-bills with a similar maturity to the life of the project will be used. The difficulty with the excess market return is its volatility over time which means that a long-run average excess market return is normally used. Finally, and perhaps most difficult of all, is the identification of the correct beta value. Usually what is used is the beta value of the industry group into which the project falls, but difficulties may arise either if the project does not fall into a neat industry group or if the project's characteristics (in relation to its revenue sensitivity and ratio of fixed to variable operating costs) are not typical of the industry. In such circumstances a considerable element of judgment enters into the determination of the beta figure.

Answer 45 AVTO

(a) Financial appraisal

The investment will be evaluated using both financial and non-financial criteria, including the possible political risk involved with investing in Terrania. However, international direct investment is sometimes undertaken for strategic reasons, which, at least in the short term, might outweigh financial considerations.

Projected cash flows:

Terranian francs (million)

Year	0	1	2	3	4	5
Sales[1]		659	735	785	838	
Labour – 300 workers[2]		228	262	288	317	
Local components		90	104	114	125	
German component[3]		41	47	52	57	
Distribution		20	23	25	28	
Fixed costs		50	58	63	70	
Total costs		(429)	(494)	(542)	(597)	
Taxable cash flows		230	241	243	241	
Taxation (20%)		(46)	(48)	(49)	(48)	
Tax saved from depreciation (v)		29	22	16	12	
Equipment	(580)				150	
Working capital (iii)	(170)	(34)	(31)	(23)	(26)	284
Remittable to the UK	(750)	179	184	187	329	284

UK cash flows (£ million)

Year	0	1	2	3	4	5
Remittable	(20·35)	4·13	3·80	3·62	5·96	4·82
Additional 10% UK tax on Terranian cash flow (vi)		(0·20)	(0·27)	(0·31)	(0·33)	
	(20·35)	3·93	3·53	3·31	5·63	
Discount factors (15%)(iv)	1	0·870	0·756	0·658	0·572	0·497
Present values	(20·35)	3·42	2·67	2·18	3·22	2·40

The expected NPV is: (£6·46) million. The expected investment in Terrania if viewed alone does not appear to be financially viable. However, the closure or downsizing of UK operations should also be considered. Closure would have a net cost, after tax, of at least £4·5 million (more if the full existing market in the EU cannot be supplied from Terrania), and might have other adverse effects on the local community that have not been quantified, and on the government in terms of extra support for redundant workers and their families. Downsizing would still have some of these effects, but would also offer the opportunity of selling to a larger market that could not otherwise have been supplied from Terrania alone.

If the UK operation is downsized, the net cost, after tax, of downsizing is £4 million, and expected annual net cash flows are £4 million, less tax at 30%, £2·8 million. Increasing these by UK inflation:

Year	0	1	2	3	4
Cash flows	(4·0)	2·86	2·94	3·03	3·12
Discount factors (12%)		0·893	0·797	0·712	0·636
Present values	(4·0)	2·55	2·34	2·16	1·98

---

[1] 50,000 × 480 × 27·44 = 658·6, etc.

[2] Labour cost has been increased by a factor of 1·2 to reflect the use of 300 workers to gain use of the rent-free factory. The cost of 50 extra workers is (3,800 × 50,000)/5 or 38 million francs. The after tax costing of renting the factory would be 75 million × 0·8, or 60 million francs. Avto would select the rent free factory as the cost is lower.

[3] 30 × 50 × 27·44 = 41·16, etc.

The total present value of cash flows from downsizing is £5.03 million over the four-year period. Downsizing results in a much more favourable outcome than total closure. If a period of longer than four years were considered the expected present value from downsizing would be even larger.

Overall the investment in Terrania plus downsizing does not appear to be financially viable, with an expected NPV of (£1·43) million. However, one major problem with the cash flow estimates is the realisable value used for the Terranian assets in year 4. If the Terranian investment is to continue beyond four years, which is implied in the information provided, then the present value of cash flows beyond four years should be considered, not the realisable value of assets. This present value is likely to be substantially higher. For example, even ignoring growth, the value of operating cash flows (TF 179 million in year 4) for an additional ten years would be $179 \times 5·019 = $ TF 898 million, rather than the TF 150 million estimated realisable value of assets.

(b)   Wider commercial considerations

Aspects of the cash flows that would need to be investigated further before a decision was made include:

- What rent would be payable for the factory after year 4?

- How accurate are the forecasts of sales, costs, tax rates etc? Sensitivity analysis or simulation analysis might be used to investigate the effect of changes in key cash flows.

- Will the investment lead to other opportunities (future options)? If so an attempt should be made to value such options.

- The strategic importance of the investment to the company.

- The political risk of Terrania. The fact that the country has had twelve changes of government in the last ten years does not necessarily mean that there is substantial political risk. Countries such as Italy have also experienced frequent changes of government. However, the degree of international indebtedness and potential lack of support from the IMF could affect the future prospects of the country. It would be useful to know the ability of Terrania to service its debt, given the problems with the banana crop and competition from neighbouring countries.

- The existence of better opportunities elsewhere. For example would it be possible to produce the DVD players in neighbouring countries where labour costs are even lower?

(c)   Impact of blocked remittances

Avto should investigate how likely further restrictions on remittances from Terrania are. If remittance restrictions are introduced Avto could partially mitigate their effects by investing in the Terranian money market, but the effect of the restrictions would still reduce the present value of excepted cash flows by approximately £1·83 million (see below) unless increased direct investment in Terrania was planned. Remittance restrictions might be avoided by increasing transfer prices paid by the foreign subsidiary to the parent company, or by trying to move cash out of Terrania by means of other forms of payment such as royalties, payment for patents, or management fees. It is likely that the Terranian government would try to prevent many of these measures being used.

ADVANCED FINANCIAL MANAGEMENT (P4) – STUDY QUESTION BANK

If remittances were blocked for four years and the funds invested in the Terranian money market.

Year 1 $179 \times (1 \cdot 15)(1 \cdot 10)^2 =$	249
Year 2 $184 \times (1 \cdot 10)^2 =$	223
Year 3 $187 \times 1 \cdot 10 =$	206
Year 4	329
Remittable at end year 4	1,007
£m equivalent	18·24
Present value £m	10·43

Present value of remittable funds (without additional UK tax) if no blockage exists is £12·26 million. The blockage would reduce the expected present value of cash flows by approximately £1·83 million.

Any final decision regarding investment in Terrania must also take into account other non-financial factors such as the nature of the country's legal system, bureaucracy, efficiency of internal processes, cultural and religious differences, and local business practices and ethics.

Appendix:

(i) Based on purchasing power parity the expected exchange rates are:

	Terranian franc per €	
Spot	23·32	
Year 1	27·44	year 1 $\frac{1 \cdot 20}{1 \cdot 02} \times 23 \cdot 32 = 27 \cdot 44$ etc
Year 2	30·64	
Year 3	32·72	
Year 4	34·94	
Year 5	37·32	

	Terranian franc per £	
Spot	36·85	
Year 1	43·35	year 1 $\frac{1 \cdot 20}{1 \cdot 02} \times 36 \cdot 85 = 43 \cdot 35$ etc
Year 2	48·40	
Year 3	51·69	
Year 4	55·20	
Year 5	58·95	

(ii) The feasibility study is irrelevant as it is a sunk cost

(iii) Working capital is assumed to increase each year in line with inflation in Terrania, and to be released at the end of year 5.

(iv) Discount rates:

Terranian investment:
$k_e = 4 \cdot 5\% + (11 \cdot 5\% - 4 \cdot 5\%) \, 1 \cdot 5 = 15\%$

UK investment:
$k_e = 4 \cdot 5\% + (11 \cdot 5\% - 4 \cdot 5\%) \, 1 \cdot 1 = 12 \cdot 2\%$

12% will be used as the discount rate for UK investments.

(v) Tax-allowable depreciation (francs million)

	Book value	Depreciation (25%)	Tax saved (20%)
Year 1	580	145	29
Year 2	435	109	22
Year 3	326	82	16
Year 4	245	61	12

(vi) Additional UK tax

Year	1	2	3	4
Sales less cash costs in Terrania	230	241	243	241
Depreciation	145	109	82	61
Taxable in Terrania	85	32	161	180
Extra 10% tax	8·5	13·2	16·1	18·0
£m equivalent	0·20	0·27	0·31	0·33

Answer 46 SERVEALOT

There are several aspects of the statement that might not be valid.

"The company aims to serve its shareholders by paying a high level of dividends."

Not all shareholders would favour a high level of dividends. Where dividends are taxed at a higher rate than capital gains there might be a preference for low or no dividends to be paid in which case the payment of high dividends might be unpopular with shareholders and have a detrimental effect on share price.

"Adopting strategies that will increase the company's share price."

This is problematic for at least two reasons. Firstly, according to financial theory a company should attempt to maximise the returns (wealth) to shareholders. Increasing the share price is not the same as maximising the returns. Secondly, the objectives of most companies are much broader than a single objective of shareholder wealth maximisation. Companies have many stakeholders, including their customers, suppliers, employees, lenders of funds to the company, and normally the government and the local community. The objectives of companies will normally be influenced by such stakeholders. Additionally environmental issues and other aspects of corporate social responsibility are increasingly influencing the objectives and strategies of companies in many countries, and there are strong ethical grounds for companies to be sensitive to such issues.

"Satisfying our shareholders will ensure our success."

As mentioned above there are many other stakeholders that the company might need to satisfy. Satisfying shareholders is not likely to ensure success as actions that satisfy shareholders might be at the expense of other stakeholders.

"The company will reduce costs by manufacturing overseas wherever possible."

This strategy is contentious, as it normally means a loss of employment, wealth generation, and possibly taxation, in the home country. It is true that costs can often be reduced by manufacturing overseas, but there is an ethical question of how loyal a company should be to its local employees and the local community.

"Adopt a strategy of attempting to minimise the company's global tax bill through the judicious use of tax haven facilities"

As long as the tax reduction is by means of legal tax avoidance then this strategy should lead to an increase in cash flow and share price. Many governments try to restrict the use companies make of overseas tax havens but they are not illegal. Government restrictions mean that it will not always be possible for companies to make use of tax havens.

Answer 47 KANDOVER

(a) **Expected after-tax profits under each transfer price**

All estimates assume no change in exchange rates. Any change would affect the profit and tax estimates.

The effective total tax rate in Petronia is the corporate tax rate of 25%, plus the withholding tax rate of 15% on 75% of pre-tax income. This is effectively another 15% × 0·75 = 11·25% tax on pre-tax income, or a total of 36·25%. In each case, as the total tax rates in Petronia are higher than the 30% UK tax rate, there will be full credit available against any UK tax liability on Petronian income.

Market based transfer price

UK parent		£	
Sales price	50,000 × 18 =	900,000	
Variable costs	50,000 × 13 =	650,000	
Fixed costs		120,000	
UK pre-tax profit		130,000	
Corporate tax (30%)		39,000	
Profit after tax		91,000	

Petronian subsidiary		P$	£
Sales price	50,000 × 250 =	12,500,000	1,602,564
Transfer price	900,000 × 7·8 =	7,020,000	900,000
Local variable costs	50,000 × 82 =	4,100,000	525,641
Local fixed costs		351,000	45,000
Petronian pre-tax profit		1,029,000	131,923
Corporate tax (25%)		257,250	32,981
		771,750	98,942
Withholding tax (15%)		115,763	14,841
Profit after all tax		655,987	84,101

Total UK and Petronian after tax profit £91,000 + £84,101 = £175,101

Period fixed cost plus variable cost

UK parent		£	
Sales price		770,000	
Variable costs	50,000 × 13 =	650,000	
Fixed costs		120,000	
UK profit		0	

Petronian subsidiary		P$	£
Sales price	50,000 × 250 =	12,500,000	1,602,564
Transfer price	770,000 × 7.8 =	6,006,000	770,000
Local variable costs	50,000 × 82 =	4,100,000	525,641
Local fixed costs		351,000	45,000
Petronian pre-tax profit		2,043,000	261,923
Corporate tax (25%)		510,750	65,481
		1,532,250	196,442
Withholding tax (15%)		229,838	29,466
Profit after all tax		1,302,412	166,976

Total UK and Petronian after tax profit £0 + £166,976 = £166,976

Negotiated cost

UK parent		£
Sales price		962,500
Variable costs	50,000 × 13 =	650,000
Fixed costs		120,000
UK pre-tax profit		192,500
Corporate tax (30%)		57,750
Profit after tax		134,750

Petronian subsidiary		P$	£
Sales price	50,000 × 250 =	12,500,000	1,602,564
Transfer price	962,500 × 7.8 =	7,507,500	962,500
Local variable costs	50,000 × 82 =	4,100,000	525,641
Local fixed costs		351,000	45,000
Petronian profit		541,500	69,423
Corporate tax (25%)		135,375	17,356
		406,125	52,067
Withholding tax (15%)		60,919	7,810
Profit after all tax		345,206	44,257

Total UK and Petronian after tax profit £134,750 + £44,257 = £179,007

ADVANCED FINANCIAL MANAGEMENT (P4) – STUDY QUESTION BANK

(b) **Advantages//disadvantages of each transfer price**

Market price

Transfer at market price means that there would be no problems with the relevant tax authorities regarding the manipulation of transfer prices, and such prices would assist in the accurate evaluation of the performance of the subsidiary.

However, if the parent company had spare capacity the use of the market price might not be optimal and could lead to incorrect resource allocation decisions (a price based upon the marginal cost of extra production could result in an increase in group profitability).

It might not always be possible to establish a market price for a component, unless the same component is sold to other customers.

Fixed cost plus variable cost per unit

This method would not earn any profits for the selling company, leaving all profits in this case for the overseas subsidiary. As the total tax rate in Petronia is higher than in the UK, this would result in less overall group income than a market based price. The UK tax authorities might not accept such a transfer price as it eliminates UK tax liability.

It might be better for the transfer price to be the fixed cost plus a variable charge that includes a profit element.

Negotiated transfer price

A negotiated price may be difficult to agree. One of the parties is likely to suffer from such a price.

The negotiated price in this example has the effect of increasing the total group after tax income by reducing the tax liability in the relatively high tax environment. However, this also means that profits are reduced in Petronia, and could affect the performance measurement of the subsidiary, and the motivation of staff in the subsidiary. It is however, possible for an adjustment to be made to reflect the artificial transfer price that has been used.

In practice, a negotiated price such as this might not be possible as the tax authorities in Petronia might insist on a market based transfer price being used to increase the tax take in Petronia.

Answer 48 NOIFA LEISURE

(a) Group's financial position

The chairman is correct in saying that revenue has doubled and that the share price has almost doubled over the period. However, during the period return on revenue has decreased from 21% to 14% and asset turnover has decreased from 0.85 to 0.75. Therefore, return on capital employed has decreased from 25% to 15%. This is largely due to a reduction in returns from hotel operations. The increase in revenue of 209% has resulted in an increase in profit after tax of only $\left(\dfrac{37}{33}\right) = 12\%$; earnings per share also shows a negligible increase of $\left(\dfrac{7.4}{6.6}\right) = 12\%$. this is accompanied by a significant increase in gearing, and therefore financial risk for the equity shareholders, to over 100% in 20X9. The current and quick ratios have also declined over the period. The overall financial position has considerably weakened during the period.

Although the share price of Noifa Leisure has nearly doubled, prices of shares in the leisure industry as a whole have increased by $\left(\dfrac{394}{178}\right) = 220\%$. The P/E ratio of Noifa Leisure was well above the rest of the sector in 20X6 but in 20X9 is below the industry figure, reflecting that the company's rating has fallen relative to the rest of the leisure sector.

(b) Financing policies

The increase in the assets of the group has been financed initially by disposal of investments and subsequently by increases in long and short term borrowing, together with a small amount of retained earnings. No equity issues have been made during the period. This has increased gearing. It may be more prudent to use a mix of equity and debt to finance expansion.

It states in the question that the euro loan has little risk. This is not the case since, although the euro is a "basket of currencies", the exchange rate between the euro and the £ could still move (the UK is currently outside "Euroland"), creating the risk of exchange losses being incurred when making interest and capital repayments. There is also the risk of interest rates increasing during the period of the loan. The group would have been better advised to use equity to finance this acquisition.

(c) Strategic objective

There are arguments for concentrating on one area of operation so as to achieve, for example, economies of scale and make best use of specialised management skills.

The group is achieving significant increases in revenue within the hotel sector but efficiency is deteriorating. Operating profit to revenue has decreased from 18% to 9%.

A high price has been paid for growth. Improvement in profit to revenue would more likely results in the other sectors, particularly the bus company, car hire and waxworks, expanding and generating much higher profit as a percentage of revenue.

The group would be better off to maintain hotels as the core business but also to recognise the importance of these other sectors and continue to expand revenue in each of them, particularly as these are often complementary to the core business.

Profitability: | 20X6 | 20X7 | 20X8 | 20X9

	20X6	20X7	20X8	20X9
$\dfrac{\text{Profit before tax and interest}}{\text{Turnover}}$	$\dfrac{67}{325}=21\%$	19%	16%	14%

$\dfrac{\text{Operating profit}}{\text{Turnover}}$ for each sector:

		20X6	20X7	20X8	20X9
Hotels	$\dfrac{36}{196}=$	18%	18%	12%	9%
Theme park		–	–	12%	15%
Bus company	$\dfrac{6}{24}=$	25%	29%	37%	39%
Car hire	$\dfrac{7}{43}=$	16%	18%	23%	24%
Zoo		–	–	–	–
Waxworks	$\dfrac{1}{10}=$	10%	27%	31%	36%
Publications	$\dfrac{3}{32}=$	9%	9%	12%	12%

ROCE:

		20X6	20X7	20X8	20X9
$\dfrac{\text{Profit before tax and interest}}{\text{Long - term funds}}$	$\dfrac{67}{268}=$	25%	24%	21%	15%
Earnings per share	$\dfrac{33}{500}=$	6.6p	7p	$\dfrac{35}{500}=7p$	7.4p
Asset turnover	$\dfrac{325}{285+98}=$	0.85	0.86	0.83	0.75

Liquidity:

		20X6	20X7	20X8	20X9
Current	$\dfrac{98}{115}=$	0.85	0.73	0.68	0.68
Quick	$\dfrac{58}{115}=$	0.5	0.4	0.4	0.3

Gearing:

	20X6	20X7	20X8	20X9
$\dfrac{\text{Total borrowing}}{\text{Shareholders equity}}$	$\dfrac{42+80}{146}$ = 83%	72%	$\dfrac{102+80+42}{192}$ = 117%	109%
With new euro loan				140%

Market ratios:

		20X6	20X7	20X8	20X9
P/E ratio	$\dfrac{82}{6.6}=$	12.4	14.8	17.1	21.5
Share price increase (%)			$\dfrac{104}{82}=27\%$	15%	32%
FT 100 share index % increase			$\dfrac{1{,}750}{1{,}500}=17\%$	3%	27%
Leisure industry share index % increase			$\dfrac{246}{178}=38\%$	40%	14%

Answer 49 TWELLO

(a) Financial health appraisal

	20X5	20X6	20X7	20X8
Profitability:				
ROCE: Operating profit/total assets	22/222	25/268	40/299	54/334
	9.9%	9.3%	13.4%	16.2%
ROS: Operating profit/sales	22/742	25/859	40/961	54/1,028
	2.96%	2.91%	4.16%	5.25%
Asset turnover: Sales/assets	742/222	859/268	961/299	1,028/334
	3.34	3.21	3.21	3.08
Liquidity:				
Current ratio:	76/104	94/103	103/150	101/163
	0.73	0.91	0.69	0.62
Acid Test:	33/104	48/103	54/150	49/163
	0.32	0.47	0.36	0.30
Trade payables/sales × 365	32 days	25 days	32 days	32 days
Financial:				
Gearing: Debt/equity	25/118	25/165	67/149	65/171
	21%	15%	43%	38%
Earnings per share (cents)	26.0	28.3	38.3	51.7
P/E ratio	11.5	12.4	11.5	10.1

With such limited information, a complete analysis is not possible. However, the following observations can be made:

Profitability: This would have to be compared with other companies in a similar business. However, ROCE does not appear to be very high, although it is moving in the right direction, perhaps as a result of the acquisition.

Profit/sales appears low, but one would need to compare this with Twello's competitors. Again, it is improving, which reduces any concern.

Asset turnover has fallen from 3.34 to 3.08 which is not encouraging. Without knowing the industry it is not possible to determine how serious this is, but if the business only produces 3% – 5% return on sales, it requires a much higher asset turnover.

Liquidity: Both current ratio and acid test appear to be low. Nevertheless, Twello has lived with these figures for four years without the share price suffering. The slight deterioration in both these ratios should not be allowed to continue. The trade payables were further studied because of the low ratios, but creditors appear to be being paid promptly.

Financial: Gearing appears not to be excessive although it has increased. EPS has risen in each of the last three years, quite substantially in the last two. This is encouraging. The share price has risen steadily, but it would have to be compared with the market generally, and the segment in particular, before any opinions could be expressed. The P/E ratio has fallen over the period.

The interest payable exceeds the interest receivable by $5 million and $6 million in the last two years. Comparing the amounts invested with the amounts borrowed, it would be worth investigating further to see if the policy of having both borrowings and investments is sound.

Overall it is difficult to draw any firm conclusions as to Twello's financial health. Whilst its liquidity and return on sales ratios might appear weak for a manufacturing company, they could be normal for a retailer.

(b) **Other information required**

(1) Twello's business.
(2) Comparable figures for similar companies.
(3) Share price movements in company sector for 20X5–8.
(4) Price level changes for 20X5–8.
(5) Cash flow statements.
(6) Current cost accounts.
(7) Chairman's statement regarding future plans.
(8) Directors' shareholdings and details of any management share option scheme.
(9) Details of any developments since the last accounts.
(10) Details of labour relations in Twello.
(11) Age and experience of management team.
(12) Information regarding the market in which Twello operates.

(c) **Advantages of deep discount bonds**

Deep discount bonds are bonds offered at a substantial discount to their nominal value. Advantages accrue to both the company and the investor.

The advantage to the company is that low interest rate is paid.

Investor advantages

(1) They are likely to remain in issue for their full life, an early call being unlikely.

(2) Gain on redemption may be treated as a capital gain, with tax advantages. Some tax authorities amortise the discount and treat this amount as taxable income.

(3) Yield to redemption can be calculated more accurately, as the annual interest received is less (therefore the uncertainties of reinvestment returns are less).

Zero coupon bonds are the extreme deep discount bond.

The redemption yield of a 4% bond issued at $50 and redeemed in 17 years' time is found by solving for r in the following:

$$\$50 = \frac{4}{1+r} + \frac{4}{(1+r)^2} + \frac{4}{(1+r)^3} + \frac{4+100}{(1+r)^{17}}$$

		$
Try 11% discount rate:		
PV of an annuity of $4 per annum for 17 years is $4 × 7.549		30.20
PV of $100 in 17 years' time is $100 × 0.170		17.00
Total		47.20
Issue		(50.00)
NPV		(2.80)
Try 8% discount rate:		
PV of an annuity of $4 per annum for 17 years is $4 × 9.122		36.49
PV of $100 in 17 years' time is $100 × 0.270		27.00
Total		63.49
Issue		(50.00)
NPV		13.49

$$\text{Redemption yield} = 8\% + \frac{13.49}{13.49 + 2.80} \times 3 = 10.5\%$$

Answer 50 SPARKS CO

Tutorial note: *Each of the measures below has been calculated using year-end figures (although mid-year averages for capital employed would be more appropriate if available).*

Return on capital employed (ROCE)

Return on capital employed (ROCE) can be measured as either operating profit before tax or net operating profit after tax (NOPAT) as a percentage of capital employed.

ROCE focuses attention on the return generated by all classes of asset. Its measurement in post-tax form as NOPAT/ (Equity + Debt) gives a measure of the return excluding the benefit of the tax shield on debt.

Post-tax ROCE, using year-end capital employed figures is:

ROCE (20X4) = 1,250 × (1 – 30%)/ (2,030 + 1,900) = 22·26%
ROCE (20X3) = 1,030 × (1 – 30%)/ (1,555 + 1,865) = 21·08%

ROCE has shown a modest improvement but a further investigation of the accounting information would be required to establish whether the improvement is a genuine improvement in the underlying performance of the business.

Marginal ROCE

Marginal return ratios measure the return generated by the latest capital reinvested in the business. Marginal return on capital employed measures the return generated on capital introduced or reinvested over the last period of account. It is measured as:

$$\Delta ROCE = \frac{\Delta NOPAT}{\Delta CE} = \frac{(1{,}250 - 1{,}030)(1 - 30\%)}{3{,}930 - 3{,}420} = 30.20\%$$

Movements in this ratio year-on-year give a clearer indication of the improvement or deterioration in the company's performance. In the case of Sparks Co, the performance on new capital is considerably better than that on the accumulated capital employed in the business.

ADVANCED FINANCIAL MANAGEMENT (P4) – STUDY QUESTION BANK

Economic Value Added (EVA™)

EVA measures that rate of value creation within a business that reflects the degree of economic "super normal profit" or residual income.

In absolute terms EVA can be expressed as a financial surplus using the following formula:

EVA = NOPAT – (WACC × Capital Employed)

Proponents of the EVA measure offer a variety of procedures for "cleaning" the NOPAT and capital employed figures to increase their economic significance and to reduce distortion through accounting manipulation. However insufficient detail is available to make any such adjustments.

EVA for the two years of account is as follows:

EVA (20X4) = 1,250 × (1 – 30%) – 6·12% × (2,030 + 1,900) = $634 million
EVA (20X3) = 1,030 × (1 – 30%) – 6·12% × (1,555 + 1,865) = $512 million

This suggests that there has been a significant improvement in EVA for the business over the two years. However reliance should only be placed on these figures once a full accounting investigation has been conducted.

EVA can also be expressed in relative terms as the difference between the actual return on capital employed and the weighted average cost of capital:

EVA% = ROCE – WACC

Where ROCE is measured as net operating profit after tax (NOPAT) divided into total capital employed.

EVA% (20X4) = 22.26% – 6.12% = 16.14%
EVA% (20X3) = 21.08% – 6.12% = 14.96%

Therefore the "value spread" has also increased over the period.

Return on equity (ROE)

Return on equity which measures the rate of return earned on the total equity funds employed

The calculation is produced as profit after tax/shareholders' funds (PAT/SF):

ROE (20X4) = 860/2,030 = 42·36%
ROE (20X3) = 650/1,555 = 41·80%

As with ROCE this return measure has shown a modest improvement over the period.

Marginal ROE can also be calculated:

$$\Delta ROE = \frac{\Delta PAT}{\Delta SF} = \frac{(860-650)}{2,030-1,555} = 44.21\%$$

Again the performance on new equity is considerably better than that on the accumulated equity in the business.

Return on fixed capital employed (ROFCE)

This measure reflects the return on the capital employed in investment in non-current assets.

If a firm's current ratio (current assets/current liabilities) is greater than one, shareholders' funds and long-term liabilities are being diverted into financing working capital which tends to reduce ROCE below ROFCE.

If the current ratio is less than one the firm is using efficient working capital management to leverage its ROCE. Hence ROCE would exceed ROFCE.

For Sparks Co:

ROFCE (20X4) = 1,250 × (1 − 30%)/4,980 = 17·57% (ROCE = 22.26%)
ROFCE (20X3) = 1,030 × (1 − 30%)/4,540 = 15·88% (ROCE = 21.08%)

The comparison of ROFCE with ROCE for Sparks Co suggests that the company is leveraging additional return through its working capital management policy. Indeed the current ratio is below one for each year (1,220/2,270 = 0.54, 850/1,970 = 0.43)

Earnings Per Share (EPS)

EPS is a key indicator of the firm's performance for its ordinary shareholders. It is calculated as profit after tax/number of issued ordinary shares.

Noting that each Sparks CO share has 25 cents par value the EPS is:

$$\text{EPS (20X4)} = \frac{860}{400/0.25} = 53.75c$$

$$\text{EPS (20X3)} = \frac{650}{425/0.25} = 38.24c$$

This is a remarkable, and potentially suspicious, rise in EPS and may be the reason that some investors fear there have been "financial shenanigans" in Sparks. Accounting policies may have been adopted to create a short-term boost in profits or discretionary expenditures cut.

Furthermore the number of shares in issue has fallen, suggesting a share buyback programme may have been introduced to further boost EPS and the share price, in turn to justify the CEO's bonus. More detailed investigation of the accounts would be necessary to discover whether the underlying business really have improved as much as the EPS.

Answer 51 WURRALL CO

(a) Pro forma statement of profit or loss for the years ended March 20X5–20X8

	$ million			
	20X5	*20X6*	*20X7*	*20X8*
Revenue	1,787	1,929	2,064	2,188
Operating costs before depreciation	(1,215)	(1,312)	(1,404)	(1,488)
EBITDA	572	617	660	700
Tax-allowable depreciation	(165)	(179)	(191)	(203)
EBIT	407	438	469	497
Net interest payable	(63)	(65)	(66)	(70)
Profit on ordinary activities before tax	344	373	403	427
Tax on ordinary activities	(103)	(112)	(121)	(128)
Dividends	(135)	(146)	(158)	(167)
Amount transferred to reserves	106	115	124	132

Pro forma statement of financial position 20X5–20X8

	$ million			
	20X5	*20X6*	*20X7*	*20X8*
Non-current assets				
Land and buildings	310	310	350	350
Plant and machinery (net)	1,103	1,191	1,275	1,351
Investments	32	32	32	32
	1,445	1,533	1,657	1,733
Current assets				
Inventories	488	527	564	598
Receivables	615	664	710	753
Cash in hand and short term deposits	22	24	25	27
	1,125	1,215	1,299	1,378
Current liabilities:				
Short term loans and overdrafts	266	287	332	320
Other liabilities	514	556	595	630
	(780)	(843)	(927)	(950)
Non-current liabilities:				
Borrowings[4]	(580)	(580)	(580)	(580)
	1,210	1,325	1,449	1,581
Capital and reserves				
Called up share capital (10 cents par)	240	240	240	240
Reserves	970	1,085	1,209	1,341
	1,210	1,325	1,449	1,581

---

[4] Refinanced with a similar type of loan in 20X6

Tutorial note: *Note (iv) of the scenario that states the firm will meet its financing needs by adjusting the overdraft. Hence the level of short terms loans and overdraft is a balancing figure in the SOFP (i.e. to reconcile total assets to equity and liabilities).*

(b)   Problems and implications of assumptions

The *pro forma* accounts are based primarily upon the percentage of sales method of forecasting. This provides a simple approach to forecasting, but is based on assumptions of existing or planned relationships between variables remaining constant, which are highly unlikely. It also does not allow for improvements in efficiency over time.

- Accurate forecasts of sales growth are very difficult. Sensitivity or simulation analysis is recommended to investigate the implications of sales differing from the forecast levels. A constant growth rate of 6% forever after four years is most unlikely.

- Cash operating costs are unlikely to increase in direct proportion with sales. The variable elements (wages, materials, distribution costs etc.) could all move at a higher or lower rate than sales, whilst the fixed elements will not change with the value of sales at all in the short run. If the company becomes more efficient then costs as a proportion of sales should reduce.

- Unless tax-allowable depreciation from new asset purchases exactly offsets the diminishing allowances on older assets, and effect of the increase in assets with sales growth, this relationship is unlikely to be precise. The government might also change the rates of tax-allowable depreciation.

- Assuming a direct relationship between inventories, receivables, cash and other liabilities to sales could promote inefficiency. Although a strong correlation between such variables exists, there should be no need to increase inventory, receivables and liabilities in direct proportion to sales.

- Paying dividends as a constant percentage of earnings could lead to quite volatile dividend payouts. Most investors are believed to prefer reasonably constant dividends (allowing for inflation) and might not value a company with volatile dividends as highly as one with relatively stable dividends.

(c)   Free cash flow analysis

Free cash flow to the firm (FCFF) will be estimated by EBIT (1 – t) plus depreciation less adjustments for changes in working capital and expenditure on non-current assets.

	$ million			
	20X5	*20X6*	*20X7*	*20X8*
Change in land and buildings	–	–	40	–
Change in plant and machinery	91	88	84	76
Change in working capital	15	27	–	56
Change in assets	106	115	124	132

	$ million			
	20X5	*20X6*	*20X7*	*20X8*
EBIT (1 – t)	285	307	328	348
Depreciation	165	179	191	203
Change in assets	(106)	(115)	(124)	(132)
Free cash flow	344	371	395	419

Tutorial notes: *The change in working capital is found by comparing each year's net current assets to the previous year's net current assets e.g. year 20X6 current assets – current liabilities = 1215 – 843 = 372 and year 20X5 = 1125 – 780 = 345. Rise = 372 – 345 = 27 = cash outflow.*

Arguably, for the purposes of forecasting cash flows, we should define working capital as net operating current assets i.e. inventory + receivables – payables. It is the change in the level of net operating current assets that explains the change in the cash position.

EBIT (1 – t) = EBIT (per forecast) × (1 – 0.3) e.g. for 20X6 = 438 × 0.7 = 307. The model answer then adds back depreciation (following the definition of free cash flow given in the requirement) but there is an argument that depreciation measures the cash required each year to maintain the firm's existing level of operations, in which case it should not be added back. In calculations do follow any definitions given in the question but add a note of any limitations in the methodology.

The present value of free cash flow to the firm after 20X8 may be estimated by:

$$\frac{FCFF_{20X8}(1+g)}{WACC - g} \text{ or } \frac{419(1 \cdot 06)}{0 \cdot 11 - 0 \cdot 06} = 8,883$$

The estimated value of the firm at the end of 20X8 is $8,883 million. From this must be deducted the value of any loans in order to find the value accruing to shareholders. From the pro forma accounts, loans are expected to total $900 million, leaving a net value of $7,983 million. If the number of issued shares is unchanged, the estimated market value per share is:

$$\frac{7,983}{2,400} = 333 \text{ cents per share, an increase of 58\% on the current share price.}$$

Based on this data the managing director's claim that the share price will double in four years is not likely to occur.

However, the impact of the performance of the economy, and unforeseen significant changes affecting Wurrall mean that such estimates are subject to a considerable margin of error.

(d) Ratios

	20X5	20X6	20X7	20X8
Gearing (%)	41·1	39·6	38·6	36·3
Current ratio	1·44	1·44	1·40	1·45
Quick ratio	0·82	0·82	0·79	0·82
Return on capital employed[5] (%)	22·7	23·0	23·1	23·0
Asset turnover	1·00	1·01	1·02	1·01
EBIT/Sales (%)	22·8	22·7	22·7	22·7
Receivables collection period (days)	126	126	126	126

It is difficult to comment upon ratios without comparative data for companies in the same industry. The current gearing level, at 42·3%, breaches the covenant limit of 40%, and it is expected to continue to do so in 20X5. Whether or not this breaches the one-year covenant is not clear, but would need to be investigated by the company and action taken to reduce gearing if the covenant was to be breached for too long a period. The receivables collection period appears high at 126 days. It is unlikely that credit would be given for such a long period, and the company might consider improving its credit control procedures to reduce the collection period. If this is successful it could also reduce the overdraft and help reduce the gearing level.

---

[5] EBIT/(shareholders equity plus long term debt). Other definitions are possible

Another ratio that would need investigating is the asset turnover. At around one this is relatively low. Unless the industry is very capital intensive, management should consider if assets could be utilised more efficiently to improve this ratio, and with it the return on capital employed.

As previously mentioned, managers might also review the company's dividend policy. Paying a constant level of earnings could lead to volatile dividend payments which might not be popular with investors, including financial institutions, that rely upon dividends for part of their annual cash flow.

Wurrall proposes to finance any new capital needs with increases in the overdraft. Overdraft finance is not normally considered to be appropriate for long term financing, and the company should consider longer term borrowing or equity issues for its long-term financing requirements.

ABOUT BECKER PROFESSIONAL EDUCATION

Becker Professional Education provides a single destination for candidates and professionals looking to advance their careers and achieve success in:

- Accounting
- International Financial Reporting
- Project Management
- Continuing Professional Education
- Healthcare

For more information on how Becker Professional Education can support you in your career, visit www.becker.com.

Becker Professional Education is an ACCA approved content provider

Lightning Source UK Ltd.
Milton Keynes UK
UKOW07f2252260116

267136UK00004B/10/P